The Degunking 12-Step Program

Here is the basic 12-step degunking process that you should follow to fully degunk your Mac:

1. Get rid of the files you don't really need (Chapter 3).

2. Uninstall programs you don't need, fix programs that cause problems, and upgrade to newer versions that are OS X compatible (Chapter 4).

3. Organize your files and folders (Chapter 5).

4. Clean up the Dock, Finder, and Menu bar (Chapter 6).

5. Clean up the Fonts folder and font gunk (Chapter 7).

6. Reduce your e-mail spam and sort through and organize Apple's Mail (Chapters 8 and 9).

7. Optimize your OS X hard drive and Install the latest upgrades and updates (Chapters 11 and 12).

8. Add hardware such as RAM, additional monitors, and external backup devices; physically clean your Mac (Chapter 13).

9. Use available and third-party maintenance tools to keep your Mac running smoothly (Chapter 14).

10. Improve security with password protected screen savers, anti-virus software, File Vault, and more (Chapter 15).

11. Back up your system on a regular basis (Chapter 16).

12. Be aware of common problems and how to fix them (Appendix).

Degunking with Time Limitations

To get the full benefits of degunking, I highly recommend that you complete all of the main degunking tasks in the order that they are presented. Performing all of these tasks will require a bit of time. If your time is limited, here are some valuable degunking tasks you can perform in the time you *do* have—whether it's ten minutes, three hours, or a half day.

Ten-Minute Degunking

If you have a very short amount of time—less than half an hour, say—you should focus on archiving, deleting, and compressing some of your e-mail and empting the Trash:

1. Move a large group of old e-mails to an archived folder, save the folder to a backup, and delete the e-mails from your current In box (Chapter 9).

2. Empty the Trash bin of Apple's Mail (Chapter 9).

3. Look for large blocks of e-mails that you no longer need and delete them. A good place to look is any folder that contains e-mail more than six months old (Chapter 9).

4. Look in the Sent folder and delete all sent e-mails with attachments (Chapter 9).

5. Empty the Trash on the Dock and in applications like iPhoto or iMovie to free up space on your hard drive (Chapter 5).

6. Think of how you want to organize your e-mail and create a plan (Chapter 8).

Thirty-Minute Degunking

If you only have thirty minutes or so, I recommend you perform three of the ten-minute degunking tasks and then get rid of files and programs stored on your hard drive that you no longer use:

1. Remove the excessive gunk in your default folders: Documents, Music, Movies, Pictures, and so on (Chapter 3).

2. Remove the programs you no longer use by dragging unwanted items to the Trash (Chapter 4). Because deciding on a program to delete might take a few minutes, focus only on deleting five or so programs.

3. Remove applications' Preferences files after removing their programs (Chapter 4).

4. Remove items from the desktop you no longer need including unzipped files, .dmg files, and .tar files (Chapter 3).

One-Hour Degunking

If you have an hour to degunk your Mac, you can go a little deeper and remove more e-mails, files and folders, and programs you no longer need. Here are the tasks to focus on:

1. Perform two of the thirty-minute degunking tasks.

2. Delete more unnecessary files by focusing on the following:

   • Remove the files you don't need from the crevices of your Mac where files hide (Chapter 3).

   • Search for files you don't need and remove them (Chapter 3).

   • Remove unused unzipped files and duplicate files (Chapter 3).

3. Uninstall more unnecessary programs by focusing on the following:
   - Remove programs installed under OS 9 that you don't use, such as extra Web browsers (Chapter 10).
   - Search for programs you didn't know you had and remove them (Chapter 4).
   - Remove programs for hardware you no longer own or don't use any more (Chapter 4).
4. Organize the pictures in the Pictures folder by renaming them and placing them in folders (Chapter 5).

Three-Hour Degunking

When you have a little more time to degunk your Mac, optimize your computer with the following tasks:

1. Perform three of the one-hour degunking tasks.
2. Fine-tune the programs you regularly use to improve their performance (Chapter 4).
3. Organize the default folders by creating additional, embedded folders and moving files into them (Chapter 5).
4. Use Disk Utility, delete the contents of the Library Caches folder, zap the PRAM, and perform other maintenance tasks to enhance the cleansing process (Chapter 14).

Half-Day Degunking

When you have limited time to degunk, your focus should be on cleaning up e-mails, files and folders, and unused programs. Having a half day to degunk allows you to clean up and tweak your desktop and Dock, as well as perform some additional e-mail degunking tasks:

1. Perform all the three-hour degunking tasks.
2. Clean up and personalize the Dock, the Menu bar, and the Finder so you can work faster and smarter (Chapter 6).
3. Configure System Preferences so that unnecessary programs don't start when you boot your Mac and use valuable system resources (Chapter 11).
4. Purchase a third-party defragmenting utility and defragment your hard drive (Chapter 5).
5. Organize your fonts, get rid of duplicate fonts, and remove any fonts you don't use (Chapter 7).
6. Go through your Address Book and remove invalid e-mail addresses (Chapter 9).
7. Set-up a separate spam filtering utility to help you reduce the amount of spam you receive (Chapter 8).
8. If spam has overtaken your In box, call your ISP and request a new address. Notify your contacts of your new address (Chapter 8).

Spare Moment Degunking

There may be times when you are working and you discover that you have a few minutes to spare. To help you degunk your Mac in your spare moments, I've created my Top Twenty list of degunking tasks that you can perform. These tasks do not need to be performed in any specific order. Simply select a task and perform it to help clean your machine.

Twenty Useful Degunking Tasks

1. Delete five icons off of your Desktop (Chapter 3).

2. Get rid of annoying pop-up messages using Safari (Chapter 15).

3. Empty the Trash (Chapter 5).

4. Uninstall one or more programs you no longer use (Chapter 4).

5. Check and repair disk permissions (Chapter 14).

6. Delete 10 of your top 30 largest e-mails (Chapter 8).

7. Clean the monitor with a moist, lint-free cloth (Chapter 13).

8. Delete the contents of the Library Caches folder (Chapter 14).

9. Check for software updates (Chapter 12).

10. Delete any user account that is no longer needed (Chapter3).

11. Check your e-mail folders—especially the Sent folder—to make sure gunk isn't accumulating there (Chapter 9).

12. Locate five 1-megabyte or larger files that you no longer need and delete them (Chapter 5).

13. Empty the Trash folder in your e-mail (Chapter 9).

14. Burn a CD of your most recent files for backup (Chapter 16).

15. Use File System Check to scan your Mac for problems (Chapter 5).

16. Personalize the default Home folders with folders of your own (Chapter 5).

17. Check to see how much RAM you have installed, and then call your local Apple store or browse the Internet to see if you can afford to add more (Chapter 13).

18. Unsubscribe from an e-mail newsletter you no longer read (Chapter 8).

19. Configure security options to protect, secure, and keep your private information private (Chapter 15).

20. See if you have any fonts you can delete (Chapter 14).

Joli Ballew

President
Keith Weiskamp

Editor-at-Large
Jeff Duntemann

Vice President, Sales, Marketing, and Distribution
Steve Sayre

Vice President, International Sales and Marketing
Cynthia Caldwell

Production Manager
Kim Eoff

Cover Designers
Kris Sotelo and Jesse Dunn

Degunking Your Mac™

Copyright © 2004 Paraglyph Press. All rights reserved.

This book may not be duplicated in any way without the express written consent of the publisher, except in the form of brief excerpts or quotations for the purposes of review. The information contained herein is for the personal use of the reader and may not be incorporated in any commercial programs, other books, databases, or any kind of software without written consent of the publisher. Making copies of this book or any portion for any purpose other than your own is a violation of United States copyright laws.

Limits of Liability and Disclaimer of Warranty

The author and publisher of this book have used their best efforts in preparing the book and the programs contained in it. These efforts include the development, research, and testing of the theories and programs to determine their effectiveness. The author and publisher make no warranty of any kind, expressed or implied, with regard to these programs or the documentation contained in this book.

The author and publisher shall not be liable in the event of incidental or consequential damages in connection with, or arising out of, the furnishing, performance, or use of the programs, associated instructions, and/or claims of productivity gains.

Trademarks

Trademarked names appear throughout this book. Rather than list the names and entities that own the trademarks or insert a trademark symbol with each mention of the trademarked name, the publisher states that it is using the names for editorial purposes only and to the benefit of the trademark owner, with no intention of infringing upon that trademark.

Paraglyph Press, Inc.
4015 N. 78th Street, #115
Scottsdale, Arizona 85251
Phone: 602-749-8787
www.paraglyphpress.com

Paraglyph Press ISBN: 1-932111-94-8

Printed in the United States of America
10 9 8 7 6 5 4 3 2

PARAGLYPH PRESS

The Paraglyph Mission

This book you've purchased is a collaborative creation involving the work of many hands, from authors to editors to designers and to technical reviewers. At Paraglyph Press, we like to think that everything we create, develop, and publish is the result of one form creating another. And as this cycle continues on, we believe that your suggestions, ideas, feedback, and comments on how you've used our books is an important part of the process for us and our authors.

We've created Paraglyph Press with the sole mission of producing and publishing books that make a difference. The last thing we all need is yet another tech book on the same tired, old topic. So we ask our authors and all of the many creative hands who touch our publications to do a little extra, dig a little deeper, think a little harder, and create a better book. The founders of Paraglyph are dedicated to finding the best authors, developing the best books, and helping you find the solutions you need.

As you use this book, please take a moment to drop us a line at **feedback@paraglyphpress.com** and let us know how we are doing—and how we can keep producing and publishing the kinds of books that you can't live without.

Sincerely,

Keith Weiskamp & Jeff Duntemann
Paraglyph Press Founders
4015 N. 78th Street, #115
Scottsdale, Arizona 85251
email: **feedback@paraglyphpress.com**
Web: **www.paraglyphpress.com**

Recently Published by Paraglyph Press:

Degunking Windows
By Joli Ballew
And Jeff Duntemann

Windows XP Professional: The Ultimate User's Guide,
Second Edition
By Joli Ballew

Jeff Duntemann's Wi-Fi Guide, Second Edition
By Jeff Duntemann

Windows Admin Scripting Little Black Book, Second Edition
By Jesse Torres

The SQL Server 2000 Book
By Anthony Sequeira
And Brian Alderman

Mac OS X v. 10.3 Panther Little Black Book
By Gene Steinberg

Mac OS X v.2 Jaguar Little Black Book
By Gene Steinberg

Game Coding Complete
By Mike McShaffry

Monster Gaming
By Ben Sawyer

Looking Good in Print, 5th Edition
By Roger C. Parker

Once again, without the support of my family and my friends, none of this would ever have been possible. I am truly blessed to be surrounded by such wonderful and encouraging people.

—Joli Ballew

ъ•

About the Author

Joli Ballew is a dedicated Mac user, digital media enthusiast, graphic designer, and Windows expert. Over the last 4 years, she has written over a dozen books including *Degunking Windows* (Paraglyph Press), *A Simple Guide to Photoshop 7.0* (Pearson Education), *Photoshop 7.0 for Screen Printers* (Wordware Publishing), and *Windows XP: Do Amazing Things* (Microsoft Press). Joli has a B.A. in Mathematics, and teaches FrontPage classes at Eastfield Community College. In addition, Joli works part-time as a graphic artist at North Texas Graphics (where Macs abound), a screen printing, embroidery, and graphics company specializing in promotional product creation. She also participates in various beta programs, newsgroups, and online communities.

Acknowledgments

Quite a few people made *Degunking Your Mac* a success. First, a special thanks to Keith Weiskamp and Steve Sayre for giving me another opportunity to participate in the Degunking series. I think we have a good thing here and I am honored to be a part of it. I'd also like to thank team members Cynthia Caldwell, Kim Eoff, Judy Flynn, Dan Young, Kris Sotelo, and technical editor Jeff Castrina for their help in putting this book out in record time.

A big thanks once again to my family, including Mom, Dad, Jennifer, and Cosmo, who always believe in me and offer support and encouragement at every turn. And a special thanks to my biggest fan, Pat Doran, who for some reason thinks I can continue to write at this pace and on any topic imaginable. This has been an exciting year for all of us, and I think our combined efforts have finally paid off!

Contents at a Glance

Contents

Chapter 3
Getting Rid of Files That Shouldn't Be There 25

Chapter 4
Uninstalling Programs You Don't Need
(and Tweaking Those You Do) 55

Chapter 8
Preventing Spam Gunk 129

Introduction

If you have been using a Mac and running OS X for a while, you might not fully realize it but your Mac might not be running as well as it used to (or as well as it should). If you've recently started using a new Mac, on the other hand, there might be things that you are doing (or not doing) that could cause problems for you down the road. Most Mac users I know love their Macs and feel that OS X is a wonderful and fast operating system, but from time to time, weird things can (and do) happen. If you don't have a good maintenance plan in place to take care of your Mac and keep it running at its best, you could even lose valuable data, not to mention a lot of time.

After you've been using your Mac for more than a few months, it might seem like it's running a little slower than it used to. It might start telling you that you don't have permission to open a file you know you created just last week. You could start to develop problems with your favorite applications (the ones that previously ran fine with OS 9). You might have a list of fonts as long as your arm and they all look alike. You might not understand why you keep getting notices for software updates, and you likely don't know what to install and what to ignore. You find other issues too.

You discover that iPhoto's Trash has to be emptied, and you wonder what other Trash cans are strewn about that you don't know about. It's likely that the number of spam e-mails you receive is starting to increase dramatically. It might seem as if every time you surf the Web, you're bombarded with more and more pop-up ads. Because you've heard about friends being ripped off through Internet scams, you might even feel a little insecure about sending and receiving e-mails and accessing the Web. Your hard drive space could even start to dwindle, and you might wish you had a new Mac again (or that you never got rid of the old one).

Of course, you don't really need a new Mac. There is a much better solution. You can degunk your Mac in just a few hours using a set of tried-and-true techniques. With this step-by-step guide, you can quickly clean your Mac, speed it up, secure it from dangerous hackers, clean up your e-mail, reduce spam, and make your Mac work as fast and as reliably as it did the day you brought it home. (Do you still remember that day? That's when you made a promise that your new Mac would save you so much time that you'd have time to get all the stuff done around the house that's been pilling up!)

Degunking Your Mac is not just another book on how to use OS X. This book is an easy-to-read and concise guide showing you, step-by-step and in plain English, how to improve the performance of your Mac and save yourself a lot of time and aggravation by setting up good maintenance procedures. I'll show you how to reorganize files that are stored all over the place, how to reduce or eliminate spam, how to manage fonts, what to do with a fragmented hard drive, how to deal with incompatible programs, and how to handle a host of other problems you don't want to discuss with your closest friends.

Why You Need This Book

I've talked with scores of Mac users, and the common problem they *all* had was what I call a gunked-up machine: They all suffered from common and easily solved performance problems. Oddly enough, I also heard that a lot of Mac users don't believe their Macs have any gunk on them at all. Once I started talking with them about the concept of gunk—slow performance, security problems, e-mail confusion, spam, font disorganization, lack of good backup procedures, and file management challenges—it ended up that almost everyone had gunk they didn't even know existed. Not to worry! As an avid and loyal Mac user, I'm here to show you how to lead a gunk-free life with your favorite computer.

Although Mac OS X is an excellent operating system, it has some peculiarities that cause it to slow down over time. Not only that, but you have to know how and where to store stuff, what maintenance to perform, and what updates to install too. *Without regular maintenance, all Macs running OS X will get gunked up.* The goal of this book is to show you how to degunk your own Mac and get it (and keep it) running like new again.

Degunking Your Mac is a unique guide that can save you hundreds of hours of valuable time. Here are some of the unique features of this book:

Shows you where gunk accumulates on a Mac and slows you down—even though you might not realize you have gunk!

Provides an easy-to-follow 12-step degunking process that you can put to work immediately.

Includes explanations, in everyday terms, of how to easily fix common problems that create gunk on your Mac.

Provides information on how to save money with free degunking tools that are easily found on the Internet.

Includes a unique "GunkBuster's Notebook" feature in every chapter to help you reduce the clutter on your Mac.

Features degunking maintenance tasks that you can perform on a regular basis to keep your machine in top form.

Provides instructions on how to degunk your e-mail and reduce the amount of spam you receive. This feature can really save you a lot of time!

Features advice on how to keep your Mac gunk-free so you won't create the same gunk again.

Shows you how to recognize when you have to do a clean install or buy a new Mac.

How to Use This Book

Degunking Your Mac is structured around a specific degunking process that you should follow in the order presented. The book starts off by explaining the importance of degunking and why operating systems like OS X require it. Each subsequent chapter describes an important degunking task, explained in plain English with step-by-step instructions.

TIP: This book is designed around a 12-step program—it is outlined in Chapter 2, begins in Chapter 3, and continues through the end of the book. I highly recommend that you follow the process in the order it is presented here. This will give you the best results for the time you spend degunking your Mac.

Once you've completely degunked your Mac, you can perform different degunking operations at different times, depending on your needs. I expect that *Degunking Your Mac* will become one of your most-used computer books, and I'll bet that it will end up on your bookshelf right next to your computer.

A Note on Mac Versions

The degunking tasks presented in this book were written to work with the current version of OS X, Panther. Some of the operations presented, such as working with the five font folders and color-coding your folders, are very specific to OS X. If you are using an older version of the operating system, though, you can still benefit from many of the degunking routines presented here. Many of the degunking tasks involve general operations—such as removing files you don't need, organizing your hard drive, and cleaning up your e-mail—that you can easily adapt to the version of the operating system you are using. Here are some of the more general (less version-specific) tasks you can perform regardless of the version of Mac you have:

Getting Rid of Files That Shouldn't Be There (Chapter 3)

Uninstalling Programs You Don't Need and Tweaking Those You Do (Chapter 4)

Organizing Your Remaining Files and Folders (Chapter 5)

Preventing Spam Gunk (Chapter 8)

Cleaning Up E-Mail Gunk (Chapter 9)

Choosing the Best Hardware for Mac Degunking (Chapter 13)

Improving Security (Chapter 15)

The Degunking Mindset

A lot of Mac users don't think their machines have gunk—but the truth is, the source of gunk is the *way* we use our Macs, not the machinery itself! All Mac users create their own gunk, mostly without even realizing it. Over time, this gunk will slow down the way you work, compromise your productivity, and make your Mac less efficient. My goal is to keep your Mac running at tip-top speed as long as possible.

The more you learn about degunking your Mac, the more you'll realize that degunking is a mindset, not just a set of technical skills. I view degunking as mostly psychology, not just technology. Rather than simply being a process that you follow when your computer slows down, degunking is a disciplined approach to managing your Mac. If you follow the basic steps outlined in this book on a regular basis, you'll give yourself an insurance policy and save yourself from encountering aggravation down the road. I also believe that *Degunking Your Mac* will make your time on your computer more efficient, more productive, and maybe even more enjoyable.

Is My Mac Really Gunked Up?

Degunking Checklist

- √ Understand what Mac gunk is and how it messes up your computer and gets in your way.

- √ Discover basic degunking tasks and how they can improve your Mac's performance.

- √ Learn how files you save can gunk up your Mac.

- √ Understand the strategy for getting and staying degunked.

- √ Understand why installing too many programs slows down your Mac.

- √ See how the Finder, the Desktop, and the Dock can get gunked up too.

- √ Learn how limited drive space can impact the performance of your Mac.

- √ Understand how unorganized data files create gunk you don't need.

B ecause you've picked up this book, I'm assuming that you have a Mac and you want it to operate as best it can. I'm not going try to convince you that your Mac is gunked up, and I won't presume you're disorganized or a packrat or that you have neglected your computer in any way. I know you love your Mac; I dearly love mine, so we have a lot in common.

My goal in writing this book is to help you fall in love with your computer all over again, not to point out flaws with the operating system, chide you for being disorganized, or scold you for giving your e-mail address to any Web site that asks for it. I want to help you get rid of spam, protect your Mac from security threats, and get rid of unnecessary programs, fonts, files, music, movies, and pictures that are bogging your Mac down and making it work too hard. I want to help you clean up your desktop, easily get updates, and organize the stuff you want and need to keep. I want your computer to feel new again. If you are like most Mac users I talk to, you probably aren't aware of how gunked up your Mac can get just from everyday use. That being said, let's move forward and see what you can do now.

What Gunk Is

On occasion, even the most Mac-savvy users encounter gunk problems—maybe you've encountered a few of them yourself. Common problems include running low on available hard drive space, getting strange errors, seeing the sad Mac face, or having to (gasp!) reboot the machine. You might also share your Mac with someone else and have no privacy, or maybe you have relatives who constantly ask you for advice. Maybe you even work at a help desk and want to impart some wisdom to the people who phone in with problems with their Macs because of being gunked up. Whatever the case, you (or someone you know) might be the victim of a fairly common problem—a gunked-up Mac!

So what exactly does "gunked up" mean? Well, the signs are common:

√ Your hard drive works too long to send a simple e-mail.

√ Sometimes you can't find that last picture you scanned and saved. (It's okay to admit this happens to you!)

√ The startup process seems to take more time than it used to.

√ The shutdown process might also be slower (assuming you shut down on occasion).

√ You've created so many folders on your Mac that you can't quickly locate the ones you need.

√ You get so much spam that it takes you way too long to get through your e-mails or locate important messages that you have previously saved.

√ You have so many old files on your hard drive (many of which you don't recognize) that your hard drive is getting full and slowing down.

√ You have downloaded a lot of music files and you don't know where to store them, so you can't keep them organized.

√ You have some programs you never use, and the ones you do use might sometimes freeze up and require you to use Force Quit.

√ There's a chance your Web cam needs an updated driver.

√ Your files occasionally open in the wrong programs.

Unfortunately, there's even more gunk to be found. Maybe your Dock is filled with things you never access and your Home folder is disorganized, too. If you're an artist, you might have 100 fonts that all look alike. You might have files that won't open and a desktop filled with icons. And you don't have a backup or a security plan. That's gunk, *mon ami*.

You might think that purchasing a new Mac is the best solution. That's just not true: you only need to degunk the one you have. To keep that beautiful Mac out of the landfill, you're going to have to take some steps to clean it up. That's the purpose of this book, and believe it or not, keeping your Mac clean and running well is fairly painless.

GunkBuster's Notebook: Still Don't Think Your Mac Can Get Gunked Up?

Consider this analogy: Your Mac is like your home. You must clean out the gutters twice a year, keep the doors and locks in working order, wash the windows, scrub the floors, and take out the garbage twice a week. You also have to throw away or recycle stuff you no longer use. You probably don't need all four of those rakes in the garage and that wheelbarrow with the broken handle, do you? Sometimes, you might even need a professional to fix the foundation or repair other serious problems. You have to take care of maintaining your house or it will fall apart. Besides that, if you don't clean up or put things away, you'd never be able to sift through the junk you have to find the junk you want.

Just as with your home, there are common "gunk" factors that bring down your Mac. There are programs you don't need, files you don't want, updates that need to be installed, backup tasks that are critical, and security issues to consider. You have to maintain your Mac, too. Your Mac is likely disorganized, cluttered, full, and feeling a little neglected to boot. Just because you use a Mac doesn't mean that you are immune from gunk and unfortunate events such as system crashes, although the Mac operating system does a better job than most operating systems at helping you manage your work and operating smoothly.

One very important thing about the degunking process that many computer users miss out on is that it's important to put into place a regular maintenance plan to keep your computer in top form. Degunking your Mac shouldn't just involve deleting a bunch of files or programs when you feel overwhelmed. You should put a process in place (and this book will certainly help you do that) to follow on a regular basis. With such a process in place, you'll be amazed at how much time and energy you'll save in the long run.

What the Experts Know

Hardcore Mac users and those geeky guys you hear on Sunday afternoon radio talk shows know how to keep their Macs in pristine condition. The good news is, you can too. The problem is that you're probably not aware of what needs to be done on a regular basis to keep both you and your Mac happy. Well, I've made it easy. By following the steps I've outlined in this book, you can improve the operation of your Mac considerably.

This process outlined in this book is divided into four key areas:

1. Basic Housekeeping 101. Here we'll focus on how to get everything back in its place and rid your Mac of all the gunk you've accumulated. (Just think about how good it feels to clean out your closet and throw away all of the stuff you don't need and separate your clothes and shoes by season!) We'll also concentrate on how you can optimize the files on your hard drive for the best performance possible.

2. Repairing Common Problems. Once you've culled down the programs and files on your Mac, you'll want to repair some basic and common problems. You can think of it as a tune-up of your system, and it can be the capstone to a core cleaning and improvement process.

3. Total Reinstall. In the most extreme cases, it's sometimes best to simply pop in the restore CD and let go of the past. Fortunately for us Mac users, it doesn't come to this very often. But as many long-time computer gurus will tell you, this is one tried-and-true way to get back to the good old days when your computer was cranked up for the first time.

4. Improving Performance and Maintenance. Once you've officially degunked your Mac, you'll want to tweak the operating system and your applications

to keep things running smoothly. You can make improvements by setting preferences so that files are saved where they should be and that backup files are created automatically, and you can enable FileVault to secure your Home folder. You can configure Energy Saver to make sure your Mac gets enough "rest" while also getting necessary updates, join the .Mac community for ultra-perks (including free programs and an area to which you can back up data), and schedule your Mac to look for updates regularly. A final set of improvements involves incorporating third-party programs that improve security, provide virus protection, and assist in overall optimization of system performance. Consider this last step as putting the wax on your newly cleaned car.

Understanding How You Got Gunked Up

It is common for a computer to slow down as it ages. Programs can take longer to load, for instance, or starting the computer can take more time than it used to. Even if you can't see any actual hardware slowdowns, at the very least I bet it takes *you* longer to find the stuff *you* need. The one situation that all computer users experience is that the more they use their computer, the more data they receive in the form of e-mails, programs, and files such as pictures, documents, video clips, and music. Data never goes away; it just seems to pile up and add to the clutter heap. This is a fact of computer life today, and the situation is only going to get worse. It seems that every few years, the average computer user spends an additional 20 percent more of their time just trying to manage data.

You might also have too many applications to sift through, too many fonts, too many Bookmarks, too much spam, and too many documents, or maybe the stuff on your computer is just disorganized. You might even have a disorganized Dock or desktop, making accessing what you need inefficient and frustrating.

Files Are Stored Everywhere

Most users have a tendency to save files and downloaded programs wherever the defaults lead them, although some users have a nasty habit of browsing to the Macintosh HD and dropping stuff there. Others simply put them on the desktop, so that it looks something like what's shown in Figure 1-1.

There are better places to put files, though, including the Documents, Movies, Music, Pictures, and Public folders. Even if you're not using the new Panther operating system that comes with these folders already created, you can always create them yourself and build your own personal organizational structure. In Chapter 3, I'll introduce where you should be saving your files, programs, and

Figure 1-1
Does your desktop look like this? If it does, you need to degunk.

downloaded media and what to do with the stuff you've already got on your hard drive.

Installation Files Are Everywhere

Most of the time, installing new programs on your Mac is either achieved by popping in a CD or by downloading and installing the program from the Internet. Programs you download from the Internet generally come in a compressed form. SIT files are StuffIt files, HQX are encoded files, and old school ZIP files are pretty common, although occasionally you'll see TAR files, which are tape archive files and, GZ files which are GZIP files. When you unstuff, unzip, or untar a program you've downloaded from the Internet, it usually turns into a .dmg file, which is a disk image file. Once the installation is complete, you'll have a myriad of unnecessary files on your desktop and on your computer. You'll learn in Chapter 3 how to clean up this mess after installation. It's important that you get rid of these unnecessary files on a regular basis because some of them can be quite large and they can really fill up your hard drive (not to mention your desktop).

Spam, Spam, Eggs, Bacon, and Spam

Everyone has spam. Spam is the bane of anyone with an e-mail account. I hate spam. You hate spam. Unfortunately, the more we try to get rid of it, the faster it comes in. Eventually, it's likely to feel a bit overwhelming. You end up with e-mail repositories teeming with irrelevant files, and those files fill up the In box and *Trash* folders and further gunk up your Mac. A gunked up e-mail program slows down the program and causes slower searches, deletions, sorts, and more.

You may have already given up on combating spam and just accepted it as part of being online and a member of the twenty-first century. No one should have to feel like that, and you shouldn't have to put up with it. As you'll learn in this book, there are strategies you can put to work right away to greatly reduce the amount of spam you receive. Many users I talk to simply throw in the towel and spend much of their precious time each day just deleting the nonsense. If you take a more proactive approach by using different e-mail addresses, setting up spam filters, using different e-mail clients, and avoiding activities that trigger spam in the first place, you could save a lot of time. You'll be a lot happier in the long run, too (and so will your Mac).

You Have Too Many Installed Programs or Fonts

Almost everyone is guilty of having too many installed programs, and most of us have fonts we just don't need. You hear about some cool utility or you need a new game to keep the kids occupied while you do your taxes, or worse yet, you give your kids permission to download their own games and software. You download a couple of media programs, a couple of messaging systems, and maybe another Web browser. You discover **www.acidfonts.com**. You install the gardening CD-ROM in the spring, the Home Improvement CD in the fall, the Genealogy CD around the holidays, and then you never use them. Chances are good you haven't uninstalled any of them either. That's gunk.

When you install a program (or screensaver, or background image, or conversion utility, or a CD that offers 1,000 fonts), you're copying files to the hard drive, you're putting more entries in your applications folder and fonts folders, you're putting more gunk on your desktop, and you're making the computer work harder when it needs to find what you really want to use. Gumming up the computer in this manner is unhealthy and causes unnecessary slowdowns. In Chapter 4 I'll show you how to roll up your sleeves and really get rid of the programs you don't need.

The Desktop, Dock, Finder, and Folders Are Overrun

Even when I brought my new eMac home, I thought the Dock was too busy. It got more cluttered and inefficient as time passed, sporting such icons as a trial version of Microsoft Office I forgot to close, iChat (which I never use), the QuickTime Player (which I don't need either), and more. The desktop got cluttered fast, too, with hosting icons for installation files, screen shots, photo images I meant to e-mail, downloaded programs, and more. Even my Finder windows got ugly: too many applications, unorganized images and music. What a mess! Hopefully, and without being too presumptuous, I'm going to now make my first assumption: you have similar problems. Does the Pictures folder in Figure 1-2 look familiar? We'll sort out the issue of keeping too many unnecessary files and organizing what you want to keep in Chapters 3 and 5, respectively.

Fragmented Hard Drive

As a computer utilizes its hard drive, it stores programs and files in bits and pieces all over the place, generally wherever it has room. Big data files and large programs often aren't stored contiguously; pieces are stored in various places on the drive, and the result is what is called fragmentation. When the reader on the

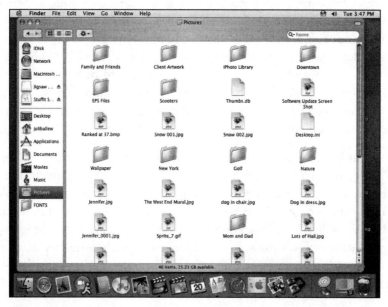

Figure 1-2
Even something as simple as the Pictures folder can get gunked up.

hard drive needs to access this data, it has to physically move back and forth to obtain and read the data it needs. Depending on how fragmented the files are, you might notice a performance hit while it gathers up all of the pieces. And the more wear and tear on your hard drive, the higher the likelihood it will crash, misbehave, or wear out too quickly.

There is a feature in Mac OS 10.3, Panther, that automatically defragments files and optimizes the file system's performance. Optimizing disk performance is different from defragmenting a drive, though. Optimization simply moves files you use a lot to sections of the hard drive that can be accessed faster than the other parts. Third-party applications can be purchased to defragment the drive, though. Although Apple believes that this is unnecessary, I believe it can help speed up a sluggish computer.

TIP: Apple has this to say about defragmenting: *"If your disk is almost full, and you often modify or create large files, there's a chance they could be fragmented. In this case, you might benefit from defragmentation."*

You're Low on Hard Disk Space

Even though newer computers come with huge hard drives, if you store lots of music, pictures, and movies on your computer and never delete or archive any of them, some day you'll run low on disk space. That's just the way it is. When disk space is low, performance suffers. Laptops are especially vulnerable to this because they tend to have smaller drives than desktops. By learning to keep only what you need on your drive, organize what you do keep, and clear out files expertly, you can ensure that you never fall victim to the dreaded "low hard drive space" syndrome.

Data Files Are Unorganized

Okay, I'm not trying to sound like a broken record here, but you really have to organize your stuff. You can't just have files stored all over the place; it causes you to be inefficient and your Mac has to work too hard to simply keep up. With that in mind, let's talk about what *other people* tend to do, and maybe you'll see a bit of yourself in there, too.

Some people put files all over the place. There are a few folks that follow the rules and put pictures in the Pictures folder, movies in the Movie folder, and documents in the Documents folder. Even so, these folders often look like what's shown in Figure 1-3.

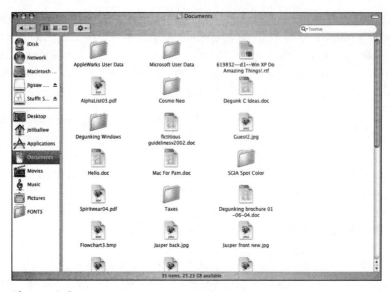

Figure 1-3
Messy, messy, messy.

Wouldn't it be nice to have all your data in the right folders, organized by type, by date, or by task? How about if you give your folders names that are descriptive while you're at it so that you don't have to open a file to see what it is? While you're on a roll, you can get rid of duplicate files, make it easier to search for files with organizational folders, and even delete files you no longer need.

In addition to organizing your own files, with your new multiuser Mac, you'll want to keep the files you share with others organized. If everyone listens to the same music, why have several copies of the same song stored on the hard drive? If you all want to see the same vacation pictures, don't upload them from the camera to everyone's account; put them in a place where everyone can access them. There's no reason to store duplicate copies; just drag the items you want to share to the Shared folder so everyone can access them! (In addition, you can move the location of the iTunes folder to a shared point too.)

Here's a pop quiz: How many digital photos do you have on your Mac that you took with your thumb over the lens, that are blurry, or that show your kids in an unflattering light? Ever thought of deleting those? Chances are good the answer is no. I bet you have a myriad of pictures with names like SNR0625.jpg and SNR0626.jpg too. That's gunk. Consider how much time you waste just looking for what you want!

Computers get gunked up because we add files all the time. We download programs we never use, we download music files, we rip our CD collection to our hard drive, and we work with PDFs, AIFFs, BMPs, DVs, MPEGs, PICTs, TGAs, AppleWorks, PowerPoint slides, JPEGs, GIFs, and Photoshop collages. Somehow, we need to do more than just dump this stuff into folders.

Bookmarks Are Unorganized

If you surf the Web a lot, you probably have a long list of bookmarks. Did you know that you can create folders for those bookmarks and organize them just as you would any folder's data? If you have a newer computer, you also have a hundred or so bookmarks you didn't even put there yourself. Take a look at Figure 1-4: the folders containing bookmarks for News, Mac, Kids, Sports, Entertainment, Shopping, Travel, Tools and Reference, and Other were already on the computer when I purchased it. These bookmarks can be removed and replaced with your own if you'd like.

Spyware Is a New Threat

Spyware is the catchall name for products and programs that, once installed, essentially report back information on your Web surfing habits to organizations that then bombard you with pop-up ads and other advertising. Spyware, for the moment, is basically a Windows-specific problem, but that isn't to say that after this book is published and in its second or third printing, that will still be the case. Spyware has become synonymous with installed programs that might or might not show up in your Applications folder and they cause the computer to suffer a performance hit as well. Spyware is generally hard to find and uninstall, and getting it off your Mac will probably require a third-party tool. You'll want to check in on Apple's Web site every so often to see if there are any threats.

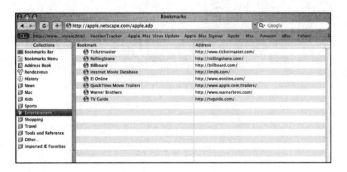

Figure 1-4
You call that entertainment?

These Cookies Aren't So Tasty

Cookies aren't programs but tiny pieces of text data that Web sites place on your computer so that they can remember your preferences the next time you visit. Overall, cookies are fairly harmless. They don't take up too much hard drive space, and they don't offer up too much information about you, unless you've previously supplied it.

However, cookies can accumulate, and after a while they can become irrelevant or useless. In addition, if you ever accidentally stumble upon a gambling or porn site, you might find cookies from them on your Mac, which can be disconcerting for some people. Imagine searching for all text files on your machine and seeing a small file name babesinfunland!

Depending on what you use—Safari, Netscape, Internet Explorer or something else—there are ways to configure your browser to accept or deny cookies and ways to get rid of them. However, legitimate sites use cookies to make your Web surfing experience better and more customized, so disabling cookies isn't a good idea for most people. (Ever wonder how Amazon knows what books you like when you log on?) Disabling cookies can sometimes lead you to throw the baby out with the bathwater, so to speak. It's your call, and in the end, you'll probably accept cookies, so it is certainly worthwhile to learn how to delete them when they start to pile up.

GunkBuster's Notebook: You're Not Automating

You can enhance productivity and security by using built-in programs such as cron (a Unix program, like Disk Utility, for scheduling events) to automate tasks you perform often. Although this is a little beyond the scope of this book, you can, if you have the time and the interest, automate Energy Saver's startup and shutdown function in conjunction with a virus checker or backup program or use the supplied AppleScript Library to help automate specific tasks. If you'd like more information on that, visit **www.apple.com** and search for Apple Scripts.

You're Gunked Up!

Chances are that if one of these things is happening on your Mac, nearly all of them are. But if you commit yourself to degunking, you can get things running pretty much the way they used to. You'll also be organized, so you can work faster, smarter, and more efficiently. The problems I just discussed will only get worse over time, and that's why your entire Mac will continue to get sluggish and disorganized if left to its own devices. It's time to get busy!

Ready for Degunking?

The most difficult part of getting your Mac back to where it should be involves dedicating a little time. As you move on and look at the different degunking techniques, you'll notice that I've arranged the tasks in the order that will likely get you the most results in the shortest amount of time. My approach will be to show you not only how to fix things, but how to get yourself on maintenance program, too, so that your Mac will always run well. If you're new to the world of degunking, don't worry. I'll walk you through it, and I promise it won't hurt a bit.

Degunking Your Mac

Degunking Checklist

√ Learn that the best degunking results can be obtained by performing cleanup tasks in a specific order.

√ Learn why good file management is a critical aspect of degunking.

√ Understand why the desktop and Finder are two places that attract gunk.

√ See how your e-mail can get really gunked up.

√ Learn how you can speed up your Mac by performing common degunking procedures such as hard drive optimization and defragmentation, removing unnecessary components, and disabling items that require complex computations.

√ Learn how securing your Mac with anti-virus software and a firewall is a necessary part of degunking.

√ Understand what you can do if your Mac doesn't respond to standard degunking procedures.

√ Learn the degunking 12-step program.

I could have called this chapter "The 12-Step Program to Degunking" because my goal in this chapter is to introduce a proven 12-step program to degunking success—a program that can really and truly get your Mac performing like new again. To get there, though, you have to understand the degunking mindset. The mindset, in a few well-chosen words, is this: The problems you're having aren't just technological, they're also psychological!

In the following chapters, you'll learn, step-by-step, how to roll up your sleeves and complete the 12 essential steps of the degunking program. The best part is that even if you have only a limited amount of time—10 minutes a day, for instance—you can start making improvements that you'll notice right away. Even better, the steps are so painless, you'll probably even have fun!

The Strategy Behind Degunking

The most important thing to understand about degunking is that you will get the best results if you follow the process outlined in this book in the order the tasks are presented. (As with other typical 12-step programs, the first step is to admit you have a problem.) Once you've accepted the fact that you are powerless over your gunk problem, continue up the 12-step ladder in the order recommended. For example, defragmenting the hard drive with a third-party application does much more good *after* deleting files and uninstalling programs. You shouldn't defrag your hard drive and then delete files later because the process of deleting a bunch of files will simply fragment your drive again. Similarly, there's no real point in performing an extensive backup of files and folders on your Mac before you've deleted the ones you don't want to keep.

If you feel tempted to skip around, keep in mind that you might not get the best results. Of course, there are some processes that can be done at any time, such as removing unnecessary desktop items, using the View commands to clean up the look of a folder, selecting a nonintensive screen saver, or installing anti-virus software. However, in my experience, users get the best results when they have an organized strategy the first time they do a major degunk.

It's Psychology, Not Just Technology!

This is my operating mantra because a gunked-up Mac is not just caused by a technological problem. The Mac operating system isn't inherently bad—in fact, it's probably the best and most reliable one out there, especially if you have upgraded to Panther. Granted, you probably need more than the 128 MB of RAM that came with your Mac or your computer may quickly get bogged down with applications you don't need (including trial applications, additional Web browsers, and applications you'll never use). But for the most part, the sluggishness you're encountering is most likely due to things within your control.

Think about this: You've probably installed system-intensive programs like Photoshop or InDesign and maybe even a set of fonts to go along with your applications. You might also have some Carbon applications loaded on your Mac. You've probably installed a digital camera and uploaded more than a few pictures, and if you have a digital video camera, you've probably got some large movie files. In addition, there's a good chance you haven't done much deleting, and that may even include emptying the Trash!

Important Degunking Questions to Consider

You should ask yourself the following questions as you use your Mac on a regular basis:

√   Does it seem that my Mac is running slower than it used to?

√   Do I add a lot of files to my Mac but rarely delete old ones?

√   How often do I look at my Home folder and subfolders to see if I'm storing files I don't need?

√   Am I keeping my documents, pictures, music, graphics, and movie files organized?

√   Do I really need all of the programs installed on my Mac? (When was the last time I even looked at some of the programs I have installed?)

√   Do I use all of the programs and utilities that load automatically when I boot my Mac?

√   Do I really need that fancy screen saver, do I need to know how large each file is, do I need file sharing turned on, and are Energy Saver settings configured correctly?

√   When was the last time I went through my e-mail and deleted the messages I no longer need?

√   Have I ever purchased a third-party utility like Norton Utilities or Tech Tool Pro and done a system check of my computer and repaired problems?

√   Have I ever defragmented the hard drive?

√   Do I have the recommended updates? Am I set up to get them automatically?

√   Do I use Disk Utility to verify and repair disk problems?

√   Do I have a firewall to keep viruses and other nasty programs from gunking up my Mac?

√ Do I know what to do if something goes wrong with my Mac because it has gotten really gunked up?

Let's put together a degunking strategy to address these issues. In the following sections, you'll learn a little about Mac components and how they get gunked up. In Chapter 3, we'll start degunking.

Organizational Techniques for Files and Folders

As I've mentioned before, one of the biggest gunk contributors are folders and the files in them. My computer is overrun with misplaced files and I bet yours is too. Take a look at the Documents folder shown in Figure 2-1. It's filled with more than just documents. It also contains JPG files, a few other folders, some PDF files, and a few BMP files. Much of this data needs to be stored in other folders. A good place to start would be to move the pictures to the Pictures folder. This is an easy task, but it's just a little time consuming so many users don't do it.

Personal data files take up a lot of space, and your computer's performance suffers when you have too many files stored on your hard drive. Degunking a Mac for the first time can be a real challenge because it's likely these personal data files are not well organized. You just can't step in and start deleting, either, because you probably don't know what half the stuff is. I myself am wondering what the Flowchart3.bmp is in Figure 2-1.

Figure 2-1
We're all guilty of storing files in the wrong place.

So, what's the plan? You should first go through all of the folders on your Mac and take inventory of what's there. Then you'll need to reorganize the data so that you can get a clear picture of what to keep and what to get rid of. In the next few chapters, that's exactly what you'll do. The strategies introduced will help you quickly deal with hard drives that need serious degunking, and I'll walk you through the tried-and-true 12-step program.

While we're reorganizing, you'll also check to make sure that your applications are stored in the right place and you'll learn to delete the ones you don't want. If you're having problems with any applications, you might find that there are upgrades available. Don't worry—you're going to love organizing your stuff. Once you're done, you'll feel like you just cleaned out your garage and put all of that broken and unnecessary stuff on the front lawn for the garbage man to take away.

TIP: *The idea of naming files with descriptive names is extremely important and will be emphasized heavily. If the files are named appropriately, you'll be able to find them much faster than when they are not. Make sure when organizing and degunking that you rename files as suggested.*

A Clean Desktop and Finder Windows

Once you've cleaned up your data files, you'll need to turn your attention to the Dock, the Finder windows, the desktop, other Home subfolders, the Applications folder, and the menus. You can tweak and organize all of these components to your heart's content. You can also personalize these components to fit your needs. This will help you work faster and smarter. For instance, why do you have iMovie on the Dock if you don't have a DV camera? Why have iTunes there if you don't listen to music on your computer? Getting rid of things you don't need or want frees up that space for something you do need. You can add just about anything just about anywhere. You can add items to the desktop, to menus, to the Dock, and to the Finder windows all quite easily. In this book, I'll show you some ways to personalize your computer in ways you never dreamed possible!

Organizational Techniques for Mail

After you've completed the file system and desktop overhaul, it's time to tackle something really big: your e-mail. E-mail programs store messages and data in a relatively simple fashion; that is, all e-mail is stored in a database, so it's fairly easy to degunk. Unfortunately, there are several e-mail programs to choose from, so it isn't a one-size-fits-all degunking process by any means. The good news is, though, that no matter what program you use—Mail, Eudora, Entourage, or something else—there are lots of general principles to manage your e-mail better, reduce the amount of spam (junk e-mail) you receive, and better organize the e-mail you keep, read, and send out.

In this book, I'll talk mostly about Apple's Mail program, but the same techniques can be applied to any e-mail client. In the degunking e-mail chapters, you'll work through the steps to delete as much e-mail as possible, set up rules to deal with junk e-mail, clean up your address book, and set up third-party spam-filtering utilities. Of course, I'll teach you how to avoid spam in the first place and how to create "disposable" e-mail addresses for Web sites that require such information.

Disable Unnecessary Components

If, after doing all this, you still think your computer is sluggish and could run a little faster, I have a few more tricks up my sleeve. There are many system components that can be tweaked to offer minimal improvements but, when combined, offer noticeable changes. For instance, you can remove extraneous extensions, preferences, or fonts you're not using. These extra files increase boot time and slow down reaction time. Application preferences can be set, too, and applications such as Photoshop can be made to open faster. You can also get rid of system-intensive desktop images and screen savers, or even reduce the color depth of the desktop for a faster redraw. You can disable Calculate All Size in the Finder windows, deactivate Remember Recently Used Items, and disable file sharing if you don't need it. There are lots of tweaks that, although seemingly insignificant when performed separately, really add up to improve your Mac's performance when combined with others.

Updates Are Important

It's important to check for updates to the operating system. Apple releases updates to make the operating system run better and faster, provide more security, and fix errors that users encounter that aren't their fault, such as security lapses or buggy program features. You can get patches for existing software, new software options, and updates to the operating system. Figure 2-2 shows what an update looks like.

Updates benefit you in several ways:

√   They reduce exposure to bugs that could cause applications to hang. This causes you to have to force-quit an application and you could lose valuable

Figure 2-2
Getting updates regularly is extremely important.

data. A bug update such as this reduces the likelihood that the operating system will encounter serious problems in the future.

√ They reduce exposure to viruses and security threats. Without these updates, your computer is vulnerable to various hacks and open security issues.

√ They verify you have the most current drivers for your hardware, including iSight, iPod, and AirPort software.

After obtaining the software updates, you'll need to configure your computer to get updates on a schedule. That way, you'll always know your computer is in the best shape possible.

Updating Your Hardware

There may come a time when all of the degunking tasks in the world won't make Photoshop run faster, won't make Mail open faster, won't let you scan at the resolution you want, or won't speed up your Web surfing. When that happens, you'll need to take a look at how much RAM you have and consider purchasing more. You may also want to purchase a backup device or add a second monitor for added functionality. You might consider moving to a cable modem or DSL. You'll also need to physically clean your Mac occasionally. And although cleaning it might not make it run faster, it'll certainly make it more enjoyable to work with.

About Security

Security is a key degunking issue, one that's near and dear to my heart, so I've dedicated an entire chapter to it (see Chapter 15). Without proper security, you're at serious risk of getting viruses and other menacing programs that can take up power and resources and even really harm your Mac. Viruses, worms, and similar threats loom. These things can make your Mac sluggish, cause it to hang, or even worse, cause it to have to be rebooted. In the worst instance, you may even need to do a total reinstall!

My goal is to get you on a first-class security regimen. A good security plan has three pieces:

√ **Anti-Virus Software**—This software will help prevent malicious computer programs from getting installed or otherwise affecting your system.

√ **Firewall**—Installation or activation of a firewall will protect your Mac from unwanted intrusion by hackers or programs.

√ **Basic Security**—Securing your Mac from intruders physically close to you is as important as securing your Mac from invisible threats. Using what is built-in to OS X, you can use a password protected screen saver, create and enable a visitor account, secure the login process, create an open firmware password, use FileVault, and use Secure Empty Trash.

Thankfully, security software is easy to install, and Apple's security features are easy to configure. As part of the 12-step program, you'll learn how to remove unwanted programs, prevent new ones from entering your system, and protect your Mac from intruders.

About Backups

If you've never lost any data to a hard drive failure, you don't know just how damaging and heartbreaking it can be. It's almost like being robbed; what you used to have is gone, and you really have no idea how you're going to replace it. If you *have* had a hard drive fail, you know your best friend that day was your latest backup.

CAUTION: *Although it's unlikely that your hard drive will crash, a good, strong bolt of lightning can bring down a computer, as can a malicious virus.*

Developing a regular backup strategy is crucial. A good backup will not only save you from losing your valuable data, but it will also save you from losing all of your setup information, preferences, critical programs, and more. As you'll learn in this book, creating backups on a regular basis and using proper procedures, will allow you to get your Mac back up and running quickly in the event of a major setback, such as a hard disk failure.

TIP: I love my .Mac membership. With my new eMac, it was only $69 (U.S.) for an entire year, and $99 (U.S.) a year after that. They offer a place to back up my stuff, and I can retrieve the data from anywhere. It's like a virtual briefcase. I use it to do a double-back-up of important files. Visit www.apple.com for more details.

Maintaining Your Mac

As you move through this book, keep one thing in mind: The headway you make during your degunking outings should be maintained from here on out. Don't spend two hours straightening out the Pictures folder only to begin saving your pictures to the desktop again! In addition to remaining organized, try to perform these tasks regularly:

√   Use First Aid every so often to check for and repair problems. (First Aid is an OS 9 program, but it can be used in conjunction with Disk Utility in OS X.)

√   Delete browser caches in your Web browsers where applicable.

√   Keep the outside of your computer clean as well as your keyboard and mouse.

√   Check for updates weekly, including updates for drivers, software, firmware, and the operating system.

√   Optimize your hard drive occasionally with third-party tools.

√   Take out the trash every so often.

√   Keep anti-virus software up-to-date.

√   Back up your files often.

√   Delete files you don't need.

√   Delete programs you install and don't like.

√   Keep the desktop clean.

Of course, there are other things that you will add to this list. The point is, once you get degunked, you want to stay degunked!

Getting a Clean Start

Eventually you'll have to admit your computer is old, tired, and too run-down to perform the way you need it to. Computers don't last forever, not even Macs. Luckily, restoring your Mac to its original condition is pretty easy. In the last part of this book, you'll learn how and what to back up, how to save your preferences, and how to reinstall your Mac operating system so it'll run like new again. In addition, if you do decide to buy a new Mac, I'll show you how to make that move as painlessly as possible.

The Degunking 12-Step Program

Here is the basic 12-step degunking process that you should follow to fully degunk your Mac:

1. Get rid of the files you don't really need (Chapter 3).

2. Uninstall programs you don't need, fix programs that cause problems, and upgrade to newer versions that are OS X compatible (Chapter 4).

3. Organize your files and folders (Chapter 5).

4. Clean up the Dock, Finder, and Menu bar (Chapter 6).

5. Clean up the Fonts folder and font gunk (Chapter 7).

6. Reduce your e-mail spam and sort through and organize Apple's Mail (Chapters 8 and 9).

7. Optimize your OS X hard drive and Install the latest upgrades and updates (Chapters 11 and 12).

8. Add hardware such as RAM, additional monitors, and external backup devices; physically clean your Mac (Chapter 13).

9. Use available and third-party maintenance tools to keep your Mac running smoothly (Chapter 14).

10. Improve security with password protected screen savers, anti-virus software, File Vault, and more (Chapter 15).

11. Back up your system on a regular basis (Chapter 16).

12. Be aware of common problems and how to fix them (Appendix).

These steps are straightforward and easy to follow. If you set aside time to follow them, you'll save yourself a lot of time, money, and aggravation in the long run.

Summing Up

Now that you know what needs to be done, it's time to get started. Degunking your Mac by getting rid of clutter will help you find things faster and keep you organized. Getting rid of programs, fonts, and other applications you don't need will help your computer run faster. Setting up a security policy will help your computer run more safely. If you follow the degunking process detailed in this book, and if you believe in the degunking mindset, you'll be amazed how great your Mac will respond! Remember, there isn't anything wrong with you or your Mac. Your computer just needs some regular attention to keep running well!

Getting Rid of Files That Shouldn't Be There

Degunking Checklist:

√ Remove the excessive junk in your Home folders: Documents, Pictures, Movies, Music, Library, and Public.

√ Remove excess junk from personal folders you've created.

√ Delete or move files that are inappropriately placed in other areas such as the Macintosh HD and the Desktop folder (the desktop).

√ Delete unnecessary .zip, .sit, .tar, and .dmg files.

√ Remove unused user accounts and their files.

√ Remove temporary files (yes, they exist) stored on your system.

√ Remove excess gunk that might be shared by multiple users on your Mac.

√ Remove unnecessary and broken aliases.

W e're now ready to begin degunking by starting with Housekeeping 101. Here you'll quickly throw out what you don't need and start organizing what you keep. To get you in the proper mindset, think for a moment about the basic housekeeping chores you do (or should do!). You take out the trash on a regular basis, put away your toys after you're finished playing with them, and fold and put away your clothes. You also have to store your valuable pictures in a photo album (or shoebox), organize your CDs, and file your important documents. These tasks are necessary to keep your house from becoming a big fat mess.

The first step you'll take in degunking your computer is to get rid of clutter (in the form of files and folders) you don't need. If you're a packrat, this could be a little painful, but I'll help you get through it! We'll now take a look at what you've accumulated on your Mac in the last few months (or years). We'll get rid of all of the personal gunk you've added and don't need—music files, digital pictures that didn't make the cut, files you unzipped or unstuffed and no longer want or need, temporary files, duplicate files, unnecessary or broken aliases, unnecessary log files, and documents that are no longer needed (like that letter you wrote to the city complaining that the tax appraisal on your house was way off).

TIP: *This book was written using the Mac OS X (version 10.3 Panther) platform. Depending on the version of the Mac OS you use, the techniques detailed may differ slightly. For more information, refer to the introduction. As we go along, I'll also try to point out things that are specific to the Panther platform to help give you the proper context.*

When it comes to storing and managing files on your Mac, your system operates like a busy train station. There's a lot going on behind the scenes that you might need to be aware of. For example, if you use a digital camera or an iPod with your Mac, your images or music files are stored in a certain place and managed in a special way. If multiple users use your Mac, special areas are set up to store and manage the files that are common to the different users. I'm bringing all of this up because to be effective at cleaning up your Mac, you'll need to understand how your Mac operates under the hood. And as you'll learn in this chapter, a little knowledge can really help you keep your Mac clutter free.

TIP: *Mac OS X, version 10.3 is also known as Panther. When referring to the operating system version, I may use any of these terms.*

Clean Up Your Home Folder

I hope you've been saving some of your files to the default folders, located inside your Home folder. With Mac OS X, the folders are:

√   Documents

√   Pictures

√   Movies

√   Music

√   Library

√   Public

You can think of these folders as default folders inside the Home folder. If you haven't been saving to these folders, if you've simply saved everything haphazardly, or if you're created folders of your own, you should start the cleaning process here. For the most part, Mac OS X tries to guide you in the right direction each time you save a file. For that reason, you're likely to have a lot of stuff in these folders.

TIP: Because the desktop is such a gunk magnet, I'll give it its own section shortly. Even though the desktop is technically a folder, I believe most people would prefer to deal directly with the desktop itself.

Deleting superfluous files might not seem necessary if you have an 80 GB hard drive, but it is. When your Mac looks for a file, it has to search the entire disk for it. The more stuff it has to sift through, the longer the process takes. Additionally, deleting unnecessary files is certainly essential if you *don't* have a large hard drive, and it's especially important if you can't remember the last time you deleted anything. Whatever the case, I'm betting the bank that you can find plenty of stuff to delete!

TIP: Not only does it take your Mac more time to sort through unneeded files, but it takes you longer also. If you have folders that are bursting at the seams with files, you'll need to spend more time looking through all of the files to locate a needed file. Those extra minutes can really add up, especially if you use your computer a lot. Get all of the unneeded files off your Mac on a regular basis and you'll save yourself from a lot of eye strain and aggravation.

GunkBuster's Notebook: Saving Files 101

Mac OS X does its best to help you put files in the proper folders by offering up your Users folder as the default location for saving files. If you've never viewed the advanced options for saving files (or don't do so regularly), or if you've never taken the time to create personalized folders and use them, chances are that you have a myriad of files scattered about with no organization at all. Therefore, when saving files in the future, it's important to know where and how to save them. Figure 3-1 shows the default Save As dialog box for saving a JPG file: notice that the default is the Users folder. Figure 3-2 shows the same dialog box with advanced options selected: notice I've chosen to save this picture in the Pictures folder. Saving that particular file in the Pictures folder makes it easier to locate later and will help keep my files ungunked.

Figure 3-1

Using the default settings might not be the best way to save a file.

Figure 3-2

Using the advanced settings and choosing a folder for saving is a better choice.

From here on out, you should make a point to name all of your files descriptively too. Give each file a name that will easily identify what it is or represents. Even music files should be named appropriately. If you have a live version of "Stairway to Heaven," the original version, and a version you created in GarageBand using your own Stratocaster and with the help of a few friends, you should make sure each name reflects those different versions. Not only that, the name you choose needs to be descriptive enough so that you will know what it means five years from now when you're looking for that first song you and your new band created on your Mac.

The Documents Folder

Mac OS X provides a Documents folder for storing documents you create. (If you're not using OS X yet, you can create your own personalized folder for documents by creating a new folder in any appropriate window.) Stop reading for a minute and open up the Documents folder and take a peek at what's in there. If you see something you don't like, or something you don't need, delete it. Here's how:

1. Open the Finder window.
2. From the left pane, select your Users folder.
3. From your Users folder, select Documents. Figure 3-3 shows an example of what you might see. And yes, I understand I'm just as guilty as anyone for having a gunked-up Documents folder!

Figure 3-3
Here's a gunked-up Documents folder.

4. Locate a file or folder you want to get rid of and drag it to the Trash. Keep in mind, though, that if you delete a folder, you also delete everything else in it.

TIP: *If you don't know what something is (and that's a good possibility if you haven't named your files descriptively), open the file before deleting it just to ensure that it isn't anything you want to keep.*

Delete to your heart's content, but *be careful about deleting something you didn't create.* Don't delete any weird folders that look like misplaced applications, and don't move anything just yet. For now, let's just focus on taking out the garbage.

TIP: *You should also look at all of your aliases. They are essentially shortcuts you've created, as you'll learn later in this chapter. Aliases are displayed with a little arrow by them. You should always check them to see if they work, and if they don't or if you don't need them, delete them or use Get Info to select a new original.*

The Pictures Folder

Now that I have you in a deleting mood, let's take a look at some other folders. The newest Macs also provide a default folder for pictures, called the Pictures folder. If you have (and use) a digital camera or create your own artwork, you probably have a lot of files in there. If you use iPhoto, you'll have a subfolder named iPhoto Library. You'll also find plenty of pictures in there. The Pictures folder isn't the only place you'll find pictures, though. As you can see from Figure 3-3, I have pictures in my Documents folder. (That's gunk, by the way.)

Delete any pictures you don't need from the Pictures folder, as well as pictures in any other folders. If you find pictures in other folders that you'd like to keep, move them to the appropriate folder by dragging and dropping.

TIP: *Don't delete pictures you've linked to other files or used in movie projects. When those files and applications are opened, your Mac will try to access those missing pictures and you'll hear about it!*

---

iPhoto and Duplicate Files

If you use iPhoto to import pictures from your digital camera, you likely have duplicate pictures on your hard drive. Why? After importing an original picture into iPhoto (thus placing it in the iPhoto Library folder), you probably then open it, make some changes, and save the new and improved image in your

Pictures folder, in a personal folder you created for your clients or for artwork, or in a specific folder for graphics files. With that process complete, you likely don't delete the original. (Of course, you might not always want to delete the original, but many times you should.) If you don't need the original, you're just creating extra gunk!

In addition to this practice, if you choose not to delete images from your camera after uploading them, the next time you upload from the same camera, you might also upload files that are already saved. This results in duplicate files in iPhoto, as the example shown in Figure 3-4 indicates.

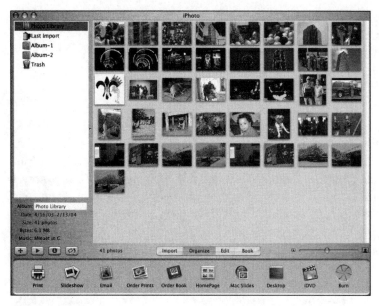

Figure 3-4
iPhoto offers a simple way to delete (and organize) picture files.

Because iPhoto is a common place for gunk, open it and delete anything you don't need. This is easier than deleting from the Pictures folder because iPhoto shows thumbnails of each picture in the iPhoto Library folder by default. It also has a place to drag images inside the iPhoto window and even has its own Trash folder. Once deleted from this application, a picture is also deleted from the Pictures>iPhoto Library folder stored in the Pictures folder.

With many of your documents and pictures now moved to the Trash, let's take a look at your movies.

GunkBuster's Notebook: Clean Up Digital Camera Gunk

You might have a bigger mess on your hands than you first thought if you have multiple cameras, or if members of your family who share your Mac have cameras that are different models. As an example, I have an old digital camera I take with me to the lake and to parties and another newer DV camera that I take to graduations, weddings, and less-volatile functions. Both cameras have their own software. With the newer camera, I use the proprietary software; with the older camera, I generally use iPhoto, but I've been known to use that camera's software too. My daughter has a camera and she uses my Mac and printer to print the pictures she wants to keep (imagine that). I'm sure she doesn't delete the pictures after uploading them. She has installed her camera's software on the computer too. You're getting the idea. We have a lot of digital camera gunk.

So, what you need to do is take a lesson from us! Don't just degunk iPhoto and the Pictures folder, but also clean up each of the software packages you have installed on your computer for each camera you have. Take inventory of your cameras and applications. Open each camera application and see where it stores pictures. Move the pictures you want to keep to the Pictures folder, create subfolders to organize them, and get them all in one place in your Users folder or a shared folder. This technique should also be used if you purchased a new camera and no longer use the old one or if you've purchased a specialty printer or piece of hardware that accepts memory cards. You may have saved some of those pictures to your hard drive too.

You'll be surprised what you'll find. I'll provide more tips on organizing your photos in Chapter 5.

The Movies Folder

Deleting movie files is a little trickier than simply dragging what you think you don't want to the Trash. With iMovie, you create a movie project file, capture video files from your camera, create clips, place those clips on the timeline, and then make a movie from the footage. Once the movie is made, you often won't need the original files, unless you plan to do something with them later or you want to archive them. So, when you start cleaning up your Movies folder, take inventory of the files that belong to a particular movie or project and decide what you want to keep and what you want to throw away.

Figure 3-5
Once a movie is complete, the original files might not be necessary.

In Figure 3-5, three items are shown: the first is the Media folder, which holds the clips created for the movie; the second is the project file itself (clicking this opens the project in iMovie); and the third is the movie itself (it has a .mov extension).

Figure 3-6 shows my Movies folder. Notice that the folder items are diverse; there is an AVI file, several MOV files, and several WMV files. AVI files are Audio Video Interleave format files and can be played by both Windows and Macintosh computers. MOV are QuickTime files and are played using the QuickTime video player. And WMV files are Windows Media Video files that can be played using Windows Media Player.

You'll have gunk in here just like you will in your Pictures folder. Once the raw footage is made into a movie, you might not need the original film. Get rid of that gunk! It takes up a huge amount of space on your hard disk.

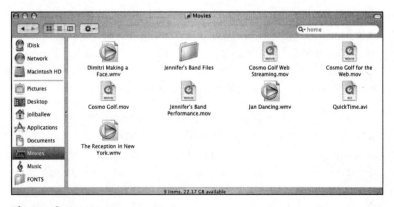

Figure 3-6
Here is an organized Movies folder.

TIP: *You can download Windows Media Player 9 for the Mac from Microsoft's Web site if you're unable to play WAV files using your installed programs.*

GunkBuster's Notebook: Understanding Where the Mac OS Looks for Files

You should really make an effort to save stuff in the right places on your hard drive. I'm not saying that because I'm obsessive-compulsive, either. Many of the applications you use are designed to look in specific locations for their files: iPhoto looks for pictures in the Pictures folder, your digital camera applications might look for pictures in another, iMovie looks for files in the Movies folder, iTunes stores its music files in the Music folder, and so on. If you start messing around and moving folders and files that are dedicated to your applications, you could be asking for trouble.

The Music Folder

The Music folder is just like any other specialized folder; it should contain only files and folders that pertain to its function—in this case, music. Depending on your hobbies and interests, you can have zero or a thousand files in the Music folder. Take a look inside to see if there's anything you can get rid of. Figure 3-7 shows mine. It's a little messy.

If you've subscribed to any file-sharing Web sites, you should verify that the music you downloaded still plays and that you have valid licenses. Some file-sharing music sites require you to pay a monthly fee, and if you stop paying, they revoke the licenses for the music you downloaded.

If you've purchased music through iTunes, you only need to worry about duplicate copies. Take inventory of the songs you've purchased from iTunes and other sites, and compare them to what you have in the Music folder. Figure 3-8 shows the iTunes folder, which is inside the Music folder with your other music. Inside that folder is the iTunes Music folder, which contains your downloaded songs.

Finally, if you've copied your own CDs to your hard drive, you might want to delete music you no longer want. If you've transferred them to your iPod and have them backed up in your physical CD library, it's probably okay to delete them here. You can always put them back if you decide to later. If you've digitized analog recordings of events from days past, you should check those files and make sure they still play too. There's no point in keeping stuff that doesn't work!

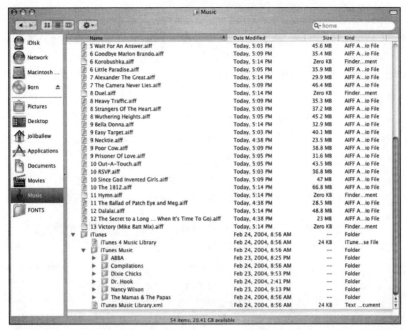

Figure 3-7

How many music files do you have?

Figure 3-8

The iTunes folder is located in your Music folder.

Tip: If you use the GarageBand software, make sure to work through those files too. There will probably be tracks, songs, and other data you no longer want or need.

Deleting music files is the same as deleting any other files. Here's how:

1. Open the Finder window.

2. From the left pane, select your Users folder.

3. From your Users folder, select Music. Figure 3-7 shown earlier presents an example of what you might see.

4. Locate a file or folder you want to get rid of and drag it to the Trash. Keep in mind that if you delete a folder, you also delete everything in it.

GunkBuster's Notebook: Locating and Deleting Duplicate Files

If you use iTunes to purchase music, chances are good that you won't have too many duplicate music files in the iTunes folder. Of course, I am assuming you don't have money to burn; if you do, you probably don't bother checking to see if you already have the music on hand before you purchase it, and you could likely have duplicate files! If you copy your own CDs to your hard drive, there is also a chance you could have some duplicates, perhaps different versions of the same song: one a live version, one from the original CD, and one from a "Best Of" collection. I'm sure you have duplicates on your iPod, but isn't that what it's for? If you ever wildly, illegally, and unabashedly downloaded songs for free off the Internet, or if you share files with friends using a file-sharing network, there's no telling what you have stored.

Because music files can be large, you should locate and delete duplicates. Much of the problem in finding duplicate files, though, is that you could have hundreds of music files to sift through, and simply sorting them by name might not offer up the information you need. The same song could be listed under various names.

To better locate duplicate music files, try these techniques:

√ Sort the songs by title, and scan for duplicate files.

√ Sort the songs by length, and scan for groups of songs with the exact same length.

√ Sort the songs by artist, and scan for duplicate titles.

√ Consider purchasing third-party software like DoubletScan or search for freeware and sharewhere at **www.versiontracker.com**.

The Library Folder

The Library folder stored in your Users folder contains things needed to personalize your Mac, such as your personal Keychain data, personal fonts, preferences files, favorites, printers, and much more. It also helps keep your personal data safe from other users who might use your Mac. Figure 3-9 shows what the Library folder *should* look like.

At this point, you should quickly check it to see if you have any stray files saved there like personal documents, music, or pictures. If you do, decide if you really need them, and move them (drag them) someplace where they're better suited, or delete them if desired. Notice in Figure 3-9 that there are no stray files in my Library folder.

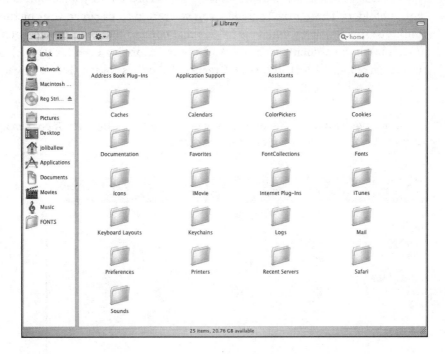

Figure 3-9
Look Ma! No lost files!

CAUTION! *The folders in the Library folder should be left alone! Don't delete or move anything you didn't create.*

The Public Folder

The Public folder in your Users folder is used to share documents and other items with coworkers on a network or others who share your Mac. It contains another folder called Drop Box, plus anything else you've put in there yourself. You can put files in there to share, or others can put files in there they want you to see. Take a look at the Public folder to see if there is anything you no longer need. If you don't share your Mac with other users, it's likely that you won't have any extra files in this folder to delete.

Personal Folders You've Created

Finally, take a look at any personal folders you've created in your Home folder and subfolders. These may be folders you've created to organize your pictures, music, or movies, or they may be folders that contain files for a project such as a scrapbook, for a client, for artwork, for publications, or even for your child's homework. Figure 3-10 shows an organized Pictures folder. (Don't forget to check out the aliases!)

TIP: *To create a new folder like the ones shown here, use Shift+Apple+N. Then, simply drag items to it. I'll talk more about that in Chapter 5.*

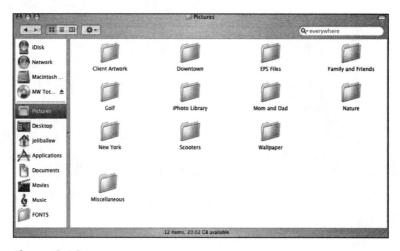

Figure 3-10
You can organize your files in personal folders you create.

Clean Up Your Desktop

Let's now concentrate on your desktop. It likely contains unneeded documents, pictures, music, movies, broken aliases, remnants of downloaded files and installations, and other gunk. The desktop is technically a folder, but you can work with it from inside the Finder or directly from the desktop itself.

In the following sections, we'll do a lot of degunking, including the following:

√ Remove unnecessary items.

√ Clean up the messes left by programs that have been downloaded and decompressed.

√ Change the text size used for folder and file names so the desktop feels larger and less cluttered.

√ Remove items using Finder Preferences.

√ Arrange items to personalize and maintain the desktop.

Remove Unwanted Items

The desktop can be a real gunk magnet. Applications and downloaded programs put stuff there. When you create a screenshot, it ends up there. Applications may also put their icons there. If you deleted any pictures, movies, or documents while working through this chapter, you probably have a lot of broken aliases too. If you deleted a file and then tried to access it using its alias, you saw a message similar to the one shown in Figure 3-11. (Figure 3-11 also shows quite a messy desktop, and the Dock is currently hidden.)

In my experience, it takes only a few days to gunk up a sparkling, clean desktop on a brand new Mac. It's certainly understandable if yours is a mess after months or years of use. So here is the desktop degunking procedure I recommend:

1. Check the aliases (the items on the desktop with arrows beside them), and then drag the broken aliases to the Trash.

2. Throw away any documents you've created or obtained that you no longer need or want, including pictures or music.

3. Focus on getting rid of stuff *you* created. Be careful about deleting application folders or files that don't look familiar. We'll talk about that other gunk shortly.

TIP: Remember, you can select multiple items by dragging the pointer over them.

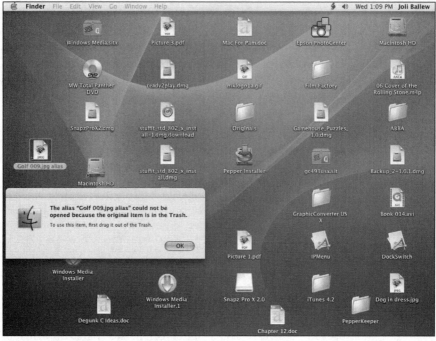

Figure 3-11
An alias will not work if its original file is in the Trash. (For some odd reason, aliases for folders do though.)

After removing the junk you don't need, drag the items you want to keep to their appropriate Home subfolder by following these steps:

1. Open the Finder and position it so you can still access the desktop.

2. Choose View>As Icons, and then choose View>Arrange>By Kind. (This only works if the Finder is set to View>As Icons.)

3. Locate any file you want to keep. If it's a document, drag it to the appropriate folder in the Documents window. Do the same for music, movies, or pictures. When dragging, hold down the mouse button while hovering the pointer over the appropriate folder; in a second or two, the subfolders will appear. Drop the file into the appropriate subfolder. Repeat as necessary. *Remember to move only files you've created!*

4. When finished, click an empty area of the desktop and choose View>Arrange>By Kind.

You'll still have items on your desktop after following the preceding steps. You will likely have downloaded installation files, icons for hard drives and network places, icons for items you really *want* to keep on the desktop, and other gunk. Once all of the personal files are in place and all broken aliases are removed, continue with the next section.

GunkBuster's Notebook: Automatically Clean Your Machine

If your Mac is severely gunked up with broken aliases, empty folders, orphaned files, and unused preference files, you might need a third-party utility to help you with the cleanup process. It can be difficult to work through every little corner of your machine looking for broken aliases and empty files and folder. Several third-party tools are available, but my favorite is File Buddy, available from **www.skytag.com/filebuddy/**. You can download this utility and use it for free for 30 days. You can purchase it for only $40 to $50 (U.S.).

File Buddy can help you with the following:

√ View file information in an Info window.

√ Find and repair broken aliases.

√ Move, delete, and copy files, including invisible files.

√ Erase files so that no unauthorized recovery can be performed.

√ Modify names of multiple files at the same time.

√ Use contextual menus to accomplish many tasks in a single step.

For even more options, visit **www.apple.com**, and search for "automatically repair broken aliases in OS X." The Web site **www.versiontracker.com** is also a good place to look for software for Mac OS X.

Clean Up Unzipped Files, StuffIt Files, Disk Image, and Tar Files

When you download programs from the Internet, most put an icon on the desktop for easy retrieval of the installation files. Once a program is installed, though, its installation files are no longer needed and can be deleted. Here are some common file extensions and icons to look for:

√ Disk drive icons—Left by installation packages. They should be dragged to the Trash once the program is installed.

√ .dmg—Indicates a disk image file. This file usually appears after the downloaded file has been decompressed.

√ .sit or .sitx—Indicates a StuffIt file, the standard Macintosh file-compression format.

√ .tar—Indicates a tape archive file, created with an older Unix utility that combines several files into a single "tape" archive, called a tarfile to simplify file transfers. These files are not compressed.

√ .gz—Indicates a gzip file, a standard Unix compression format.

√ .tar.gz or .tgz—Indicates a compressed archive of files.

√ .zip—Indicates a WinZip file, a common compression format for Windows computers.

You might also run across other file types, including Arc (.arc), Arj (.arj), BZip (.bz), Compact Pro (.cpt), LHa (.lha), Rar (.rar), and Unix Compress (.Z), although these file types are less common. You can safely delete all of these files. However, if you paid for the software and you want to keep it in case you have to reinstall it later or because you don't want to have to download it again, save the files with a .dmg extension.

TIP: *You can trash any files or folders that say Installer on them (as long as they've been installed). I have several on my desktop, including Windows Media Installer and Pepper Installer.*

Miscellaneous Items

To deal with the miscellaneous items on your desktop, you'll have to look at each one and determine if it is a functional application or a duplicate copy of something and if it is something you really need. You might find that you have folders that contain applications that don't work because you failed to purchase or register them, that the folders are duplicates of other folders stored elsewhere on the hard drive, or that they are items you simply don't need or want anymore. If they are applications that are not already in the Applications folder, you can drag them there; if they are copies, they can be dragged to the Trash. You might also have icons for a disk that can be ejected from the CD or DVD player. Figure 3-12 shows a desktop that has now been really cleaned.

GunkBuster's Notebook: Cleaning Up After Performing a Download and Decompression

You'll likely get tired of manually deleting the files that end up on your desktop after you download and install a program. There is an easy solution you can apply to deal with this. You can configure StuffIt Expander to delete such files automatically:

1. Double-click the hard disk icon on the desktop.

2. Open the Applications folder.

3. Open StuffIt Expander, and double-click the StuffIt Expander icon.

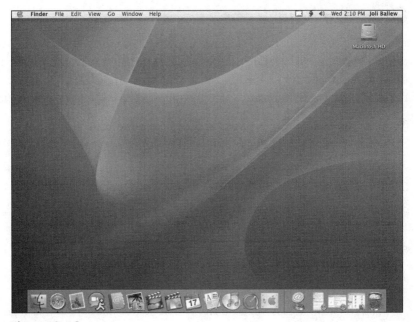

Figure 3-12
Now that's a clean desktop!

4. From the menu bar, choose StuffIt Expander>Preferences> Expanding.

5. Select both Delete After Expanding options. Click OK.

This is a good maintenance technique.

You can also tell Safari not to put downloads on the desktop at all. To create a dedicated download folder to hold all of your downloads, follow these steps:

1. Select the Finder. From the menu bar, select Go>Home.

2. From the Action menu, choose Select New Folder, and name the new folder Downloads.

3. Open Safari, and choose Safari>Preferences. Click General.

4. In the Save Downloaded Files To area, use the arrow to select Other.

5. From the new window, select the folder you just created, and click Select.

6. Close the Safari Preferences dialog box.

Organize Your Icons

Although I like a clean and uncluttered desktop, the ease of accessing things directly from there always lures me back in. The truth is, you're going to have stuff on your desktop, and at times it's going to seem cluttered. You can make it less disorderly and easier to maintain simply by setting the desktop's view options.

To make more room on your desktop and configure it so that it can be easily maintained, follow these steps:

1. Click an empty area of the desktop.
2. From the menu bar, choose View>Show View Options.
3. Use the Icon Size slider to make the desktop icons smaller.
4. Use the Text Size window to configure the text size.
5. Use the Label Position options to tell OS X where to put the labels for icons, on the bottom or on the right.
6. Select any of the following:

   √ Snap To Grid—Keeps items on an invisible grid so they are always aligned.

   √ Show Item Info—Shows information about the item underneath its name.

   √ Show Icon Preview—Shows icon preview when available. This is useful when scanning image files such as TIFF files. (Your Mac has to work a little harder to do this.)

   √ Keep Arranged By—Keeps the icons arranged by name, date modified, date created, size, kind, or label. This is a good tool if you regularly access items from the desktop and want to keep it organized. (If you choose this, Snap To Grid will be unavailable.)

7. Close the Desktop dialog box.

Remove Items from Your Desktop Using Finder Preferences

Another way to clean up the desktop involves removing items that are normally on it by default. With OS X, there's really no need to have the Macintosh HD icon on the desktop all of the time, unless you're just used to accessing things that way. You can just as easily open the Finder window and select the Hard Disk icon from there. The same holds true for CDs, DVDs, and iPods, as well as connected servers.

To remove unnecessary disks on the desktop:

1. Click an empty area of the desktop.
2. Choose Finder>Preferences from the menu bar.

Figure 3-13

Remove system icons you don't want.

3. Choose General, and deselect any items you desire. Figure 3-13 shows your options.

4. If you want the Finder window to open a different folder (not your Home folder) by default, make that selection from the New Finder Windows Open area.

5. Close the dialog box.

GunkBuster's Notebook: Maintaining Your Desktop

To organize the future gunk you plan to store on the desktop, follow these steps:

1. Create folders using the handy Shift+Apple+N keyboard short-cut.

2. Name the folders as if they were folders in a filing cabinet so that you can tell easily what's in each one. You might consider descriptive titles such as Taxes, Clients, Artwork, Poetry, Music, Films in Progress, and Hot Projects.

3. Move your stuff to the folders.

Remember that you're trying to organize your files and folders, so the more you can organize your folders like a filing cabinet or filing system, the better off you'll be.

TIP: As you progress through degunking, you'll learn how color-coded labels can help you get organized too. I'll talk about using them in Chapter 5, but for now, let's just try to get some basic organization done.

Clean Up Other Folders

Besides your Home folder, there are other folders that might need attention. Your Mac has a second Library folder that contains installer packages that can be deleted. Your system also provides a Shared folder that may contain files and folders. Some people also have data saved directly to their hard disk. Let's look at how to best clean these three areas.

The Second Library Folder

We already cleaned up the Library folder in your Users folder. A second Library folder is stored on your Macintosh HD though, and there are most likely items in there that you can safely delete to recover some hard disk space. This Library folder contains things your computer needs to work properly, such as fonts that everyone can access, logs, screen savers, scripts, desktop pictures, and similar items. I do not want you to delete any of these things! The data I want to address is data that has been misplaced that you've added. This folder should not contain anything you've personall created, like documents, pictures, or movies. here's how to locate and delete (or move) these misplaced files.

Here's how to locate and delete these unnecessary packages:

1. Double-click the Macintosh HD icon on the desktop.

2. Open the Library folder. This folder contains items for all users who access your Mac, such as screen savers, fonts, scripts, desktop pictures, user pictures, and more.

3. See if there are any misplaced files that you created or added.

4. Drag the items to their appropriate place on the hard disk.

The Shared Folder

The Shared folder is not in your Users Home folder like most of the folders I've previously discussed. Why? It doesn't actually belong to anyone; it is there for all the users on your Mac. It is the one folder each user can access, which makes it an easy target for gunk.

As I said, the Shared folder is a folder everyone has access to. If you wanted to, you could move your iTunes library there so that all users of the machine could access the songs you've downloaded. You might also create a Pictures folder in the Shared folder to store pictures that everyone can access, or a Movies folder to share your creations. Other users on the machine can do the same and add their own creations. Your budding musician might put his GarageBand creations there, and your budding movie maker might add movies. Unfortunately, many of the items put in this folder by other users are duplicates, and a good movie can take up a gig or so of space. Your budding musician will likely keep his own copy of his GarageBand creation in his personal Music folder for editing and future versions. You can imagine the gunk here.

There's a distinct difference between this Shared folder and the Public folder's Drop Box in your personal Users folder though; you are in control of your personal folder and can choose No Access if desired. You can also set the permissions to Read & Write, Read Only, or Write Only. The Shared folder's options, on the other hand, are grayed out and cannot be changed by just anyone.

Follow these steps to access the Shared folder and see what's in it:

1. Double-click the Macintosh HD icon on the desktop.
2. Open the Users folder.
3. Open the Shared folder.

Take a look at what's in there. Ask users of the computer if they still want to share the items they've added, and if not, delete those items. If junior has a newer version of "Stairway to Heaven," delete the old one and urge him to share the new one. If everyone has seen the movie your budding filmmaker has created, delete it. I'm sure she has a copy in her personal Movies folder, burned to a CD, or stored on a PDA. In addition, check the Fax folder. Delete any faxes that aren't needed. Finally, organize this folder with subfolders as detailed in this book and in previous sections.

GunkBuster's Notebook: Using the Shared Folder as a Gunk Buster

With a little bit of setup, the Shared folder can become a great degunking mechanism instead of just operating like a gunk magnet. Instead of saving your digital pictures, iTunes music, or movies in a single Users folder, you can store them in the Public folder so everyone who uses your Mac can access them. If you have several users, you might have lots of duplicate files and a lot of wasted space because each user has their own private copy of the same item. If you use iTunes, for example, you might even be paying for duplicate files!

To move a folder such as iTunes to the Shared folder, simply move the folder (iTunes is currently in a single user's Music folder) to the Users>Shared folder. Once that's done, anyone can open iTunes. Choose iTunes>Preferences>Advanced, and click the Change button to choose the relocated iTunes Music folder. You can also do the same with other folders. Now everyone who uses the computer can access the purchased music.

Clean Up Your Hard Disk Window

It's not uncommon for people to save some of their data directly to the Macintosh HD. For some reason, dragging a file off of the desktop straight to the HD icon is just too easy to pass up, even when you know it's not the best way to store your stuff. If you're a Mac user from way back, you might even do it out of habit. That's not really the best place for your data in OS X because your operating system is designed to take a more active role in where files are stored and how they are managed. You should now take a moment to look at what you have stored directly on your hard disk. This is easy to do:

1. Double-click the Macintosh HD icon on your desktop, or open it using the Finder.

2. There should only be operating system folders there. There should not be any stray files, folders you've created, or any other gunk. You should see Applications, Library, Users, and System and, depending on the operating system version and computer manufacturer, possibly folders named User Guides and Information, Applications (Mac OS 9), and an OS 9 System Folder.

3. If you see stray documents, pictures, movies, fonts, installation files, music files, client files, personal artwork, and similar items, drag them from this folder to their appropriate place in your Users folder. Once you have cleaned up this area, you'll want to try to be more disciplined about saving your files directly to the hard disk.

In addition to personal information, you may find items you don't need that came with your Mac. As I mentioned earlier, you may see a folder named User Guides and Information or something similar. After looking at the information stored there, you may decide you don't need the folder at all. My User Guides folder contains three rather large PDF files. I read them and deleted them. I won't suggest that you go mucking around in the other folders right now. Don't delete any applications yet (that's covered in Chapter 4). You also shouldn't delete anything from the Library folder or do anything else with the Users folder (I'll cover that in the next section). Also, leave the System folder, the OS 9 System folder, and Applications (Mac OS 9) folder alone for now (if you have them). I don't want you to mess anything up. Our main goal in this chapter is to recoup some hard drive space and help the hard drive function better.

GunkBuster's Notebook: Removing Unnecessary Language Files

If you only speak one language and you don't think you'll ever need the other languages that are installed on your Mac, you can delete them and free up hundreds of MBs of hard disk space. There are a myriad of software applications to help you do this, including J. Shrier's Monolingual and Bombich Software's Delocalizer. I chose J. Shrier's Monolingual to clean mine, and it worked great. Figure 3-14 shows the program in action.

Figure 3-14
Monolingual in action.

Here's how to obtain and use Monolingual:

1. Visit **http://homepage.mac.com/jschrier/** and click Download.

2. When the download is complete, open the Monolingual.dmg file and double-click the Monolingual icon.

3. In the Monolingual dialog box, select the language files to remove. Click Remove.

4. Type in your administrator's password and click OK.

5. Read the warning, and click Continue or Stop.

6. Wait while the process completes.

Clean Up the Users Folder

If other users have access to your Mac and they have their own accounts, you can bet they have left some of their own gunk around. The problem is that their gunk won't be as obvious to you. If you're really serious about degunking, you'll have to pass this book around so they can clean up their Home folders. If you previously had other users who accessed your Mac but no longer do, well, that's a different story. I'll show you how to get in and delete their old junk once and for all.

Deleting User Accounts

If you have a user who no longer accesses your Mac, you should delete the user account and the unnecessary files that go along with it. You'll have to be an administrator or have an administrator's password to perform these steps: as with installing applications and deleting important files and folders, only administrators can delete user accounts and user data.

To delete a user account, follow these steps:

1. Open System Preferences. Generally, it's on the Dock.
2. Open Accounts.
3. Select the account you want to delete, and click the Delete User symbol (the dash at the bottom of the dialog box).
4. You will be prompted with a warning that the contents of the user's Home folder will be saved in the Deleted Users folder in case you need that information again. Click OK to choose that option. If you do not want to save the user's data, click Delete Immediately.
5. If you choose OK instead of Delete Immediately and decide later to get rid of the saved data, simply drag the Deleted Users folder from the Users folder to the Trash.
6. When you empty the Trash, the file will be gone forever. If you do not empty the Trash, you can still retrieve the discarded DMG file.

If You Share a Computer

If you share your Mac with others and you use OS 10.3 or higher, you might have Fast User Switching enabled. Fast User Switching is a nice utility because it allows users to log off so another can log on without having to close open programs or working documents. Unfortunately, if the logged-out user leaves an application like Photoshop running, the Finder open, Safari open, and application files like Word and Excel files open, the CPU has to manage those items while you're using the computer. That's going to cause your Mac to take a performance hit, and you'll probably notice it. While Fast User Switching is nice, it's usually better to disable it.

To disable Fast User Switching (Panther and higher only), follow these steps:

1. Open System Preferences.
2. Open Accounts.
3. Deselect Enable Fast User Switching, as shown in Figure 3-15.

Search and Find Elusive Temporary Files

Programs create temporary files. These files are generally created in case you need to recover unsaved data after an unexpected crash. Temporary files are supposed to be automatically deleted when an application is closed or when your Mac is restarted. However, these files typically do not get deleted and remain somewhere on the hard drive when a program requires a Force Quit, when a program unexpectedly crashes, and after system crashes.

The operating system also creates temporary files. Some temporary files on your disk may be left over from system errors that you've already forgotten about. After a crash, these temporary files are placed in the Trash in a folder called Rescued Items. If you find a Rescued Items folder in the Trash, you can delete the files in it. Most of the time, temporary files are useless.

You can try to search for elusive temporary files and delete them, but this doesn't work very well. Temporary files are usually invisible, so to successfully locate the temporary files on your system, you'll need a third-party utility like FileBuddy, Norton Utilities, or DiskTop.

Figure 3-15
Disable Fast User Switching from System Preferences.

GunkBuster's Notebook: Working with OS X's Maintenance Schedule

Mac OS X does its own background maintenance and deletes temporary files on its own. The tasks run by default at 3:15 A.M. every day, 4:30 A.M. on Saturdays, and 5:30 A.M. on the first Sunday of every month (it uses your time zone). When background maintenance is running, the OS automatically deletes temporary files, cleans up log files, and removes unnecessary system files. This automatic maintenance keeps your Mac running smoothly.

However, these maintenance tasks won't run if your Mac has been shut down for the night, and they won't run if your Mac is in Sleep mode. If you turn your computer off at night or put it to sleep, you'll need to get a third-party utility to help you catch up during the day when the computer is idle. There are several available, including MacJanitor, which is free; OnyX for Jaguar and Panther, which is also free; and others, all of which are available at **www.versiontracker.com**. However, if you'd rather not gunk up your Mac with additional programs, simply turn off Sleep mode on the appropriate days and times and let your Mac catch up!

If you do decide to use a third-party utility, you might as well get one that will let you schedule when to run these maintenance utilities and perform other maintenance tasks too. Panther Cache Cleaner, from **http://northernsoftworks.com**, is one such program. For under $10 (U.S.), you can take control of the following:

√ Tune Internet and File Cache settings.

√ Improve startup performance by eliminating duplicate or orphaned login items.

√ Maintain system health by automating maintenance chores.

√ Repair disk permissions.

√ Kill and restart the Finder.

√ Use in all user accounts.

√ Repair OS 9 permissions.

√ Execute Mac OS X maintenance scripts.

Manage Aliases

As I mentioned earlier, aliases represent a duplicate of an original icon for an application, document, or other item. (For all of you newly converted PC users, an alias is pretty much the same as a shortcut you create in Windows, except aliases are smarter.) Aliases can be created and placed in any folder on your Mac to provide access to the original item. An alias requires very little hard disk space because it is simply a link to another item on the computer. Creating aliases allows you to access the original file or folder from inside any folder.

Aliases are pretty smart too. You can rename the alias or the original file or folder, move the alias, or move the original and the alias will still open the original file or folder (well, most of the time). You can even use an alias to create a shortcut to another hard disk. Figure 3-16 shows an example of an alias.

Figure 3-16
Aliases can be created for files, folders, or applications.

Problems with broken aliases occur when the original file is no longer available, most likely because the item was moved to the Trash. However, you can accidentally burn an alias (instead of the original files or folders) to a CD or DVD and create your own broken aliases in that manner. The point is, if you use an alias to access a file, if that file is missing or on another non-networked computer, you won't find it. If you burn an alias of a file to a CD or DVD, take that to another computer (or worse, a meeting), and try to open the file, it won't be there. If you encounter a broken alias, you can delete it or try to repair it.

From the contextual menu of an alias (hold down the Control key and click the alias's icon), there are two extremely useful options for working with aliases. You can choose Show Original to locate and access the original file, or you can choose Get Info to select a new original for a broken alias. If you only need access to the original, select Show Original. To select a new original for a broken alias and thus repair the alias, do this:

1. Hold down the Control key and click the alias's icon.

2. From the menu that appears, choose Get Info.

3. In the Get Info dialog box, choose Select New Original.

4. From the Select New Original dialog box, locate the original file or folder and click Choose.

5. Close the Alias Info dialog box; the alias is repaired.

TIP: *Remember that an alias is just that—an alias of the original file. Don't burn an alias to a CD and head out to a presentation. You'll be in for a shock when all you get is a broken alias warning box.*

Summing Up

In this chapter you started degunking. You deleted documents, pictures, movie files, and music that you don't need anymore or that were duplicates. You learned how to systematically clean up your desktop and keep it clean using some clever maintenance tips and tricks. You learned how to get rid of users who no longer access your Mac and how to locate temporary files, and you learned a little about aliases and how to delete them or repair broken ones. Let's now move on to degunking applications!

Uninstalling Programs You Don't Need (and Tweaking Those You Do)

Degunking Checklist:

√ Remove the programs you no longer use by dragging them to the Trash.

√ Remove a deleted application's preferences file.

√ Remove programs you don't even know you have.

√ Remove spyware and adware.

√ Remove downloaded applications you don't need or want.

√ Remove programs for hardware you no longer own.

√ Tweak the programs you want to keep.

√ Understand the differences between Classic, Carbon, and Cocoa applications and the importance of upgrading to OS X.

f you've deleted all the unnecessary documents, pictures, movies, and music from your computer (and anything else you may have run across, including saved chats, sticky notes, DVD project files, and faxes), you've taken a gigantic step forward in reducing the amount of clutter on your Mac!

As you've learned, when you reduce clutter, you improve the performance of your system. You also improve your personal performance and efficiency because all of the junk has been put in the Trash and you no longer have to sift through it to find what you want. The next step after removing unnecessary personal items is to remove programs and applications you don't use and their related preferences files.

In addition to removing programs you *don't* use, though, you can remove programs you *can't* use, such as the image application you installed with your first Web cam. You don't need that now that you have iSight. You can also look for programs that you installed with printers you no longer own or programs for an old scanner or digital camera you no longer use. You may also have programs that have expired (as shown in Figure 4-1), beta programs you tested and didn't like, or programs you tried but didn't buy. Finally, if you've recently purchased the newest version of Photoshop, you might no longer need or want Photoshop Elements or similar programs.

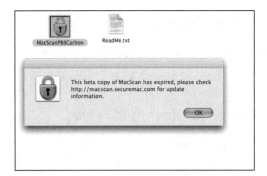

Figure 4-1
Some programs simply don't work anymore, for whatever reason.

You Mac came preinstalled with things you might not need. Although I'm not recommending it, you can delete iMovie, iTunes, iDVD, iPhoto, iCal, and other built-in applications if you desire. You can certainly delete Tony Hawk's Pro Skater 4, the trial version of Microsoft Office that expired months ago, and similar programs as you deem necessary. Finally, you should scan your computer for adware or spyware programs and get rid of any you find. Although this is not yet a major issue with Mac users, it will be in the future, so it's best to get on that bandwagon now.

CAUTION! Your Mac probably came with a restore disk, so if you need to reinstall any of the deleted applications that came with your Mac, you may be forced to reinstall the entire OS. There is a trick to installing a single application and it can be done, but it's a little complicated, so be careful of what you delete!

Remove Programs You Don't Use

It's important to delete programs you don't use anymore because unnecessary programs take up disk space and require you to search longer for the things you want. They also clutter up your Applications folder and may affect how long it takes your computer to boot up, depending on how the applications are configured. After looking around, you might decide to delete the following:

√ Working programs that you no longer want (genealogy, gardening, home projects, games, and similar applications)

√ Beta programs you downloaded and installed that you didn't like or that don't work properly

√ Programs that need to be registered and whose trial versions have expired

√ Freeware or shareware programs that you don't need

√ Applications that came with older, broken, or unused Web cams, scanners, or printers

√ Programs that shipped with your Mac but you never use

√ Applications in the Applications (Mac OS 9) folder on the HD (if you have one) that were installed but are never used

Cleaning Out the Applications Folder

Let's start by using these steps to clean out the Applications folder (a likely place to find program gunk you don't need):

1. Open the Macintosh HD.

2. Open the Applications folder. (After you've worked through these steps, return here, open the Applications (Mac OS 9) Folder if you have one, and repeat the steps again to clean out that folder.)

3. Expand the folder to show all of the applications. You can also use the View>As Columns option to see the applications in column view. (Press Option+Command+D to hide the Dock so you can see the entire window.) Figure 4–2 shows a sample Applications folder. This folder is pretty clean; yours might have many more applications.

4. Browse through the applications that you installed or that came preinstalled on your Mac, noting third-party applications only.

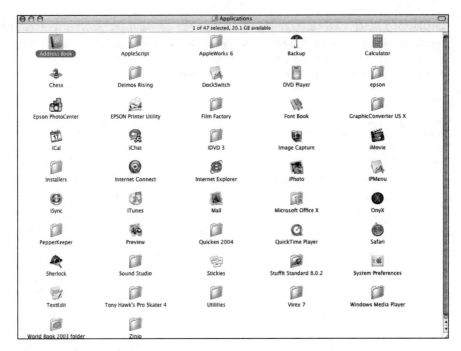

Figure 4-2
Open the Applications folder to view its contents.

5. Open any program you are not familiar with so you can determine what it is and if you need it.

6. For now, only delete the *third-party applications* you don't want. Don't delete iCal, iDVD, iPhoto, or anything similar. Also, don't delete items you might confuse for third-party applications such as Address Book, Font Book, Internet Connect, Preview, and TextEdit. As an example (and for the purpose of helping you choose which programs to delete), I will get rid of the following applications:

√ Deimos Rising—This is a game that came installed with my eMac. I don't want to play this game and can therefore delete it. It also generated a crash report when I tried to quit the program after playing a short game to verify that I wasn't interested.

√ Graphic Converter US X—This program always prompts me to buy the program when I open it. I would buy it if I want to continue using it, just to be fair to the makers of the application. I haven't used it in two months and plan to buy Photoshop next week.

√ Microsoft Office X—This is a trial version of the program and includes Microsoft Entourage, Excel, PowerPoint, Word, MSN Messenger, and more. I don't plan to purchase this software, and it has expired. (Even when it was in its trial version if offered limited functionality.)

√ PepperKeeper—I used this program to keep track of my child's homework assignments a while ago. I don't use it anymore.

√ Tony Hawk's Pro Skater 4—I'm 40 years old. 'Nuff said.

√ Zinio—I don't even know what this is. Upon opening the program and accepting the license agreement though, I see it's a magazine reader application. I'm not planning on reading magazines on my Mac, so I can delete this.

Get the idea? Just delete the items you don't want and don't need. At this particular juncture you only want to delete third-party applications that you recognize and no longer want.

TIP: Some programs have uninstall options inside the folder. Microsoft Office X, the trial version on my computer, has an icon to "Remove Test Drive." If that's available, use it, and then drag the whole folder to the Trash when the uninstall routine is finished.

Deleting Preferences Files

A preferences file contains the information an application needs to keep track of your customized settings. The preferences file is what the program uses to remember that you don't want to use automatic bullets or numbering and what file type you want to save in by default, among other things. Once an application has been deleted, you don't need those files gunking up your Mac. You'll need to delete the preferences file associated with the deleted program manually; if you don't, you're just keeping unnecessary gunk around. Preferences files are located in the user's personal Library folder, in a folder called Preferences. You'll learn how to delete them next.

Figure 4-3 shows the Preferences folder for user joliballew. Notice there are preferences files (they end in .plist) for applications I just deleted. You'll find similar preferences files on your Mac. To delete these unnecessary files, follow these steps:

1. Open the Finder and select your user name.

2. Open the Library folder and then the Preferences folder.

3. Work through the list, deleting files associated with programs you have previously deleted.

4. To delete the file, Control+click it and choose Delete.

CAUTION! Don't delete preferences files if you don't know what program they're associated with!

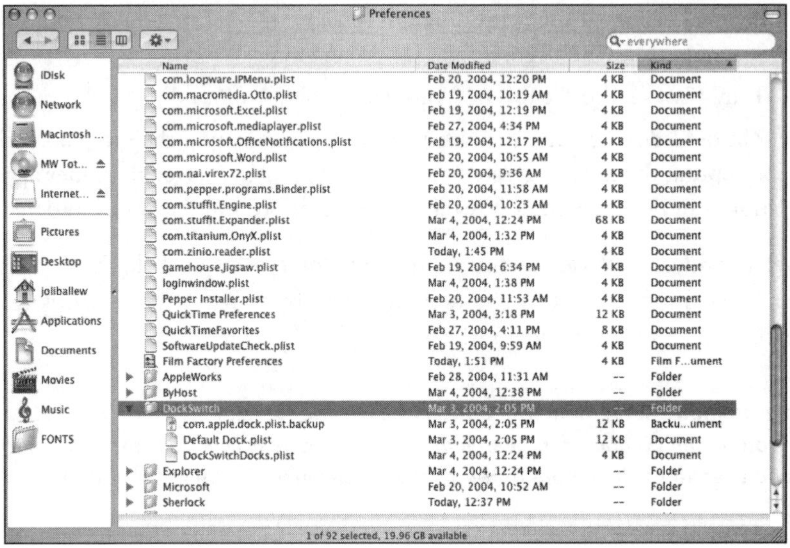

Figure 4-3
Preferences files are gunk once their associated applications have been deleted.

There are two more Preferences folders. Besides the one in your Home folder, there's another in the hard drive window whose files can only be deleted by an administrator. There's probably not enough gunk in there to warrant risking deleting them, but you can open and browse around in there if you want. Just don't delete anything if you don't know what it does! The third Preferences folder is inside the System>Library folder and can't be trashed by anyone.

TIP: *If you have a System 9 System Folder on your Macintosh HD, open it and look at the Preferences folder there too. Remember to only delete preferences files for programs you recognize and have previously deleted.*

GunkBuster's Notebook: Preferences Files Can Cause Problems

A corrupt preferences file can cause a program to behave erratically. It can, for example, cause crashes when the program opens or when a document needs to be saved. Deleting a preferences file can thus be used to troubleshoot an application.

If an application is behaving erratically, log in using a different user account, open the program, and see if you can replicate the problematic behavior. If you can't, the problem may lie with your

personal preferences file. To test that theory, log back on using your user account, delete the preferences file for that program, and then restart the program. On restart, the program will create a brand new preferences file, which should solve the problem. (You'll have to re-create your preferences if this solves the problem.) If the problem still exists, salvage the old preferences file from the Trash and continue troubleshooting.

Remove Programs for Hardware You No Longer Own

If you've had your Mac for a long time, you probably have software installed that works with hardware you no longer own. This hardware is likely a Web cam, a printer, or a scanner, but it could also be hardware that just never worked right, such as a digital camera or a used CD burner. Take a look around your computer and take inventory of what hardware you actually have. Then, open the Applications folder and see what you can get rid of. I'm betting you'll find old printer and scanner software, at the very least.

I make mention of printers and scanners specifically because they are the worst culprits for gunk. Almost every printer and scanner past and present comes with programs for enhancing photos, converting them to different formats, publishing or e-mailing them, and similar tasks. If you use a different program to perform editing tasks (which you probably do), these programs are unnecessary. They're doubly unnecessary if you no longer own or use the hardware.

TIP: Don't forget about broken or lost PDAs, software for an old digital camera, pen/camera/Web cam/coffee maker all-in-one hardware, and similar items.

Don't Need iApps?

I keep seeing articles in magazines encouraging users to delete iApps they don't need. These include iMovie, iTunes, iSync, iPhoto, iCal, and iChat, as well as games like Chess and additional browsers such as Internet Explorer. That may be all well and good in theory, but in reality, most Mac users are going to have a hard time reinstalling those iApps if they are deleted and needed later. You can always download Internet Explorer, but if you want iMovie back, you might find yourself in a fine predicament.

Although you can delete just about anything you want, including items you think you might never need like iTunes or iMovie, my approach is to let them be. You just never know when you'll be put in charge of filming a wedding, when a guest will arrive and need their iTunes fix, or when your newly graduated college student will move back in and want to know where iChat went. If you must, though, open your Applications folder and drag the offending programs to the Trash.

TIP: Don't toss out utilities from the Utilities folder. You'll likely need them at some point. Example of utilities include Font Book, Bluetooth File Exchange, Grab, and Internet Connect.

Find Programs You Don't Even Know You Have

If you haven't opened each of the applications that you have installed on your computer, you may still have programs you don't need. The only way to know what an unfamiliar program does is to open it, use it for a moment, and see if you still need it. If you don't, trash it! My rule of thumb is that if I have an application on my computer that I haven't used in a year and I've forgotten all about it, I probably won't ever use it again.

TIP: Don't forget to check out that Applications (Mac OS 9) folder, if you have one!

In addition to programs you can see, there might be some programs installed on your computer that you can't view. If you've used illegal music file-sharing Web sites, visited porn sites, or agreed to install software from similar Web pages, spyware or adware may have installed itself on your computer without your knowledge. With a Mac, the chance of becoming infected is pretty slim, not only because of the password requirements but also because hackers and bad guys would prefer to spend their time infecting a PC user's computer rather than your Mac.

At the time this book was printed, there were no widespread spyware and adware threats and no spyware or adware programs that I would deem effective against future threats. This is not to say that in a few years these threats won't be real. You should occasionally visit **www.versiontracker.com** and search for spyware utilities. Chances are good there will be free ones available that will allow you to verify that there are no unknown programs on your computer.

TIP: To see every software program installed on your Mac, open Macintosh HD>Applications>Utilities>System Profiler and select Software>Applications.

Tweak Programs You Do Need

Once you've pared down the programs you have installed on your computer, you should tweak the ones you have for optimal performance. Almost all programs have preferences that can be set, options that can be configured, and different options to view the files and folders. When you close the program and open it again, it almost always remembers your preferences.

In addition to configuring a program's preferences, you can further enhance an application's performance by doing the following:

√   Configuring the applications View options

√   Understanding the differences between Classic, Carbon, and Cocoa applications and upgrading when possible

√   Continuing with the degunking processes in this book

Configure Program Preferences

Every program you install has some preferences that can be configured for optimal performance. If it's a game, you might configure the screen resolution (and close all open programs while playing); if it's a word processing program, you might configure autocorrect options or add words (like *degunking*) to the dictionary; or if it's a Web browser, you might configure it to open to a specific Web page every time. Whatever the application, you should search for and configure preferences or options.

Table 4-1 offers some of my favorite tweaks for the applications that come with Mac OS X Panther. As you explore these tweaks, take a look at each application's additional options and preferences settings. You will probably find other tweaks to enhance performance.

Table 4-1   Tweaks for Panther and iLife Applications

Application Name	Tweak	Procedure
GarageBand	Optimization	GarageBand>Preferences>Audio/Midi>Optimize For and select an option.
iChat	Saving received files	iChat>Preferences>General>Save Received Files to>Other. Browse to and select a specific folder for saving received files. Do not save them to the desktop (the default).
iDVD	Deleting unnecessary files	iDVD>Preferences>General>Delete Rendered Files On Closing A Project.
	Turning off annoying music	From the iDVD interface, select Customize. In the window, choose Settings, and click the Audio button to turn off the default music.
iMovie	Smoother motion	iMovie>Preferences>Advanced>Standard Quality (Smoother Motion).
iPhoto	Opening a photo in a specific editing program	iPhoto>Preferences>General>Double-Click Photo:>Opens Photo In, and then click the Select Application button. Select the appropriate program from the Finder window.
	Changing thumbnail view size	Open iPhoto, move slider to change thumbnail view.
iTunes	Creating smart playlists	File>New Smart Playlist. Create criteria for a playlist that will be automatically updated based on your personal preferences.
Preview	Enhancing speed	Preview>Preferences>General. Select from Show Image Only and Show Name Only and configure the thumbnail size by moving the Thumbnail Size slider.
Stickies	Creating transparent stickie window	Note>Translucent Window.
Virex (only with a .Mac membership)	Avoiding slow starts	Virex>Preferences. Deselect Automatically Scan At Login.

Configure View Options

You can also configure your programs to show files and folders in a specific view, and you can configure Safari with tabs of your choice. Let's take a quick look at the view options for some of the common applications first. As with the preferences section earlier, take some time to experiment with the options so you'll know what's available. The more you know, the faster and smarter you can work!

Here are some tips for getting the most out of some common applications:

√   In iCal—Switch the view to see what is on the calendar for a day, a week, or a month.

√   In iPhoto—Switch the view to Film Rolls for better organizational options and faster opening of the application.

√   iTunes—Turn the Visualizer off if performance suffers when playing music or listening to the radio.

For any applications, where applicable, choose to view smaller thumbnails or no thumbnails at all, choose not to obtain information from the Internet automatically, turn off animations or visualizations for better performance, and reduce the text size of the file names to increase the amount of items that can be viewed in the Finder.

TIP: *For even better performance, open System Preferences>Appearance, and in the Font Smoothing Style choices, select the option that best describes your monitor (CRT, Flat). In addition, enable Use Smooth Scrolling; this makes documents more legible while you scroll.*

Safari's Enable Tabs Feature

If you spend a lot of time surfing the Web, you'll appreciate Safari's tabbed browsing feature. This feature allows you to open multiple Web pages and switch between them using tabs you define and create. Want to degunk the way you surf? Configure the tabbed browsing feature to include your most-visited Web sites and have access to them from the interface itself! They'll always be ready, too, and will make a great addition to the browser for anyone with a fast Internet connection. (Having multiple pages open at once can slow down a dial-up connection, so you'll have to weigh the pros and cons if you haven't upgraded to cable or DSL yet.)

Here's how to enable Safari's tabbed browsing feature and create your own tabs for your favorite sites:

1.   Open Safari, choose Safari>Preferences, and click the Tabs button.

2.   Select the options Enable Tabbed Browsing, Select New Tabs As They Are Created, and Always Show Tab Bar. This is shown in Figure 4-4. Close the Preferences window.

3.   Open any Web page by typing its URL or click a link to a Web site from an open page. Notice that the new tab is placed under the existing ones. By default, any time you type a Web address or open a new link, the new Web address will take over the current tab.

Figure 4-4
Enable tabbed browsing using Safari's Preferences options.

4. To create a new tab and leave the old tab intact, Control+click the new link or Web address. Choose Open In New Tab. A new tab will be created.

There are also other choices—you can choose Close Tab to delete a tab or use Command+click to bypass the menu option to create a new tab automatically. Once you have your tabs set up, you'll wonder how you ever got along without them!

TIP: Even better than the tabs is Safari's built-in feature to block pop-up windows. To enable this feature, choose Safari>Block Pop-Up Windows.

The Operating Environments: Classic, Carbon, and Cocoa

The Apple you have grown to know and love has changed. The Mac OS X operating system is drastically different from its predecessors, and for the better! This is a good move for Apple and will greatly enhance all subsequent versions of Macs and the applications written for them. For the moment, though, we're all in a little bit of limbo while we wait for manufacturers to catch up with this new technology. In a few years, all of the kinks will be ironed out; for now, though, we have to be extremely patient while the creators of the software get their applications updated and catch up with the changes Apple has made. (You'll also need to prepare yourself to purchase or upgrade to the new applications as they become available.)

If you're new to OS X, be it Jaguar or Panther or some version beyond that, and you're a veteran Mac user, you're probably a little confused. Why all of the change? Why won't older programs run normally in OS X? Why is there an Applications folder for OS 9 on the Macintosh HD? And why does Classic start up when an older program is run? It's understandable that you're confused! (If you are a new

Mac user entirely and have recently made the switch from Microsoft, you've probably been through this before when upgrading Windows 98 to Windows XP; it's kind of the same thing.)

In a nutshell, Apple wanted to revamp the operating system and make significant changes. These changes were created to enhance performance and security and allow the management of multiple users on a single computer. Apple also wanted applications to run independently of each other so that if a single application crashed, the computer would not need to be rebooted. The entire architecture of the OS has changed to support these features.

For these changes to be made, the operating system itself had to be dramatically altered. Altering the operating system so dramatically has caused application manufacturers to also alter how they write current and future programs. In order to keep from causing massive and immediate conflicts, though, Apple left an out for software companies who did not have the resources or money to completely redo their applications and created an environment where older applications could be run in OS X. That's the Classic environment. However, they also want to encourage companies to update their software when possible, so Apple has two other types of programs manufacturers could write, Carbon and Cocoa.

Applications and OS Versions

There are three kinds of applications that can be run on your OS X computer: Classic, Carbon, and Cocoa. An introduction to these terms is a necessary addition to this chapter because they describe different types of applications for your Mac.

Classic applications are older applications that have not been updated and might never be. Companies go out of business, users get used to a particular program and don't want to upgrade, and others simply don't want the expense of purchasing additional software. When these Classic programs are opened in Mac OS X, Mac OS X launches the Mac OS 9 Classic environment. The Mac OS 9 Classic environment is just what it sounds like: it turns your brand-new OS X computer into an OS 9 retro machine. The application can run fine in this environment, although you won't have access to all of the cool stuff in OS X.

Carbon applications are updated versions of Classic applications. They can run in OS X (and many can also run in OS 9). Carbon applications also support OS X's crash protection and other features, but in reality, a Carbon application is just an adapted version of the Classic version. The application will feel like OS X, though, and that's a start. Many companies have produced carbonized applications so that they can quickly adapt to OS X and make their products compatible. Apple allowed Carbon to exist as a stop-gap measure to ease the transition from the old OS to the new one.

Finally, Cocoa applications are created from scratch by manufacturers to run on OS X. The iChat, iPhoto, TextEdit, Stickies, Mail, and other included applications with OS X are Cocoa applications. For the best performance possible, you should move to Cocoa applications as these programs become available. For more information on Cocoa applications, visit Apple's Web site or the Web site of your favorite application.

TIP: *Chapter 10 is all about optimizing OS 9 and details Classic mode in depth.*

Summing Up

In this chapter you learned how to locate and get rid of unwanted applications, including beta applications, unnecessary programs, and unnecessary Mac OS X applications. Getting rid of unnecessary applications frees up hard drive space and guarantees that those programs aren't running in the background and using up system resources. You learned a little about the future spyware and adware threats and how to move forward to protect yourself. You also learned how to tweak the programs you want to keep by setting preferences and view options. Tweaking a program so that it meets your needs saves you much time and effort when you're working. And finally, you learned the differences between Classic, Carbon, and Cocoa applications and why upgrades are necessary.

Organizing Your Remaining Files and Folders

Degunking Checklist:

√ Organize the Home folders by creating additional embedded folders, and then move or copy files and other folders into them.

√ Label files and folders for color-coded organization and easy access.

√ Compress and archive data you don't access often.

√ Use the File>Find command to locate any additional unwanted data.

√ Empty the Trash, including the trash inside applications such as iPhoto and iMovie.

√ Use OS X's Secure Empty Trash command.

√ Understand how hard disk fragmentation occurs and how to defragment your hard drive.

Now that you've deleted unnecessary files and applications, it's time to organize what you have remaining on your hard drive. Comparing this to our housecleaning analogy in the first few chapters, this part of degunking is like cleaning out the garage: You need all of the stuff in your garage, but you don't want to trip over it each time you need to use the car. You want to be able to find stuff easily when you most need it.

In this chapter, you'll learn how to create folders for organizing your desktop and Home folders. You'll also learn the difference between copying and moving data and when to do each. You'll learn about Panther's options for color-coding folders and some neat tricks for getting data where it should be. (Did you know that iTunes has a command under the Advanced menu to consolidate your music library automatically? It does!)

After you get everything where you want it, I'll show you how to find out how much hard disk space the Trash is taking up, and then I'll show you the best ways to empty the Trash. With your files now organized and the Trash empty, we'll defragment your drive. Once that is done, your Mac should be zipping along at breakneck speed.

Better Organize the Home Folders

The simplest way to organize your data is to create personal folders inside of the Home folders and move existing files into a folder that details its contents. For instance, all of the pictures of your vacation to Italy should be in a subfolder named Italy Trip, and all of the documents that pertain to taxes should be in a folder named Taxes. You could even have subfolders inside of the Italy Trip folder named Florence, Rome, and Venice, or you could have subfolders inside the Taxes folder named 2004, 2005, 2006, and so on. As discussed earlier, the default folders you can access from your Home folder, including Desktop, Documents, Movies, Music, Pictures, and Public, make excellent places to store data. By creating your own subfolders inside these folders, you can create a tree structure that organizes your data in the same manner a filing cabinet would.

TIP: Unless you've personally partitioned your hard drive or you run a dual-boot system, you'll most likely have one hard disk partition where you store data, and that's it. If you've tweaked your system or have other special circumstances, you might have a separate partition just for data. Either way, you'll want to determine on what partition data should be saved before continuing if you have more than one partition. You can view your disk drives from the Finder window.

Personalize the Home Folder

Your Home folder is the best place to start organizing. Take a look at Figure 5-1. It shows a fairly degunked Home folder. Notice that the default folders are there, along with folders I've created, including Book Chapters, Book Screen Shots, Client Artwork, Downloads, Hot New Ideas, Personal Artwork, and Taxes. Some of these have subfolders, too. Many of these folders could have been created in the Documents folder or the Pictures folder, but I prefer to have them here. In addition to the folders I have created, I'm using ones that were there already, and I've deleted a few I didn't need, including Magazines. Of course, how you choose to organize your work is up to you.

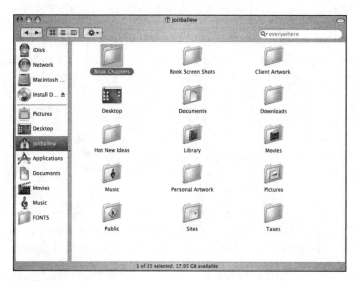

Figure 5-1

An organized and totally degunked Home folder makes finding data easy.

While your Home folder might not look so organized, it's easy to start the cleaning and organizing process here. Just take a look at the data you've decided to keep. Do you have tax information, personal letters, artwork, poetry, music you've created with GarageBand, letters of complaint, receipts or confirmations from bills you've paid online, or other data? Take inventory and decide on some categories, and then follow these steps to create folders (you'll use these same steps to create subfolders and folders in other default folders, including the Desktop folder):

1. Open the Finder and select your user name.

2. From the Action menu, choose New Folder.

3. Type a name for the folder and press Return on the keyboard.

To create a subfolder in any folder, open that folder and perform the same steps. With the appropriate folders created, you can now move forward and start organizing!

GunkBuster's Notebook: Organizational Ideas for the Creative

When creating folders and subfolders, take a moment to think about what you use your Mac for the most. The hardware you have connected to your Mac generally gives you a clue there. Do you have iPods, digital cameras, DV cameras, or musical instruments hooked up? If so, you should start there. If you need a little help deciding what folders to create, what to name them, and where to store them, consider these ideas:

√   If you have a digital camera and take a lot of pictures, create folders with subfolders that are named after the type of pictures you've taken: Weddings, Vacations, Wild Parties, Building Our Home, and folders for each of your children and each of your pets.

√   If you are a freelance artist or run a graphics company, create folders that contain artwork for specific companies or clients. You might also have folders for artwork in progress, finished artwork you can archive, and artwork ideas.

√   If you have a scanner and are the family genealogist, create a folder named Scans and create subfolders for each branch of the family tree.

√   If you use an iPod regularly, create a folder on your desktop (or an alias to your Music or iTunes folder) so that you can access those files quickly.

√   If you create GarageBand projects for fun or profit, organize your GarageBand tunes by date created, by name, by client, or by song.

√   If you have a DV camera and take a lot of video, create subfolders inside the Movies folder that are named after the type of movies you've created.

The idea is to take a good, hard look at what you use your Mac for and create folders that represent who you are and what you do.

Personalize the Desktop

You can create folders inside the Desktop folder too. The new folders will appear inside the Desktop folder in the Finder and on the desktop. Creating folders that stay on the desktop might be easier or more desirable if you use the desktop often and plan to continue doing so. There are two ways to create folders on the desktop; perform the steps in the previous section for the Desktop folder or use the following steps:

1. Click an empty area of the desktop.

2. Choose File>New Folder, or use the Command+Shift+N key combination.

3. Type a name for the folder.

The technique of placing folders directly on the desktop allows you to continue to save items to the desktop in the default fashion and then quickly move them to the desired folder easily and quickly when you're ready to store them. Not that it matters, but I prefer a clean desktop, simply because it looks nicer and forces me to use the Finder. My Finder folders are organized and make locating things quick and easy. Using the Finder every time helps me keep things organized.

Move Data into the New Folders

After creating the folders to store your data, you'll need to move the data into them. Notice I've used the word "move." If you copy the information, it will be in two places. Having data in two places complicates things and uses up unnecessary space on your drive. There's no point in copying your pictures into subfolders if you're going to leave a copy somewhere else. If you want to have multiple access points to your data, you should consider using aliases. Creating an alias for your data isn't considered moving it either. (Recall that an alias is simply a shortcut to the data.) In this section, let's concentrate on moving data from where it is to where you want it.

To move data from one folder to another on the same disk—for instance, from the Pictures folder to a subfolder you've created inside of it—follow these steps:

1. Open the Finder, your Home folder, and then the folder that contains the files to move.

2. Select the files to move by clicking or dragging over the pictures with the mouse.

3. Drag the items to the new folder. To place the items in a subfolder inside the folder, hover over the folder for a second and wait for the subfolders to appear. Drop the file while hovering over the appropriate folder.

TIP: To copy the file instead of moving it, hold down the Option key while dragging.

This procedure is one you'll use often. Drag and drop from the desktop to folders you've created to keep data organized, or drag and drop between folders to get organized. You can also use the Edit menu to copy and paste a file. Copying and pasting a file isn't moving it, though, so be careful!

This process is in contrast to dragging files between disk partitions. If you try to use the previous procedure to move a file from one disk or partition to another disk or partition (for instance, from your computer to iDisk, part of a .Mac subscription) or to a backup device such as an external drive or Zip disk, the file will not be moved—it will just be copied. This is because Apple figures if you're dragging from one disk to another, you're probably backing up the data, not moving it. Figure 5-2 shows a copy to iDisk in progress. For more information on iDisk, visit **www. Apple.com** or refer to Chapter 16.

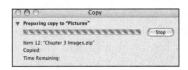

Figure 5-2
You'll see this progress window when you copy a file from one disk to another.

CAUTION! If you try to copy the contents of a CD to your hard drive by dragging, you'll only get an alias of the drive and not the actual contents of the CD. To get around this, hold down the Option key as you drag.

Organize Documents

Just like your Home folder, your Documents folder can be personalized with subfolders. My personal Documents folder has several subfolders, listed here; you might want to use these or create folders of your own:

√   Received Faxes

√   Saved Chats

√   Personal Documents

√   Work in Progress

√   Archived Data

√   Finished Projects

√   Classes

√   eBooks

√   Miscellaneous

Remember, you're trying to organize your documents just as you would if you used a filing cabinet. Organizing files with this in mind will help you create a system that is truly usable. When I need to view a received fax, for instance, with this setup I can simply open the Received Faxes folder and locate what I need quickly.

TIP: *You can rename folders easily just by clicking once on the name (the folder name will turn blue) and then typing in a new name.*

Organize Your Pictures

The pictures on your Mac can be organized in a number of ways. If you've transferred your pictures from another computer, say a PC or another Mac, they may simply be stored in the Pictures folder and might not be organized at all. If you use iPhoto, you might know that you can create themed albums, assign custom keywords, add comments to pictures, and sort and organize them in any number of other ways. If you use a third-party picture organizer instead of iPhoto, you have additional choices, depending on the software used. Because I can't assume you are using iPhoto religiously, for now I'll simply introduce some basic organizational ideas for your Pictures folder and libraries. These ideas can be transferred to other software programs including your digital camera's software. You can use the menus included with the application to create new folders or albums and to move data into them.

Organizing pictures is the same as organizing the Documents or the Home folder. Take inventory of what types of pictures you have, create folders for them, and then move the pictures into them. Because I do a lot of graphics work for clients, I have folders upon folders of EPS files. Figure 5-3 shows an extremely organized Pictures folder.

TIP: *I dragged the Pictures folder from my Home folder to the sidebar of the Finder for easier access.*

Notice in the first column of the Pictures folder, shown in Figure 5-3, that there are several subfolders: Client Artwork, Downtown, EPS Files, Family and Friends, and so on, each of which contains data, subfolders, or both. The EPS subfolder that is selected has multiple subfolders. (These EPS files are clipart.)

TIP: *When there are multiple subfolders, as shown in Figure 5-3, viewing the folder contents using column view is generally better than viewing thumbnails.*

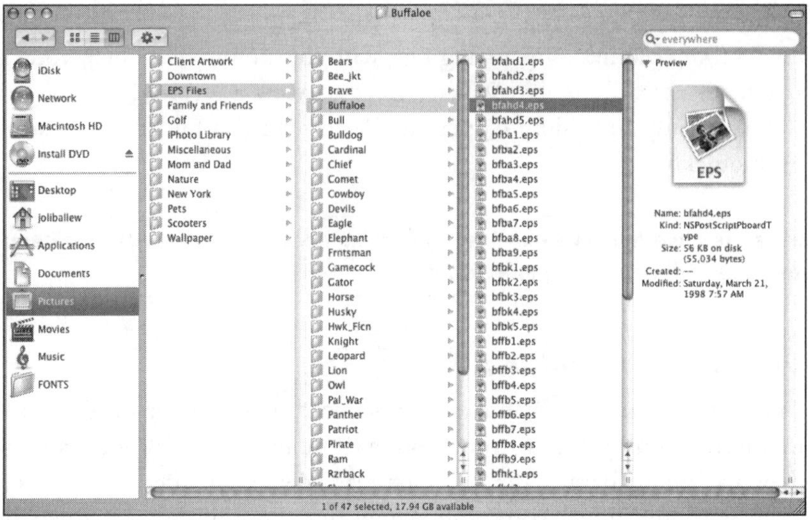

Figure 5-3

Now my pictures are organized!

GunkBuster's Notebook: Get Organized with iPhoto's Smart Album Feature

Using iPhoto's Smart Album feature, you can create albums that chronicle an event such as a vacation or party, or you can create an album that holds specific types of pictures, such those of sunsets, animals, a sport, or an invention. iPhoto's Smart Albums feature lets you specify what you want a particular album to hold, and the albums are updated each time you add pictures to iPhoto.

Follow these steps to create a new Smart Album:

1. Open iPhoto and choose File>New Smart Album.

2. In the Smart Album Name text box, type a name for the new album.

3. To have iPhoto add photos that match specific criteria, make appropriate selections from the available menus. For example, to create an album that contains all of the photos in your library that you have rated as 4 stars or higher, choose My Rating, choose In The Range Of, and choose four stars in the first window and five in the second.

4. To add additional criteria, click the + sign.

5. Click OK when finished.

Organize Your Music

Music can be organized a number of ways too. Of course, you can create subfolders in the Music folder and move your music into them, just as you did with Documents and Pictures, but you can also do quite a bit of organizing using iTunes. You can create playlists to support a mood, an artist, or an event or organize the songs to fit on a CD. You can even create smart playlists to automatically change, based on how much you listen to specific songs in your library.

As always, take inventory of what you have and see how it can be organized. Here are some ideas for sorting songs in iTunes via the Edit>View Options choices:

√ By artist

√ By genre

√ By song size

√ By rating

√ By how often its been played recently

√ By year

√ By date downloaded or acquired

√ By kind

√ By album

GunkBuster's Notebook: Use iTunes Consolidate Library Option

Okay, I know some of you have music scattered everywhere. If organizing all of your music by dragging and dropping seems like too big of an undertaking, iTunes offers a simple, albeit somewhat ineffective, way to locate all of your tunes and copy them to the iTunes folder. Once they are copied to the folder, you can organize and categorize to your heart's content.

Unfortunately, you may have noticed that the word "copy" was used instead of the word "move." As you know, when a file is copied, it makes a duplicate. That's gunk, and if you're really overwhelmed by the enormity of your degunking tasks, this is a good place to start. Once the files are copied, you can then begin deleting duplicate files from other drives or media and start the degunking process in earnest. You'll also have all of your files in one place, making backing up your entire music library much easier.

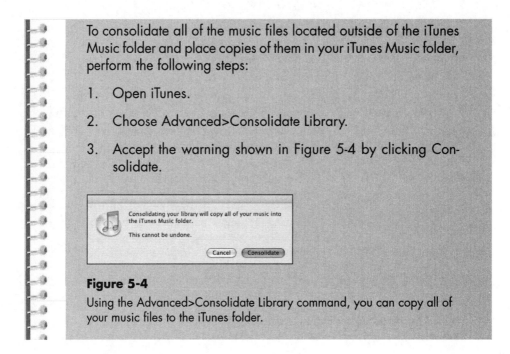

To consolidate all of the music files located outside of the iTunes Music folder and place copies of them in your iTunes Music folder, perform the following steps:

1. Open iTunes.

2. Choose Advanced>Consolidate Library.

3. Accept the warning shown in Figure 5-4 by clicking Consolidate.

Figure 5-4
Using the Advanced>Consolidate Library command, you can copy all of your music files to the iTunes folder.

Organize Your Movies

You have to be careful when organizing, moving, and deleting movie files. That's because if you open a project that needs a specific source file and that file is gone or can't be found, you'll get an error and might not be able to open, play, or finish the project you've worked so hard on. Your best bet with the Movies folder is to create subfolders ahead of time and save the files in their proper places while working and creating them.

Once a project is complete and has been exported and saved in a final movie format, you can safely delete or organize the source files and other files used to create the movie. However, if the project is still in progress, I'd suggest leaving all the files where they are until the project is complete. Once the project is complete, consolidate and compress the files required for it. You can always trash them later.

CAUTION! *One minute of DV footage takes up about 220 MB of hard disk space, so multiple movie projects can quickly fill up even the largest of hard disks.*

Organize Your Graphics Files and Artwork

If you're like most Mac users I know, you probably use your Mac to create or use graphics files and artwork. Because of the size of these files, they can really gunk up your Mac. If you use your Mac to create publications, newsletters, brochures, and so on, you probably have a lot of images (and possibly duplicate ones) that you use with applications like InDesign to compose final documents. In creating projects like publications and brochures, it's easy to get yourself into the situation of having your art files spread all over your hard drive. This can make them difficult to find, use, and archive, and it might even cause you to delete the wrong files when you go about removing files after you finish a big project.

Getting your graphics and project files organized can be quite time consuming. You might have applications that save your files in strange places, or you might have project files that you've saved to network drives. You might also have files you've linked into other files so the information will be up-to-date each time you access it but you have no control over where these files are saved. Because of these things, you can't just go about randomly moving project files into "Art" or "Project" folders. If a file you need is moved and the application, document, or presentation can't find it, you'll get an error about that missing file.

TIP: *Linked files are those that are used in a document but that aren't actually part of the document and are located elsewhere on the hard drive. One such example is an Excel file in a PowerPoint presentation. Linked files are used so that when the document is opened and the linked file is accessed, the latest version of the file is obtained.*

So how do you go about getting these types of issues resolved? The best way to start is to get all of a project's files into a single folder. Then, you'll want to do the same with other projects and their files. Once you've done that, you'll have everything together and you can access, share, and archive the project easily.

Look at one of your projects, such as a brochure you created in InDesign or Photoshop. It likely consists of various images, text, and marketing information. Open the main project file and look at its contents. Is there a linked spreadsheet? Is there an image that was obtained from and is stored on a network drive? Is the original project file stored in some weird folder you've never heard of? Is there text that is linked from a document that is changed daily or weekly? If so, you have to decide what you can and can't move and if it's worth the time and effort to try to consolidate it. Linked files will give you the most grief, especially if they're out of your control. Here's a general outline for organizing a project that has files stored all over the drive:

1. Open the main project and take inventory of the files that are linked and the location of the original files. If those files are on your hard drive, you can move them; if they're on a network drive and out of your control, you may be out of luck.

2. Use Get Info to find out where the image files are stored.

3. Use the application's Preferences, Options, or Custom choices to find out where files created in that program are saved.

4. Locate and make a copy of any static file saved on a network drive.

5. Create a folder on your hard drive with a name that represents the project.

6. Move all of the files, linked files, images, any music files, and copies of networked documents to this folder.

7. Open the main project and look for missing files. Locate and copy or move these files to the new folder.

8. Change the default location for saving files in the application's Preferences, Options, or Custom menus.

If you have all of your files on your own hard drive, it is possible to move them all to one folder. You might have to relink linked objects, and you might have to make copies of certain images, but it can be done. For all future project files, start off right by saving the files all in a single folder as detailed in the GunkBuster's Notebook next.

> ### GunkBuster's Notebook: Create Project Folders and Use Them
>
> The next time you start a large project, open the Documents folder and create a project folder for your new project's files. Open the application and create a new document, presentation, or spreadsheet. Choose File>Save As and save the file in the folder you just created. As images, music, and documents are embedded or added, either move the files needed to the new folder or copy them there. If you need to link a file that isn't used by another document or file, move the linked file to the folder before linking it. If the linked file is used by another application, consider copying the file or leaving it in its original location. You don't want to move a file that another application or project depends on.
>
> As you continue to work on the project, put all correspondence, edits, and changes in the new project folder. You'll find that this greatly reduces the time it takes to locate files, save them, or make changes to images or music that you've added.

Take Advantage of Labels

If you've been following along from the beginning, I'm betting that you're pretty darned organized right now. You probably have your documents, pictures, movies, and music organized into folders and subfolders, and you probably have created folders inside your Home folder or on your desktop for you most-used data. You might have even consolidated a few projects that had files scattered all across your hard drive. You're not going to believe this, but there's one more trick up my sleeve to get you even more organized—labels.

Using labels is a colorful way to highlight a folder's name for easy recognition. This will make finding your files faster and easier. Figure 5-5 shows how I've labeled the personal folders in my Users folder:

√   Blue—Data for books I'm working on

√   Green—Web sites I've created and work on regularly

√   Purple—Personal artwork I've created for my clients and my Pictures folder

√   Red—Folders with data needing immediate attention

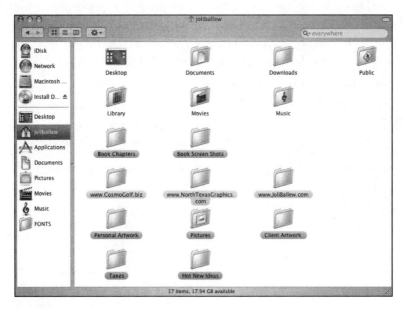

Figure 5-5
Use labels to further organize your stuff.

Color-Code Files and Folders

Creating a color-coded system is easy. Just decide what colors you want to assign to what categories of folders or files, select the item or items, and then from the Actions menu, select the appropriate color from the Color Label choices. You can then sort your data by these labels. Here's the play-by-play:

1. Open the Finder and the folder that contains the data to color-code and select it with the mouse. The data can be a file or folder, or it can be multiple files or folders. (You might even open the Pictures folder and color-code your favorite pictures or the music folder and color-code your favorite music.)

2. With the data selected, click the Action menu. (That's the icon that looks like the little sprocket.)

3. In the Color Label section, select a color. Notice as you hover your pointer over the color you see the name of the label. By default, it is the color's name, but we'll change that shortly. (You can also Control+click the item.)

4. Click an empty area of the folder to deselect the files or folders and see the changes.

Change Label Names

You can also change the label names to be something more descriptive than Red, Orange, or Yellow, for example. Changing the names to indicate what each color represents will help you apply the correct color the next time you apply a label color. To change the label's names, follow these steps:

1. Open the Finder to your Home folder.

2. Choose Finder>Preferences>Labels.

3. Click inside the label names boxes to change any name. Figure 5-6 shows my new label names. Close the dialog box when you're finished.

Figure 5-6
Changing the label names will make it easier to keep your computer degunked.

GunkBuster's Notebook: Keep Folders Small for Easier and Faster Opening

A folder with fewer files in it will open faster than a folder with lots of files. It simply takes your Mac less time to obtain the information and offer it to you if there's less data to locate. It also takes longer to browse through a folder with many files in it to find the file you actually need. A folder (or subfolder) that is 650 MB or less in size or can easily be burned to a CD. A folder that is 100 MB or less can easily be backed up to the iMac storage area on Apple's Internet servers (if you have a .Mac membership). For these reasons, it is generally a good idea to keep folder size to a respectable limit.

If you want to find out how big a folder is, perform the following steps:

1. Open the folder to check.

2. Choose View>List View.

3. If the sizes are not already listed, choose View>Show View Options, and select Calculate All Sizes and This Window Only. Close the dialog box.

4. You can now calculate how large the folder is. (You can click the Size tab to sort by size.) Figure 5-7 shows an example.

5. When finished, choose View>Show View Options, and deselect Calculate All Sizes. (Leaving it checked only makes your Mac have to work harder than it should each time the window is opened.)

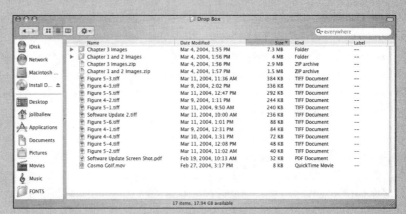

Figure 5-7

Here, the size of images in my Mac's Drop Box folder are calculated.

Compress and Archive

There is one more way to take control of your documents, files, and folders, and that is to organize, compress, and archive items you need to keep but rarely need to access. Simply select the items to compress and archive and then use a Control+click or use the Action menu to select Create Archive. The resulting file will be a ZIP file that can be opened by either your Mac, another Mac, or even a PC. Compressed files and folders take up far less hard disk space than uncompressed ones. Compressed files are also much easier and quicker to transfer to other users when you use a network or the Internet via e-mail.

To use the Create Archive command, follow these steps:

1. Open the folder that contains the items to compress. Select the items.
2. Choose File>Create Archive, or from the Actions menu, choose Create Archive. You can also use Control+click.
3. The archive will be named Archive.zip.
4. You can rename the ZIP file by clicking it once.
5. After the file is compressed, you can delete the original (uncompressed) file if desired. If you do not delete the original file, you'll have two copies of the data.
6. You might also want to create a folder just for archived files. This folder can be backed up for further security.

And that about does it. There really isn't that much more to organize or get rid of. There are a few Trash containers you might not know about, and perhaps a few stray files, but as far as degunking your own stuff goes, you're almost finished! When you're ready, move on to the next section, where you'll learn how to empty the Trash from applications such as iPhoto and iMovie, locate and delete the few files you've yet to uncover, empty the Trash from the desktop, and finally, defragment your hard drive!

Empty the Trash

It's time to take out the garbage. Just as with cleaning the house, it takes some time to gather up all of the trash, put the bags together, and then tote them out to the garbage can. So far, we've been collecting the trash; it's time now to complete the trash-gathering tasks and take the leap. Before we empty the trash we've collected, though, we need to make a final pass to see if there's anything we missed. There are a few hiding places for garbage that haven't been addressed, like the iPhoto Trash and the iMovie Trash. These Trash receptacles are not unlike the smaller trash cans in the bathrooms and offices of your own home!

Empty the iPhoto Trash

If you've ever used iPhoto to manage your pictures, import images from a digital camera, or browse through the iPhoto library, you'll want to see what's in the iPhoto Trash. If there's anything in there, you should empty the Trash now:

1.   Open iPhoto.
2.   From the Source pane on the left side of the interface, select Trash.
3.   If there are images in the Trash, select File>Empty Trash. Click OK to verify that you want to permanently delete these items.
4.   Quit or close iPhoto.

Empty the iMovie Trash

If you've ever used iMovie to manage your videos, import video from a digital camera, or create a movie, you'll want to see what's in the iMovie Trash. If there's anything in there, you should empty the Trash now:

1.   Open iMovie.
2.   Choose File>Empty Trash. Click OK to verify that you want to permanently delete these items.
3.   Quit or close iMovie.

TIP: If any of your third-party programs has a Trash option inside its interface, check to see if those Trash files need to be deleted.

Find Elusive Files

Because Macs are so tidy and easy to use, chances are good you've collected almost all of the gunk you've created on your own and moved that gunk to the Trash. However, depending on how long you've been collecting gunk and where you've hidden it in the past, there might still be some remnants hanging around. In this section, we'll look under the beds and behind the desks and see if we can scrounge up any dust bunnies that have been hiding there. To locate stray files, you have two good options: the Search bar or the Find program.

Locating Stray Files with the Search Bar

The Search bar is an extremely convenient tool for locating lost or stray files because you can add the Search bar to the Finder window and make it available 24/7. You search using this tool by typing in all or part of the file or folder name. The Search bar isn't nearly as powerful as your second option, the Find program, but it'll do in a pinch when you've lost a specific file and know its name. You'll have to manually add the Search bar if you want it to appear in the Finder windows, though, so let's do that first:

1.   Open the Finder and maximize it.

2.   Choose View>Customize Toolbar.

3.   Drag the Search bar to the Finder's toolbar.

4.   Click Done.

By default, searches entered in this window will search the entire hard disk. However, you can select the flippy triangle inside the window to narrow the search to part of the hard drive. Figure 5-8 shows this option.

Type the name of the file you are looking for into the Search bar, and watch the results magically appear. You can search for just about anything by its name and then sort through the results by clicking the headings in the Finder window. You can also select any item in the list and see where it is stored or double-click it to open it. You can delete the file by dragging it to the Trash and even rename the file if desired.

TIP: Use the Search bar when you know the name of a file or part of its name or when you need to locate a file you've misplaced and know it is on the hard disk.

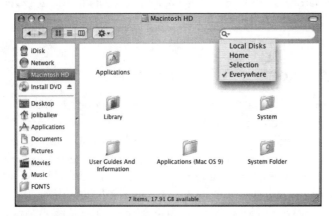

Figure 5-8

Use the Search bar to search for missing or stray files or folders.

Using the Find Program to Locate Stray Files

The Find program is a much more powerful tool for locating stray or unnecessary files because it allows you to search for files by specific criteria, including by name, by size, by creation date, by suffix, or even by a phrase inside the document. You can also define where it searches just as you can with the Search bar. The Find program offers a good way to locate lost JPG files, MP3s, Photoshop files, Final Cut files, and more.

To access the Find program, select Finder, and from the File menu, choose Find. Configure the Search In window to define where to perform the search, and in the Search For Items Whose area, configure other search criteria. In Figure 5-9, I'm searching for stray files with the .jpeg extension that have been modified between January 2004 and May 2004.

To simply locate stray files you don't want or need, search by their extension as I've done in Figure 5-9. Remember to delete only what you created and don't need. Don't delete any files of unclear origin. You don't want to delete anything important. Some extensions (that I haven't discussed earlier) that you can search for are listed in Table 5-1. These files extensions represent only a few of the file types you'll find on a Mac and do not represent all available file types.

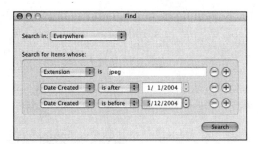

Figure 5-9
Use the Find program to locate any kind of file using almost any criteria.

Table 5-1   File Types for Macs

File Extension	Description
.ai	Adobe Illustrator file
.doc	Microsoft Word document
.dot	Microsoft Word template
.eps	Encapsulated Postscript file
.gif	Graphics Interchange Format. Image format generally used on the Web
.htm, .html	Hypertext Markup Language

(continued)

Table 5-1   **File Types for Macs** *(Continued)*

File Extension	Description
.jpg, .jpeg	Joint Photographic Experts Group. Image format generally used with digital camera files
.pdf	Adobe Acrobat file
.pict, .png	Common image file format. Pict is the native image file format for Macintosh; PNG, Portable Network Graphics, is intended to be the patent-free replacement for GIF.
.ppt	PowerPoint file
.pst	MS Outlook Export file
.rtf	Rich Text format file
.txt	Text file
.xls	Microsoft Excel file
.zip	WinZip (compressed) files

You can also search for file extensions that have been previously discussed, including .sit, .tar, .mp3, .aiff .gz, .gzip, .au, .wav, .avi, .mov, .mpg, .qt, and others.

Make a Final Pass

Restart your Mac and make sure everything runs well before continuing. Open your remaining programs and working projects, and verify that all your necessary files are there. If you accidentally deleted any files you need, rescue them from the Trash before emptying it.

GunkBuster's Notebook: Determine the Size of the Trash in OS X

Just for kicks, let's see just how much hard drive space your Trash is taking up so that we can see how much space we can free up by emptying it:

1. Open the Finder and choose Go>Home.

2. Choose View>As Columns.

3. Choose Go>Go To Folder.

4. In the resulting window, type **.Trash** and click Go.

5. Select the .Trash folder and choose File>Get Info.

Figure 5-10 shows that my Trash folder is using 5.16 GB on my hard disk. Emptying the Trash will free up a large amount of disk space!

Figure 5-10
My Trash is gunking up 5 GB of space!

TIP: There are plenty of third-party sites that offer ways to tweak the Trash. I like www.kanzu.com. Using Kanzu software, you can create new Trash icons, securely delete files, force-empty the Trash, and more.

Ready? Empty!

There are plenty of ways to empty the Trash, but the most straightforward is to select the Finder and choose Finder>Empty Trash. You'll have to verify that you want to empty the items in the Trash permanently. You can also use Shift+Command+Delete or Control+click the Trash icon. The latter doesn't ask you to verify that you want to empty the Trash, though, so be careful.

There's no hard and fast rule to tell you how often to empty the Trash; it all depends on how much you delete. I tend to empty the Trash about a week after deleting applications or projects, which is generally long enough to decide if I've made a mistake or if I deleted files I actually need. Here are some general guidelines:

√   Empty the Trash at least once every two weeks.

√   Don't empty the Trash immediately after making a large deletion, such as an application, artwork, or several files. You might find you need them later.

√   Empty the Trash if it gets larger than 1 GB.

√   Empty the Trash before selling your computer.

√   Don't empty the Trash if you've deleted something and are getting error messages.

GunkBuster's Notebook: Secure Empty Trash

Although emptying the Trash removes the items from the Trash can and frees up valuable disk space, the data still remains on the hard drive. The space is available, but it will not be technically *erased* from your hard disk until something is written over it. A fairly adept user who has access to your Mac could still recover the data by using an application such as Norton Utilities. If you are really concerned about security—perhaps you're the type that shreds all your documents before putting them in the trash can at home—you might opt to use Secure Empty Trash.

When you choose the Secure Empty Trash option from the Finder's File menu instead of Empty Trash, the OS actually writes gibberish over the areas of data you've deleted. The deleted data won't even be recoverable by the CIA or the IRS!

Follow these steps to use Secure Empty Trash:

1. Select the Finder.

2. Choose File>Secure Empty Trash.

3. When prompted, choose OK to verify that you want to erase the items.

4. Wait while the Trash is emptied.

Disk Fragmentation

You can count on one thing: If you've moved files around, deleted programs and applications, and emptied 5 GB worth of trash, your hard drive will be a mess internally. You might think that you've really cleaned up your hard drive because you've deleted a lot of files and really reorganized your data, but that's only what you see on the outside. When I say it's a "mess," I don't mean disorganized by our standards. I mean that the files on the actual hard drive are *fragmented,* or disorganized by the hard drive's standards.

Here's basically how a hard drive works. A hard drive is a circular disk, kind of like an LP record. As data is saved to the disk, the disk spins and the data is written sequentially, starting with the first open space it finds. If that space isn't big enough, the rest of the files' data is stored somewhere else. As you install and uninstall programs and add and delete files, the holes for data on the hard disk become plentiful and you end up with files stored everywhere on the drive.

When you open a file that is stored on the hard disk in several different places, the disk has to spin many more times to collect the data and put the pieces together. The more the disk spins, the more wear and tear on your machine, which causes problems and degrades the performance of your hard drive.

When this happens, the computer's response time slows down because it simply takes longer to obtain and organize the data than it would if the files were stored contiguously. After a computer is *defragmented,* the files are stored (more) contiguously and the computer's hard disk has to spend less time spinning around and looking for files. This makes for better performance and less stress on the computer. Figure 5-11 shows a representation of a hard disk.

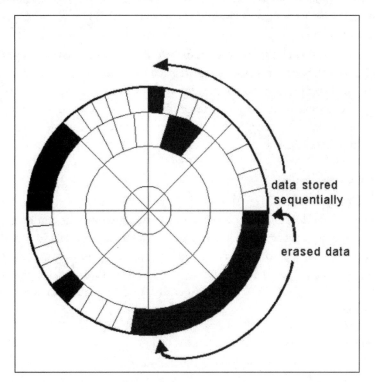

Figure 5-11
This is how a hard drive looks and how data is stored.

Defragment the Drive with Third-Party Utilities

Macs don't come with their own defragging utilities yet. However, there are several third-party ones that will do the trick. Norton Utilities 8.0's Speed Disk is one, and this program will reorganize the files on the disk and make sure files that belong together are placed together. This will improve the responsiveness of your Mac and will offer noticeable improvements for fragmented drives.

So, take my advice and run out and purchase a defragmenter, install it, start the defragmenting process, and head off to bed. Defragmenting is almost always as simple as opening the program and clicking the Defragment Now button. It's no big deal at all and requires only seconds of your time. It'll take a good amount of time to complete, though, so make sure you can be away from your computer for a while.

TIP: Always read the manufacturer's instructions. Before running any defragmenter, back up your data, turn off all screen savers, close all open programs, and disconnect from the Internet. Disable anti-virus software if you have it.

Some final thoughts on defragmenting: Analyze your disks three times a year or so to make sure they are not becoming fragmented. You can do that with the third-party utility you purchased for defragmenting. Make sure you run a defragmenting program after deleting large blocks of data, such as emptying a 5 GB Trash can. And finally, remember that an organized hard drive runs better than an unorganized one, so try not to get gunked up once you're degunked!

Summing Up

In this chapter, you learned how to organize your remaining documents, pictures, music, movies, and artwork, including how to create a folder and subfolder system. You also learned about Panther's color-coding options and learned to create labels and personalize label names. Once your files and folders were organized, you learned various ways to empty the Trash and, finally, to defragment the hard drive.

Clean Up the Dock, Finder, and Menu Bar

Degunking Checklist:

√ Clean up and personalize the Dock so you can work faster and smarter.

√ Add and employ secret menus to the Dock to locate and open items faster.

√ Clean up and personalize the Finder toolbar.

√ Clean up and personalize the Finder window.

√ Clean up and personalize the Apple menu and the Menu bar's menulets.

While degunking a computer generally means making *it* work faster and smarter, sometimes you must configure it to make *you* work faster and smarter. Configuring your Mac to help you work more efficiently involves a few different processes because there are multiple things that can slow you down while you rush to meet tomorrow's deadline.

Consider these annoyances and productivity busters that likely impact you on a regular basis:

√   You have so many items on the Dock that you must get out your reading glasses to make them out.

√   The Dock contains items you never use.

√   The Dock gets in your way and hides the information bar in an application like Photoshop or it prevents you from clicking the Contact Us link at the bottom of a Web page.

√   Each time you open a text document, it opens in the trial version of Word instead of AppleWorks where you'd like it to.

√   The Finder shows icons and there are just too many to sort through. You should be viewing the items another way, perhaps as a list.

√   The applications are buried in the Applications folder and it takes too long to locate and open each one.

If you really thought about it, these scenarios represent just the beginning.

Teaching your Mac how you want it to act and look is very important, and it is something that many users overlook, especially when it comes to fine-tuning the Mac for greater productivity. Do you have too many icons on the Dock? Remove them. Do you use the same programs every day? Add them to the Dock or the Finder toolbar. Do you need an icon for your display properties on the Menu bar? Add it. In this chapter, we'll focus on getting you working more efficiently by personalizing what you access every day.

Clean Up and Personalize the Dock

The Dock is like the kitchen counter space in your home. It's a small area, but you place lots of items there, ready for use because you know you'll need them daily. In the kitchen, you probably have a can opener, a microwave, and a coffeemaker, but you might also have tools you don't use very often, like a blender, food processor, or Crock-Pot. When you start preparing a meal, you add more items as you need them (pots, pans, flour, milk, spices, and other ingredients). Your counter, in the midst of cooking dinner, may become so crowded that you have difficulty finding what you need. If you organized everything first, you might find that putting the blender, food processor, and Crock-Pot under the sink frees needed space and really doesn't hamper your performance.

The same thing happens with the Dock. It looks good when your Mac isn't in the middle of a big project, but it can become quite cluttered when you are working, especially if you have several applications and documents open. Each time you open an application, it places its icon on the Dock. This clutter can definitely hamper your productivity. When cleaning up the Dock, you need to keep one thing in mind: The more applications you open or icons you add, the smaller the icons get and the more clutter you have to sift through to find what you want. That being the case, why have icons on the Dock for applications you don't need or use?

Remove Icons

Take a few minutes to look at your Dock, take inventory of your software and hardware, and write down what you use your Mac for on most days. Now, take a look at the Dock and see if there's anything there you simply don't use that often. If you don't have a DV camera, you probably don't need iMovie. If you don't listen to music, you probably don't need iTunes. You can remove any icon you don't want by dragging it off of the Dock to an empty area of the desktop. (You can always drag it back from the Applications folder if you desire.) Here are some ideas:

√   Remove the System Preferences icon; once preferences are set, they're set. If you need to change preferences later, go to HD>Applications>System Preferences.

√   Remove any application you don't use weekly, including GarageBand, iMovie, Address Book, iPhoto, iCal, and QuickTime Player. These can be located later in the Applications folder.

√   Remove the Preview icon. Preview opens automatically when you need it. You might not want its icon gunking up your Dock.

√   Remove any folders you've added that you no longer use. (These are on the right side of the Dock).

Figure 6-1 shows a gunked-up Dock; Figure 6-2 shows a personalized Dock that has really been cleaned up.

Figure 6-1
A cluttered Dock.

Figure 6-2
A clean Dock.

Add Icons

Because the Dock is the center of Mac OS X, you'll want it to be as personalized as possible and include the items you use most often. From the Dock, you can launch programs, switch between programs, quit programs, and more. Of course, with the little black triangles underneath running programs, you can also see which ones are immediately available.

Just as important as removing unnecessary programs and folders from the Dock is adding customized programs and folders. Here are some ideas for personalizing the right side of the Dock:

√ Add the Applications folder—Open the HD and drag the Applications folder to the right side of the Dock.

√ Add your Home folder—Open HD>Users and drag your Home folder to the right side of the Dock.

√ Add your Documents folder—Open the Finder, open your Home folder, and drag the Documents folder to the right side of the Dock.

√ Add the Shared Documents folder—If you share your computer with others, and you use the Shared Documents folder to share data, open the HD>Users folder and drag the Shared documents folder to the right side of the Dock.

You can also add items to the left side of the Dock:

√ Add Internet Explorer—If you use Internet Explorer instead of Safari, open the Applications folder and drag its icon to the left side of the Dock.

√ Add a favorite program—If you use Photoshop, BounceBack, Elgato EyeTV, or other third-party applications daily, open the Applications folder and drag their icons to the left side of the Dock.

√ Printer utility—If you need daily access to your printer software, drag its icon to the left side of the Dock.

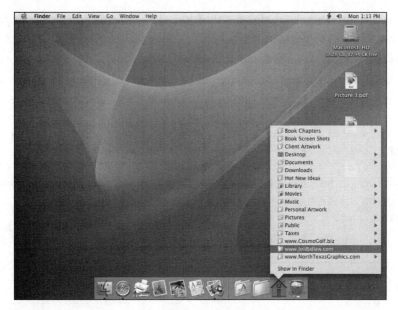

Figure 6-3

A customized Dock makes finding commonly used items easy.

Figure 6-3 shows one way to configure a Dock. Mine has Safari, my printer software, Mail, iPhoto, AppleWorks, the Applications folder, the Shared folder, my Home folder, and the Trash icon.

TIP: If, after opening a program, you decide you want to leave its icon on the Dock permanently, Control+click the icon and select Keep In Dock. The icon will remain in the Dock after the program has been closed.

Auto-Hide, Shrink and Enlarge, Move, Magnification, and Effects

There are several ways to personalize the size and feel of the Dock:

√   You can use Auto-Hide to remove the display of the Dock and then bring it back whenever you need it.

√   You can shrink or enlarge the Dock.

√   You can move the Dock to another area of the screen.

√   You can change how the Dock's icons are magnified when the pointer is moved over them.

√   You can even configure what effects are used when applications are minimized.

All of these options are configured from the same area of your Mac's interface, so let's take a look at that now:

1. Open Applications>System Preferences>Dock.

2. To change the Dock's size, move the Dock Size slider. You'll see the changes immediately.

TIP: *If you just want to resize the Dock, you can click and drag the dividing line on the Dock itself up and down. This saves opening System Preferences.*

---

3. To change how icons are magnified when the mouse is used to hover over them, check Magnification and move the slider to the right or left to configure it. Use your mouse to see the changes immediately.

4. To change the Dock's position on the screen, select Left, Bottom, or Right.

5. To change the effect used when applications are minimized to the Dock, select Scale Effect or Genie Effect.

TIP: *When a program is minimized, it disappears in a "genie in a bottle" fashion. If you'd like programs to go away faster, switch from Genie Effect to Scale Effect.*

---

6. To turn off animations when programs are opened, uncheck Animate Opening Animations. (The less work your Mac has to do to perform a task, the faster it will do it.)

7. To hide and show the Dock automatically when the pointer is moved over the area of the screen where the Dock usually resides, check Automatically Hide And Show The Dock. (To manually show the Dock only when necessary, leave this unchecked and use Command+Option+D as needed.)

8. Close this window.

TIP: *If you feel as if the Dock is always in the way, or if it ever prevents you from viewing a necessary part of a program's interface, such as an information line that runs across the bottom of the screen or the last part of a Web page, you'll want to hide the Dock.*

GunkBuster's Notebook: Use Secret Menus

Secret menus offer shortcuts to help you work with the Dock and programs more efficiently. I don't think that Apple meant for its users to refer to these hidden pop-up menus as *secret* menus, but the term is used by a lot of people. (They might as well be called *under-appreciated menus, wow-what-did-I-click-to-get-this menu,* or *menus nobody knows about.*) What you'll see in a secret menu depends on what type of item you're clicking, though, so let's take a look at the menus.

Open iPhoto, Mail, Safari, and any other program you use often. Work your way through the open programs (the ones with black triangles underneath them), and click their icons while holding down the Control key. You'll see a variety of choices:

√ Hide—Minimizes the program.

√ Show In Finder—Opens the Finder window and shows where the program is located.

√ Quit—Closes the program.

√ Keep In Dock—Keeps the icon for this program in the Dock after the program is closed.

Specialty programs have other choices. For instance, Safari has search options and information about pages that are loading, and Mail has the options Get New Mail and Compose New Message. You'll also see shortcuts for open documents or projects, which can be extremely helpful when more than one document or project is open at the same time. Figure 6-4 shows an example of three open documents in AppleWorks.

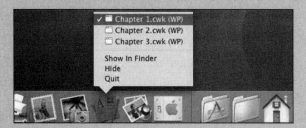

Figure 6-4
Secret menus offer various bits of information.

Third-Party Applications

I don't want you to go overboard with this section and start downloading and installing a bunch of third-party applications that you'll never use; that would go against the entire degunking principle of this book. However, if a third-party application can help you work smarter and faster without bogging down your computer or costing you an arm and a leg, it may well be worth it. In this section, I'll introduce some of my favorite third-party applications and detail what they do.

ClearDock

Visit **www.unsanity.com** for ClearDock, a free program that removes the semi-transparent white background from the Dock so that you can see what's underneath it. This is an especially powerful tool if you need and like the Dock and want to leave it on the desktop all the time. You can also change the colors of application triangles too. You'll have to download and install the Application Enhancer if you haven't already; you'll be prompted for what to do at the site.

Dock Extender

Dock Extender is useful if you're an experienced Mac user and have dozens of applications open at a single time and if you work on multiple projects simultaneously. Available from **www.codetek.com** for $20 (U.S.), this program helps you organize your applications and documents into as many as 10 different menus, all of which are a single mouse click away. Menus can have submenus, labeled separators, and more. Being able to organize your work and access it quickly is a positive step toward degunking!

TinkerTool

TinkerTool does a lot more than just help you tweak the Dock, and it's a great addition to any Mac if you want to fine-tune the operating system. You can move the Trash icon to the desktop, use transparent Dock icons to show hidden applications, place the Dock at the beginning or end of any screen border, set the Dock minimization effect to a "suck in" animation, and more. If you don't need or want these tweaks, by all means, don't gunk up your machine with this program. However, if you're a die-hard Dock user, use this program to take a little more control.

Clean Up and Personalize the Finder Windows

Finder windows make it easier than ever to locate the items you want. With the Applications folder, your Users folder, and the Desktop folder all in one place, you can not only find the things you want quickly, but you can use the Finder to your advantage to help you stay organized. Fortunately, you can personalize the Finder windows in any number of ways too.

Every Finder window has a row of buttons, icons, and navigation options across the top and a toolbar along the left side. A single click takes you where you want to go in almost all instances. However, if you use the Dock or the Menu bar to navigate your Mac religiously, you might not be so impressed with what's available from the Finder. In fact, it may seem as if it's just too big and unwieldy to serve its intended purpose. If that's the case, there are options to hide or shrink the Finder window.

If you like the Finder window and use it often, hiding and shrinking might not be your main concern. If the Finder is your window to the world of Mac, you'll be more productive if you add, rearrange, or remove icons; add folders to the toolbar; set advanced preferences; and customize everything "Finder." It can be personalized to your heart's content. With that in mind, let's see how you can become more productive by tweaking the Finder.

Move and Shrink

Moving, shrinking, enlarging, repositioning—all of these basic tasks are performed with a simple mouse click, keystroke, or basic click-and-drag of the mouse. Here are some tips and tricks for making the Finder more user-friendly:

√   Shrink or enlarge the entire Finder window by dragging from the bottom right corner.

√   View the contents as a list or as columns using the View menu options or the icons on the Finder itself.

√   Hide the sidebar and the toolbar by clicking the small, white oval in the top right corner of the Finder window. You can also choose View>Hide Toolbar. (The sidebar displays the icon and text name—e.g., the Applications folder's icon and the word "Applications"—but you can drag the bar between the sidebar and Finder window if you want to see only the icons and not the text. This will save you a little horizontal space while still making that information available.)

√   Using View>Show View Options, change the text size to 10 pt. and remove columns for size and kind and any other data you don't need.

√   Use the separators between the panes (when in list or column view) to resize a specific pane's size.

Figure 6-5 shows a very efficient Finder window. I used the View option, List, and 11 pt. text size. I removed the columns labeled Date Modified, Date Created, Size, Kind, Version, Comments, and Label and resized the window by dragging. I left the toolbar on the left for easy access to other areas of the hard disk. Now that the window is smaller, I have more desktop space for working and viewing desktop icons.

Figure 6-5
Personalize the Finder so it is not only effective but also small.

Add, Rearrange, or Remove Icons

Personalizing the icons available from the Finder menu allows you to add your most-used tools right to the Finder. The default icons that run across the top of the Finder window include Back and Forward, Action, and View. You can add a number of other icons if you desire, and you can choose to add them as text, as an icon only, or as both. Compare Figure 6-5, which has the default icons (plus Search), to Figure 6-6, which contains additional icons.

Want to personalize the Finder like this? Here's how:

1. Open the Finder.
2. Choose View>Customize Toolbar.
3. Drag any icon from the dialog box to the top of the Finder window. Get Info is an especially useful addition, as is iDisk if you have it.
4. Click Done.

TIP: *If you're concerned about the Finder and desktop real estate, configure the newly added tools as Text Only.*

You can also drag other items to the Finder window; they don't have to be available from just the Customize Toolbar options. Items you can add include files, folders, programs, or anything, really. Just as you would add items to the

Figure 6-6
Adding tools to the Finder window makes it even easier to work with.

Dock for easy access, you can add them here for easy access too. If you prefer to hide the Dock and use the Finder, consider these additions to make the Finder more effective:

√ Open the Finder's Applications folder and drag iPhoto, iMovie, iDVD, or any other program to the Finder interface.

√ Open the Finder's Network folder, open a workgroup folder, and drag the icon for a computer on the network to the Finder. You'll have easy access next time you need to access the shared documents on that computer.

√ Open the Finder's Documents folder and drag the subfolder you use most often to the Finder interface.

√ Highlight a Web page in Safari and drag it to the desktop. Open the Finder and drag this new Internet location file to the Finder window.

TIP: To remove any item you've added to the Finder, choose View>Customize Toolbar, and then drag the items away from the Finder.

Finally, with the icons or text (or both) added to the Finder window, open View>Customize Toolbar, and then drag the items to situate them as you please. Click Done when finished. Figure 6-7 shows an example of a personalized and extremely effective Finder window. I love this because I'm more comfortable with the Finder than the Dock, which I can now auto-hide, and then I'll simply use the Command+Tab key combination to move between open applications and the Finder windows!

Figure 6-7
The Finder can take the place of the Dock if configured correctly.

Add Folders to Bottom Half of the Sidebar

You can add folders to the bottom half of the sidebar finder by dragging the folders there. This doesn't move the folders—it only creates a new way to access them. For instance, if you have a subfolder that you access regularly inside the Documents folder and you want to access that folder from the left side of the Finder window, simply drag it there. Removing it is as simple as dragging it away from that area.

Miscellaneous Cleanup

There are a few miscellaneous organizational, personalization, and cleanup tasks that still need to be addressed, and these last-minute tweaks will, as the others in this chapter, help you work faster and smarter and with less frustration! If you've ever opened a JPG file from a friend and had to wait 2 or 3 minutes for Photoshop to open before you could view it, you know the types of frustrations I'm talking about. One of the last-minute tweaks in this chapter will include assigning a particular file type to a particular program.

I'll also show you how to use an inexpensive third-party application called FruitMenu to personalize almost any aspect of menus and menu options, including disabling animated menu fadeouts, displaying submenus in smaller fonts, adding or removing items from the Apple menu, and more. Remember, the less your Mac has to do, the better! Following that, you'll learn even more ways to customize your Mac, including dragging icons to the Menu bar and creating menulets.

File Name Extensions

A file's extension tells your Mac what program to use when you ask it to open the file. By default, files with a .doc extension will open in Microsoft Word, files ending in .xls will open in Microsoft Excel, files with a .mov extension will open in QuickTime Player, files ending in .jpg will open in Preview, and files with a .cwk extension will open in AppleWorks. If you want to change the default program a file opens with, you can. You can also revert back to the defaults if a program you've recently installed has taken over the job of opening a particular file type.

Assigning Documents to Programs

Let's say once or twice a week your mom sends you pictures of her dog doing tricks or sporting a new hairdo and you're supposed to ooh and ah over her by writing back and stating how cute she looked in her new winter outfit (the dog, not your mom). Those doggie files used to open automatically in Preview and opened in about a second. Unfortunately, since you installed Photoshop, every time you open one of your mom's pictures, Photoshop opens, quite slowly, and to the dismay of your poor, hard-working Mac, reluctantly pulls up the picture for your viewing (dis)pleasure. You'd give anything if you could just make those JPGs open in Preview again. You can—here's how:

1. Open Finder and locate any file that's opening in the wrong program. This might be an RTF file that opens in TextEdit instead of Word, or a JPG that opens in Photoshop instead of Preview. Select the file by clicking once, but do not open the file itself.

2. Choose File>Get Info, or if you've added that command to your Finder window as detailed in the previous section, click the Get Info icon.

3. In the Info dialog box, expand Open With by clicking the triangle, and from the Open With choice, select the new program you want this particular file to open with. Figure 6-8 shows an example.

4. If you want all other files of this type to open with this same program, click Change All. Verify your choice by selecting Continue in the resulting dialog box.

5. Close the information dialog box.

Apple Menu

There used to be an Apple Menu Options control panel, but no more. However, you can still tweak the Apple menu using FruitMenu, a $10 shareware application from **www.unsanity.com**. (When I downloaded FruitMenu, I had a 15-day grace period.)

The FruitMenu application lets you do all kinds of neat things, including the following:

√ Add any contextual menu item to almost any contextual menu.

√ Edit the Apple menu.

Figure 6-8
You can tell your Mac what program to use when opening a specific file type.

√   Assign hotkeys to particular menu items.

√   Show submenus in a small font.

√   Show hidden files.

√   Add aliases to the Apple menu.

TIP: Don't download, install, or purchase third-party applications you don't need; they'll gunk up your machine. However, for the purpose of making the Mac more productive and taking control of its menus, these types of programs can be quite effective if you decide you need them.

Menu Extras

Think of the Menu bar and the area for menu extras as a second, advanced Dock. Menu extras are the small icons located on the Menu bar next to the clock on the right side, and these represent items you can always access that directly involve the system, such as AppleScripts and the speaker volume. Figure 6-9 shows the default menu extra area for an eMac.

Figure 6-9
The menu extras are located on the far right side of the Menu bar.

There are scripts available in the Script menu that allow you to interact directly with the system, such as InfoScripts>Current Date & Time, Internet Services>Current Temperature By Zip Code, and Mail Scripts>Import Addresses. It's a little more difficult to add items here than it used to be; you'll have to locate the actual command in System Preferences and check the appropriate box in most instances. However, it's worth the trouble if you want to access system items here.

Here's an example of locating the correct check box for adding an item to the Menu bar:

1. Open System Preferences>Sound. (If System Preferences is no longer on the Dock, access it from the Applications menu.)
2. Check or uncheck Show Volume In Menu Bar. This is shown in Figure 6-10.
3. Open System Preferences>Show All>Displays.
4. Check or uncheck Show Displays In Menu Bar.
5. Open System Preferences>Show All>Date And Time. Choose the Clock tab.

Because the items available seem to change with every version of Mac OS X, experiment with other system preferences to see what's available.

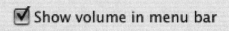

Figure 6-10
When adding items to the Menu bar, look for choices in the program's preferences file.

Summing Up

Configuring the Dock, Finder windows, and Menu bar to contain the things you need on a daily basis helps both you and the computer work faster and smarter. With things where you need them, you will be more productive. In the same vein, avoiding having to sift through things you *don't* need or don't use also makes you more productive, so moving items from the Dock in addition to adding them provides immediate speed improvements.

By cleaning up and personalizing the Dock, the Finder windows, and the Menu bar, by downloading and installing third-party productivity tools, and by making sure that files open in the right program, you've made even more progress toward degunking your Mac!

Fonts and Font Gunk

Degunking Checklist:

√   Understand the various places where fonts are stored and why, especially the new folders in OS X.

√   Use the Font Panel to choose, change, preview, and group fonts.

√   Use the Font Book to further organize fonts.

√   Delete duplicate and unnecessary fonts.

√   Move fonts from OS 9 to X.

√   Use third-party applications to manage fonts.

Fonts have long been a nightmare for Apple users. In fact, just understanding where fonts are stored and why almost requires a Ph.D. If you're a font fanatic, if you download fonts from the Internet or purchase font collections, if you've installed various graphics programs, or if you're a professional artist, Web designer, or printer, it's very likely you've got a lot of font gunk. Font gunk can cause programs to open slowly, use up unnecessary RAM, slow down the boot process, and if you've tried to take control of fonts by moving them around yourself, even cause system crashes.

With OS X, working with fonts is a little easier than it used to be. However, there's the new issue of multiple font folders, not knowing where to install fonts, and when multiple graphics applications are installed, duplicate fonts. You might even have missing system fonts or other problems. If you've never installed a font, you might not have a lot of font gunk; OS X takes pretty good care of its fonts if you're not messing around with them. However, if you work with fonts religiously or if you've installed your share of applications, you definitely need to take a look at this chapter and find out how to manage or eliminate your font gunk.

This chapter is not a primer on fonts, font types, or how to use fonts. I don't want to waste precious space detailing the differences between bitmap, PostScript, and TrueType fonts and when you should or shouldn't use each type; there are plenty of books that cover this topic. If you don't know about font types already, if you don't use Adobe Type Manager or have a PostScript printer, chances are good you don't need to know that information anyway. If you do, there's probably very little I could teach you about fonts in the space I have here. What this chapter is about, then, is getting rid of the font gunk that almost every Mac user has by using the following tools and performing the following tasks:

√ Learn the reason for all the font folders on your computer, why there are so many, and in what folder you should install (or delete) fonts.

√ Use the Font Panel to choose, change, and group fonts.

√ Use the Font Book to create collections, preview fonts, and enable, disable, and delete fonts.

√ Move fonts from OS 9 to OS X.

√ Use third-party font management programs to further control fonts.

Where Fonts Are Stored

Five Font Folders. Say that five times fast. When you're finished with that tongue twister, see if you can wrap your brain around *why* there are five font folders (or more if you share a computer with other users). It's important to understand the organizational structure for fonts that Apple has mapped out for you if you're ever going to take control of the font gunk on your computer.

Private Fonts

The fonts in <*your user name*>>Library>Fonts folder contain your private fonts. (If you share a computer with other users, those users will also have their own private Fonts folder.) Fonts in this folder can be accessed only by you, the user to which they belong. As the owner of the folder, you can add your own custom fonts, delete fonts, and customize to your heart's content. No one else has access. Figure 7-1 shows an example of my private Fonts folder.

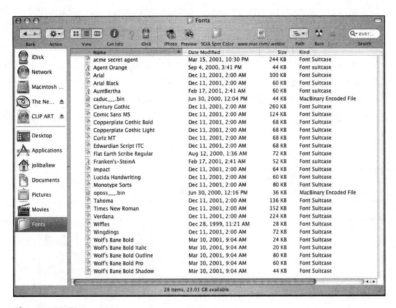

Figure 7-1
A user's private Fonts folder contains fonts only they can use.

TIP: If you are the only person who uses your Mac but you have multiple users created and active, you've got a lot of gunk (including font folders) you don't need. If you're sure that a user is gone for good, delete the user and the user's folders.

Library Fonts

The Library fonts are in the Library>Fonts folder. Fonts in this folder are available to everyone who uses your Mac. Only users who are administrators can make changes here. For the most part, this should be considered the main font folder. To install a font that everyone can use, install it here.

Network Fonts

Network fonts are those fonts available to you only if a network administrator has configured a separate and distinct font collection on a network server or other computer and you have access to that folder. This folder, if it is available, is located in the Network>Library>Fonts folder. Many times, these folders are set up so that all users in a corporation can access standard, agreed-upon company fonts, allowing everyone to create documents, graphics, and e-mail following company standards.

System Fonts

System fonts are located in the System>Library>Fonts folder. Figure 7-2 shows a sample System Fonts folder. These fonts are used by the operating system and are necessary for the Mac to function correctly. This font folder holds the fonts used for menus, dialog boxes, and icons. If they're moved or deleted, you'll find yourself in a world of hurt. In fact, if a font that a system application needs is missing, the application may very well crash on opening. You should avoid mucking around in here for that reason. To borrow a line from one of my favorite movies, *Turner and Hooch,* "This is not your room."

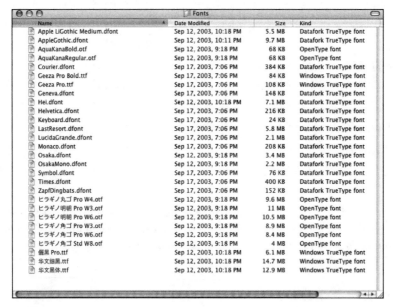

Figure 7-2

Don't muck around in the System Fonts folder.

Classic Fonts

If OS X needs a font and can't find it by looking in the user's personal Fonts folder, the Library Fonts folder, the Network Fonts folder, or the System Fonts folder (almost always in that order), it looks in the Classic Fonts folder. That folder is located in Mac OS 9 System Folder>Fonts. This folder also holds the fonts used by the system when you run OS 9. I'll address moving those fonts later in this chapter, and we'll revisit it briefly again in Chapter 10, "Optimizing OS 9."

Organizing Fonts

Now that you know where your fonts are, it's time to take a look at what fonts you have. I'll venture a guess that you have lots of fonts you don't want or need. You might not know this, but many companies such as Microsoft and Adobe install their own fonts as you install their programs. If you've ever purchased a font collection, you might even have special folders and font viewers as well. If you've ever visited a Web site and downloaded fonts, you can be sure those are hanging around somewhere too.

Having unnecessary fonts, fonts with only minor differences (such as a bold, italic, and normal versions of the same font), fonts that are the same but have different names, unorganized fonts, or duplicate fonts not only slows down your system and how fast you work, but it can also cause system crashes. It's important to take control of your fonts before they get out of hand!

We'll start here with the easiest of all font tasks: organizing them. To begin, let's take a look first at the Font Panel and font menus, and then we'll look at grouping fonts and finally we'll examine which fonts to delete and why.

Two Ways to Select Fonts

When using older applications, or when using an application that has simply been made compatible for OS X (a Carbon application), choosing a font for a particular piece of text involves selecting a font name from a formatting window or palette or from a font menu, as shown in Figure 7-3. It's common to access fonts this way in applications created by Microsoft, Adobe, and AppleWorks, as well as any older programs you have installed. Selecting a font from an alphabetical list works pretty well as long as you don't have hundreds of fonts, but for the most part, wading through a long list of fonts with no preview is incredibly inefficient.

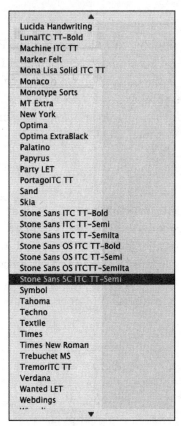

Figure 7-3

For older applications, you'll need to wade through fonts like this.

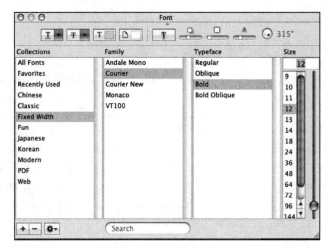

Figure 7-4

For newer applications like TextEdit and Mail, you'll get to use the new Font Panel.

For newer applications, there's something much better. For programs specifically created for the Mac OS X operating system (Cocoa applications, programs that have been written specifically for OS X to be Mac OS X compatible), the Font Panel is used instead of the familiar drop-down lists.

With the Font Panel, you can use one interface to choose fonts, their size, and their type; manage collections; and edit your collections by putting fonts in specific groups. You can even choose Show Preview from the Actions menu to see a preview of the font you've selected. To use the Font Panel, you'll have to use a Cocoa application such as TextEdit or Mail or a third-party application that was specifically created for OS X.

To make OS X work better and to help you work faster, it's imperative that the fonts displayed in the Font Panel and in font menu lists are organized. That's what we'll talk about in this section.

TIP: If your fonts look fuzzy on the screen, open System Preferences, click the Appearance icon, and chose a higher number for the section Turn Off Text Smoothing For Font Sizes ____ And Smaller. Experiment to get the right on-screen effect.

Organizing the Font Panel

Because most of you have recently upgraded to OS X, or will soon, and because you will also be moving to Cocoa applications now or in the near future, I'll introduce the Font Panel first. (If you are still using OS 9, you can skip this part and move on to the next section. Or if you're thinking of upgrading, you can visit **www.mac.com** and click the Mac OS X tab for additional information.) The Font Panel allows you to work with and choose fonts using an extremely powerful interface. From one area, you can do the following:

√   Edit font characteristics from inside a powerful user interface.

√   View and choose a font.

√   View a font in various sizes.

√   Change the characteristics of a font.

√   Add ordinals, change the glyph characteristics, enable or disable ligatures, and more.

√   Delete collections of fonts.

By organizing what you see in the Font Panel, you can save lots of time and frustration. You can put all the fonts for a particular client in a folder specifically created for that client, drag and drop fonts from one folder to another (create a link to Comic Sans in the Fun folder, for instance), access recently used fonts from the Recently Used folder, delete folders and collections, and change a font's default characteristics.

To get started, open TextEdit from the Applications folder, type a few words and select them, choose Format>Font>Show Fonts, and from the Collections pane, select a folder from the Collections pane, select a font family from the Family pane, and select a typeface and size from the Typeface and Size panes. Figure 7-5 shows an example. (If you aren't seeing the preview of the font, from the Actions menu, select Show Preview.)

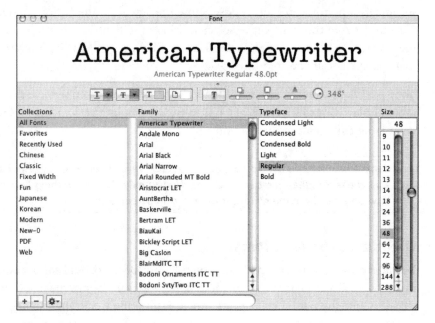

Figure 7-5
Open the Font Panel and select a font.

Once the Font Panel is open, it's easy to add fonts to the Favorites folder, design collections, edit font characteristics, show characters, manipulate a font's typography and color, and manage fonts.

To add a font to the Favorites folder, follow these steps:

1. Open TextEdit and choose Format>Font>Show Fonts.

2. In the Collections pane, select All Fonts (or any other folder that contains the font you want to add to the Favorites folder), and choose the font to add.

3. From the Actions menu, select Add To Favorites. (This does not actually move the font—it only creates a type of font alias.)

Follow these steps to create your own font collection:

1. Open TextEdit and choose Format>Font>Show Fonts.

2. In the Collections pane, select All Fonts.

3. From the Actions menu, select Manage Fonts. The Font Book opens.

4. From the Collections pane, select All Fonts. Click the + sign on the bottom left to create a new collection.

5. Type a name for the new collection.

6. Choose any other folder that contain the fonts you'd like to add to the new folder.

7. Drag any desired fonts to the new folder. Figure 7-6 shows the Font Book (accessed from the Font Panel) with a new folder and fonts. Close the Font Book.

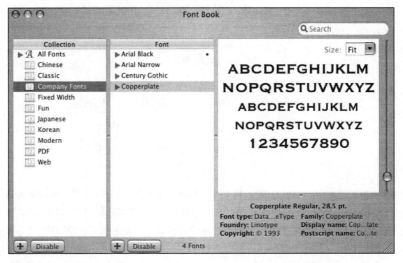

Figure 7-6
From the Font Panel's Actions menu, select Manage Fonts, and from Font Book, create a new collection and add fonts to it.

TIP: When you create a collection, it will also appear in the FontCollections folder of your personal Library folder.

Now, the next time you use TextEdit, Mail, or another Mac OS X–compatible Cocoa application, that folder and its fonts will be available.

Here's how to edit a font's characteristic:

1. Open TextEdit, type and select a few words, and choose Format>Font>Show Fonts.

2. In the Collections pane, select All Fonts (or any other folder that contains the font to edit). Select the font you want to use.

3. From the Actions menu, select Edit Sizes. Verify that Fixed List and Adjustable Slider are selected. In the size list, select a font size that you want as the default. Click Done. (Notice that you can use the slider too.)

4. From the Actions menu, select Color. Choose a new color from the Colors dialog box. Close the box.

You can select and add characters from the Actions menu by selecting Characters; you can configure typography settings if they're available for a font from the Actions menu by selecting Typography. Many times, typography settings consist only of enabling or disabling ligatures. (A ligature is a set of letters that join together when printed.) Sometimes, the letters of a font are close to one another, as in *fi, ff, fl,* and enabling ligatures provides a cleaner look on the printed page.

To delete a collection, follow these steps:

1. Open TextEdit and choose Format>Font>Show Fonts.

2. In the Collections pane, select the collection to delete.

3. Click the − (minus) sign in the bottom left corner.

4. Verify that you want to delete the collection by choosing Delete. (Deleting the collection does not delete the font.)

As you can see, degunking your machine goes way beyond simply deleting your old pictures and videos or organizing folders. Degunking is also required for things you've never suspected could get gunked up or never thought you had much control over, like your font folders. By keeping your fonts and the Font Panel organized, you can increase productivity, stay organized, and keep fonts how they should be kept: organized and easy to locate and use.

Cleaning Your Font Menu

Font menus can get quite messy and gunked up, and selecting a font almost always becomes a major headache sooner or later. Working through long lists of fonts just to find the single font you want can be quite trying. Font menu clutter is a major headache and makes working from the menu completely inefficient. If you are still using older applications that aren't Font Panel compatible, you'll want to work to clean up your font menu gunk.

Figure 7-7 shows an example of gunk in a font menu. Notice the Bodoni font has seven entries and the American Typewriter font has four. If you aren't a professional artist, Web designer, or graphic designer, you should consider removing or disabling those fonts you can live without. I, for one, can live without the seven versions of Bodoni. Make a mental note of the fonts you don't like or need, and I'll show you how to disable or delete them later in this chapter.

```
Agent Orange
American Typewriter
American Typewriter Condensed
American Typewriter Condensed Light
American Typewriter Light
Andale Mono
Apple Chancery
Arial
Arial Black
Arial Narrow
Arial Rounded MT Bold
Aristocrat LET
AuntBertha
Baskerville
Baskerville Semibold
Bertram LET
Bickley Script LET
Big Caslon
BlairMdITC TT-Medium
Bodoni Ornaments ITC TT
Bodoni SvtyTwo ITC TT-Bold
Bodoni SvtyTwo ITC TT-Book
Bodoni SvtyTwo ITC TT-BookIta
Bodoni SvtyTwo OS ITC TT-Bold
Bodoni SvtyTwo OS ITC TT-Book
Bodoni SvtyTwo OS ITC TT-BookIt
```

Figure 7-7
Font menus can collect lots of gunk by offering similar font options.

Some programs offer the option to show a font in its own format. Microsoft products and AppleWorks are two of those. Although choosing to show the fonts in the list as it would actually appear can slow the menu down as it opens, the time saved by being able to see the font before selecting it is worth the extra split-second it takes the font menu to appear. Figure 7-8 shows an example of such a menu. Notice that you can tell how similar some of these fonts are and, thus, that they are probably unnecessary.

So, how do you get rid of the font menu clutter? There are a couple of ways. You can disable or delete fonts you don't need, or you can use one of several utilities to organize the font list, including one very powerful program entitled Adobe Type Reunion Deluxe. This program cleans up font menu gunk by grouping styles of fonts together in the menu. Instead of one long menu list, you'll have two: the name of the font followed by the additional entries for that particular font. You won't have to worry about deleting or disabling fonts if you use a utility such as this.

Installing and Deleting Fonts

Although you can buy and install as many fonts as you want, having too many fonts will cause applications to start slowly and will require you to sort through unnecessary fonts to find what you want. Upon first opening a program and accessing fonts,

Figure 7-8
Showing fonts as they would actually appear helps you be more productive, even
though it takes a split-second longer to open the menu.

you'll also notice it takes some time to get that long font menu to open. As you
acquire fonts, then, make sure you really need a new font and that the font is not just
a variation of one you already have. Make sure it doesn't look like a font you have,
either. Graphite and Tek look almost exactly alike; Chancellor and Penman do, too.
There's likely no reason for a nonprofessional artist to have both.

When deciding what to delete, use Font Book (as detailed in the next section)
to preview fonts and font types, and make a list of what you can get rid of or
disable. Fonts and collections can be disabled and deleted from inside Font
Book, or you can remove them by dragging from your personal Fonts folder. If
you're an administrator, you can delete them from the Library Fonts folder, but
as always, I'll urge you to leave the System Fonts folder alone. There are only a
few fonts in there anyway. (I'll assume that if you have a Network Fonts folder,
your network administrator will be taking care of those fonts. We'll discuss OS
9's fonts a little later in this chapter.)

Font Book

You may be thinking that all of this font talk—especially dealing with five folders,
the Font Panel, font menus, and now a Font Book—is just too much stuff to deal
with. You may also be thinking that locating and organizing fonts is just too much

trouble to go through to knock off a split-second from the time it takes a menu to open, a couple of seconds off of the time it takes to open Photoshop or AppleWorks, or a few extra seconds off the time it takes to locate a font in a menu. It's actually worth it in the long run, though, and if you follow my advice in the rest of this chapter, I think you'll see a big difference in the operating performance of your Mac. Organizing fonts and deleting the ones you don't need can really make a difference. Think of it this way: even though it will take you an entire Saturday to put up shelving in the garage and half of Sunday to get all of your tools stored properly, you'll save countless hours from here on out when you need to locate one of those tools. It'll be right where it should be, easy to locate, and ready for use.

The Power of the Font Book

The Font Book offers several other options, and it's quite a powerful tool. Here are just a few of the things you can do inside Font Book:

√   Install and preview fonts.

√   Configure preferences for newly installed fonts.

√   Search for fonts by name.

√   Locate duplicate fonts.

√   Activate fonts and font collections you like; deactivate fonts and font collections you don't like.

√   Access advanced controls for typography, as well as the Character palette.

√   Organize fonts in collections.

√   Get font information.

√   Remove fonts.

√   Remove collections.

TIP: The Font Book can also be accessed from the Applications folder.

Preview Font Families

In order to decide what fonts to disable or delete, you need to know what the fonts look like. Here's how to preview fonts:

1.   Open Font Book from the Applications folder. Click All Fonts.

2.   In the Font pane, click the flippy triangle next to each font name to see the variations available for each font. Select a variation to view it. Figure 7-9 shows an example.

3.   Select a size or move the slider to view the font in various sizes.

4.   Make a note of the fonts you want to get rid of or disable.

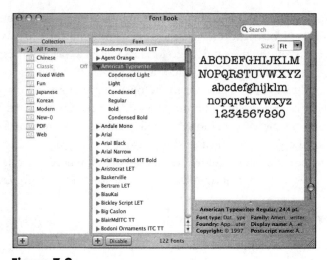

Figure 7-9
Some fonts have several variations, adding to the level of font gunk on your Mac.

Figure 7-9 shows that the font American Typewriter has 6 variations, including Condensed Light, Light, Condensed, Regular, Bold, and Condensed Bold.

Enable/Disable Fonts and Font Collections

You can enable or disable fonts and font collections that you no longer want or need, which will shorten the lists of fonts you have to sort through when using the Font Panel or the font menus in applications. Disabling a font does not free up hard drive space, though; the font is still on the computer, but it does help clean up font menus and the Font Panel by removing the listing. (Well, you have to quit and restart most applications, but it does remove the listing eventually.) Disabling a font grays the font out in the Font Book; enabling the font reverses this move.

TIP: If you ever are positive you have a font that you can't find, take a look at the disabled fonts in the Font Book.

To disable a font, open Font Book, and in the Font pane, select the font to disable. Click the Disable button underneath that pane. Choose Disable again when asked to verify.

To disable a font collection, open Font Book, and in the Collection pane, select the collection to disable. Click the Disable button underneath that pane. Click Disable again when asked to verify.

To disable any collection as well as all of the fonts in it, choose Font Book>Preferences, and in the choices after Disabling A Collection Turns Off, choose All Fonts In The Collection. Figure 7-10 in the next section shows this option.

Tweak Preferences

When the Font Book is open, you have access to the Font Book Preferences dialog box from the Font Book menu. Preferences allow you to state how fonts you install will be shared, if at all. If you do not share your Mac, there's no need to change the default settings, so leave the Font Book preferences as shown in Figure 7-10.

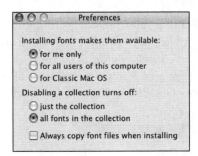

Figure 7-10
If you don't share your Mac, choose to install fonts for your use only.

If other users access your Mac and have accounts, and if you want those users to be able to access the fonts you install, select For All Users Of This Computer instead.

Delete Fonts

It's important to delete fonts you don't need because having too many fonts not only slows down how fast *your computer* works, it slows down how fast *you* work. There's no reason to have multiple versions of the same font or fonts that are the same but have different names. Although it'll take a little time, deleting unnecessary fonts is an extremely important degunking task.

You have fonts in lots of places on your hard drive, five folders in fact. To remove a font, an administrator must remove it from each of these folders. Remember, when OS X looks for a font, it works through all five available folders; the font will continue to be available as long as your Mac can find it in one of the font folders. Because the operating system needs certain fonts, though, we're going to concentrate on fonts you've added or acquired by installing programs. (I still don't think I want you mucking about in the System Fonts folder.)

Delete Fonts You Don't Want

To delete a font completely, or as near to completely as we're going to get right now, you need to remove it from both your personal Fonts folder and the Library Fonts folder. If it's available in the Classic OS 9 Mac folder, you'll have to remove it from there too. If the font is in the System Fonts folder, we're going to let it be. Deleting a file such as TrueType HelveticaNeue.dfont from the System-level Fonts folder will cause iCal to crash on opening, among other problems. I certainly don't want to be the one to encourage you to bring on a problem such as that!

To delete a font file from a "safe" folder, follow these steps:

1. Open Font Book.

2. Click the flippy triangle next to All Fonts to show the categories User, Computer, and Classic Mac OS. Select User, as shown in Figure 7-11, and then select a font to delete. Make sure it's a font you've added yourself or are sure you won't need later; you don't want to delete any font that you'll need often, such as Arial, Century Gothic, or Times New Roman.

Figure 7-11
Notice the three categories of fonts: User, Computer, and Classic Mac OS.

3. From the Menu bar, choose File>Remove Font. Click Remove to verify you want to remove this font file. Removing a font from your user Font folder does not remove it from any other folder. If the same font is present in another folder, it must be deleted from there as well.

4. Under All Fonts, select Computer.

5. Select a font to delete. Make sure it's a font you've added yourself; you don't want to delete any font that you'll need often.

6. From the Menu bar, choose File>Remove Font. Click Remove to verify you want to remove the font.

7. Under All Fonts, select Classic Mac OS 9.

8. Select a font to delete. Make sure it's a font you've added yourself; you don't want to delete any font that you'll need often.

9. From the Menu bar, choose File>Remove Font. Click Remove to verify you want to remove the font.

Just for kicks, I performed the preceding steps to delete Arial Black, which was available from all three folders. Arial Black is not in the list of fonts in the System Fonts folder and is thus removed from my Mac completely. You could work through your font folders and delete duplicates in this manner if you really want to remove as much gunk as possible.

TIP: You can always recover the font file from the Trash and drag it back to the appropriate Fonts folder if the Trash has not been emptied. You can even drag it back into the Font Book. (Because recovering missing fonts from the original disks is difficult, I suggest backing up any deleted fonts before emptying the Trash; if you ever need them again, you'll have them.)

Delete Duplicates

When OS X needs a font, most of the time it looks first in the user's personal Fonts folder, then the Library Fonts folder, then the Network Fonts folder, and then the System Fonts folder. If it isn't available in those folders, it looks in the Classic Fonts folder. If you have duplicate fonts, OS X will generally use the first font it finds without causing any problems at all. However, third-party applications may not look for fonts in that order. This can cause problems for the application, can change the way the text looks on the screen, and can cause formatting problems when the document or graphic is printed. In addition, if the font has a duplicate, especially a duplicate in the same folder, sometimes an application gets so confused it can't even open the file or program at all and crashes. What's worse, though, is that duplicate fonts can even keep your Mac from booting up! To make a long story short, it is *not* a good idea to have fonts that are duplicates in the same folder. It's also not good to leave font conflicts unresolved.

Welcome to Font Book's bullet symbol for denoting font conflicts and Font Book's Resolve Duplicates command. If you think you have a problem with duplicates, or even if you don't, perform the following steps to find out and resolve any font conflicts:

1. Open Font Book.

2. Select All Fonts.

3. Scroll down the font list looking for bullets denoting conflicts. Figure 7-12 shows an example.

4. If you find a font with a bullet beside it, expand it by clicking the flippy triangle to see what's listed for the font.

Figure 7-12
A bullet in Font Book denotes a duplicate font.

5. In the bulleted list that appears, select a font that has a bullet beside it (there may be several).

6. Choose Edit>Resolve Duplicates. Verify you want to disable the font selected by choosing OK when prompted.

7. The bullet will disappear and the conflict will be resolved. Repeat these steps until all conflicts have been resolved.

Once you've finished with the All Fonts folder, take a quick peek in the other folders—Users and Classic Mac OS—to make sure no other conflicts appear.

TIP: *If you can't find Font Book, it's because you don't have it. You will need to upgrade to the latest version of OS X to get it.*

Moving Fonts from OS 9

If you have made the move from OS 9 to OS X and you want to move your OS 9 fonts to your OS X font folders, you can do so easily using Font Book (assuming you have 10.3 or higher). If you're using an earlier version of OS X, it's the same concept, but this process will involve dragging and dropping between folders instead of using Font Book.

Follow these steps to move fonts using the Font Book:

1. Open Font Book.

2. Expand the All Fonts folder.

3. Make a mental note of which fonts are in the User folder and the Computer folder. You don't want to move fonts that are already in either folder and cause conflicts as the result of duplicate fonts.

4. Choose the Classic Mac OS folder.

5. Select the font or fonts to move. Select noncontiguous items in the list by holding down the Command key while selecting; select contiguous items by holding down the Shift key while selecting.

6. Drag the selected files to the Computer folder.

To move fonts by dragging and dropping between folders, follow these steps:

1. Open the OS 9 System folder. It's available from the Macintosh HD.

2. Open the Fonts folder.

3. Choose View>As List.

4. Move that folder aside while you locate the folder to move the fonts to in OS X.

5. Open the OS X System folder. It's available from the Macintosh HD.

6. Open Library>Fonts. These are the fonts that are available to everyone who uses the computer. You'll drag the fonts to this folder. (You could drag the fonts to your personal Fonts folder, but the main Fonts folder is generally a better choice.)

7. Position this folder so both folders are accessible.

8. Drag the desired fonts from the OS 9 Fonts folder to the OS X Fonts folder. Don't move fonts that would create duplicates.

9. Close all windows when finished.

You can also disable OS 9 fonts, delete them, and manipulate them as desired.

Font Management Programs

If understanding where fonts are stored, organizing fonts into groups, disabling and deleting unnecessary fonts, and moving fonts from OS 9 to OS X isn't enough control for you, there are several extremely powerful tools available from third-party companies to help you manage fonts more effectively. While it would be difficult to compile a comprehensive list of the available applications, I can introduce some of the more popular ones here.

Extensis Suitcase

Extensis Suitcase is a rather expensive program ($100 U.S.) available from **www.extensis.com**, but it's well worth the cost if you need more control over your fonts. With Extensis Suitcase, you can do almost anything, including the following:

√ Preview fonts in lots of different ways to compare fonts and font similarities or differences.

√ Activate fonts in a number of ways, including directly from the Preview pane.

√ Automatically activate fonts for the most popular Mac OS X applications.

√ Use the Quick Find feature to find a font matching specific criteria.

√ Automatically scan fonts for font corruption and repair.

√ Resolve duplicate fonts easily.

√ Use the included utility, FontDoctor, to diagnose and repair font problems.

Pacifist

If you did not heed the warnings in this chapter and somehow deleted a necessary system font and this caused your Mac or one of its applications to crash and burn, you'll need to reinstall the missing font to resolve the issues caused by removing it. If there's no backup copy, you'll have to either reinstall OS X or use a third-party utility. Pacifist, from **ww.charlessoft.com** ($20 U.S.), can be used to extract the font from your OS X CD, saving countless headaches.

Fontifier

Fontifier, available from **www.fontifier.com**, is a free application that can take your handwriting and turn it into a font that can be used with any word processing program or graphics application. Once you've downloaded and installed Fontifier, you can print out the template sheet, write each character, scan the template, name the font, and send the file to the Fontifier Web site. Your file will be turned into a TrueType font that you can then download and install. It only works on OS X, though, but it's a blast!

Summing Up

Font gunk can really slow you down. Too many installed fonts makes finding the one you want nearly impossible and slows down how quickly programs open; conflicts with fonts can even bring down your Mac. If system fonts are missing, applications might not open or the computer might fail to boot. Keeping your fonts clean, organized, and in good working order is a must.

In this chapter, you learned where fonts are stored and why, how to organize your fonts into groups for easier access, how to delete and disable fonts you don't need, and how to resolve conflicts when duplicate fonts are installed. You also learned to move fonts from OS 9 to OS X, and we looked at some third-party applications that will help you manage your fonts better.

Preventing Spam Gunk

Degunking Checklist:

√ Create three different e-mail accounts—primary, backup, and disposable—to minimize spam.

√ Choose a primary e-mail address that is not vulnerable to dictionary attacks.

√ Don't use your primary e-mail address on newsgroups, with vendors, on the Web, or anywhere else.

√ Do not use "unsubscribe" options to get rid of spam.

√ Choose, use, and update a separate spam filtering product to reduce spam.

√ Take advantage of Mail's Junk Filtering options.

√ Learn about mail proxies and free and low-cost spam filtering utilities.

E -mail is the glue that holds your personal and business computing together. Unfortunately, this glue is a magnet for gunk. Just a little careless-
ness will attract an unimaginable amount of gunk in the form of spam. Spam is
one of those phenomena for which prevention is the very best cure. In this
chapter, you'll learn how to degunk your Mac by preventing spam from entering your In box in the first place.

Spam is unsolicited e-mail. It's generally from companies you've never dealt
with or heard of, although one purchase from a legitimate site can result in
spam as well. Much of spam is fraudulent—pleas for help from Nigerian royalty,
get-rich-quick pyramid schemes, penis or breast enlargement offers, offers for
prescription drugs without a doctor's visit, and so forth. Chances are you're not
interested in any of these things.

As you'll learn here, you can minimize spam by performing some preventative
maintenance and by using a little common sense. The object is to prevent spam
first, keep what you do get under control, and formulate a plan for reducing or
eliminating spam altogether. We'll do that in this chapter. In Chapter 9, e-mail
housecleaning will be covered in more detail, and you'll learn how to clean up
and organize your legitimate mail and deal with spam that gets through your
defenses.

Choose the Best E-Mail Addresses

Choosing the proper e-mail address is crucial for spam prevention. If you want
to take control and minimize the amount of spam you get, it's important to
have three e-mail addresses:

√   Primary

√   Backup

√   Disposable

Your primary e-mail address is the one you give your closest friends and colleagues. It's the address you'll use to receive legitimate correspondence. This is
also the place you'll be fighting spam the hardest and with the most resources.
Make sure you tell your friends and colleagues not to share this address with
anyone. One well-meaning friend who types in your primary address at a greeting
card Web site can get you on a spammer's e-mail list that will only be propa-
gated to others.

Your backup e-mail address should be a second e-mail account that doesn't
have anything to do with the first but that you're able to use just in case your
primary address goes down. You should choose one that also has spam filtering

tools of its own. This might be from MSN, Yahoo!, or a similar vendor. Figure 8-1 shows a welcome message and a link to the Bulk folder for my Yahoo! account. Notice that there are 177 unread messages in the Bulk folder; these are all spam. However, in a pinch, I can ask friends and colleagues to use this address if my primary address is unavailable.

Figure 8-1
When choosing a backup address, choose a company that offers spam filtering options, and have suspected spam sent to a folder for that purpose.

Finally, you'll want a disposable address (or addresses). These are addresses you can cancel at any time and lose nothing. These disposable addresses can be obtained free from various sites on the Internet. Use these addresses when corresponding with vendors, when registering at Web sites, and for similar communication. When the spam finally forces your hand and the address becomes useless, discontinue it.

Set Up Your Primary E-Mail Address

You should be able to get e-mail from your primary address from anywhere, whether you're using your laptop in another country, using a friend's computer, or using your PDA at a wireless hotspot. Here are some guidelines:

√ Your primary address should not be the e-mail address that you get when you sign up for a broadband Internet connection at home. Some of these providers do not allow access when connecting via a wireless Wi-Fi hotspot or from a dial-up connection.

√ If you connect using a dial-up network like AOL, that address is suitable as a primary address. AOL and similar networks have dial-up points of presence around the country, and you can get in from any of them.

√ The best primary e-mail address to have is one associated with a Web hosting account. Most Web hosting firms offer some number of e-mail addresses (usually 5 to 10). These multiple addresses are good if you ever have to change for spam reasons.

√ You should be able to access your e-mail from the Internet; .Mac accounts offer a fine way to do this.

√   If you have a Web site, use the e-mail address associated with your domain name. It looks professional and people can remember it easily. There will be more on that later.

Set Up Backup and Disposable E-Mail Addresses

The address you obtain from your broadband provider makes a good backup address, as does an address from one of the free Web mail sites. Here are some guidelines:

√   Use your broadband ISP e-mail address or an account with a well known e-mail provider like AOL.

√   Obtain a disposable account from any of the free Web mail services such as MSN or Yahoo! (More on using disposable e-mail addresses shortly.)

Avoid Spammer Dictionary Attacks

Spammers pay virtually nothing to send out an e-mail. They can send out millions of e-mails in a single day, so sending out e-mails that don't actually make it to any recipient doesn't bother them much. Hence the popularity of the dictionary attack. Spammers simply pick a domain, say mac.com, and send out e-mails that look like this:

√   Abe@mac.com

√   Abby@mac.com

√   Al@mac.com

√   Alan@mac.com

√   Albert@mac.com

√   Andrew@mac.com

√   Andy@mac.com

√   Ann@mac.com

√   Anna@mac.com

So the problem, as anyone can see from this list, is that if you have a common ISP, and if you combine that with a common name, you're going to get hit hard with dictionary attacks. There's hope, though. Avoiding dictionary attacks is simple, if not foolproof, by following these guidelines:

√   Make sure your e-mail name is not a recognizable word. For instance, instead of Bob@mac.com or Wells@mac.com, try BobWells@Mac.com, or better yet, make up a word, such as BobsTheBest@mac.com.

√ Stay away from words that aren't in the dictionary but are well known, such as Gandalf or DrSpock.

√ Stay away from words that are in the dictionary. Period.

√ Don't use random letters like akslf@mac.com. This looks like a spammer's address and may cause your e-mail to be passed over and deleted by your recipients' spam filters.

√ Don't think a middle initial will help. BobG@mac.com can be caught by spammers. In recent years, spammers have been cycling through first names and middle initials looking for e-mail addresses.

The basic idea is to choose a name that would be hard to guess, the same way you'd choose a password that is difficult to figure out. For even more protection, put a number or two in there: BobWells2@mac.com.

Use Your E-Mail Address Carefully

If you're not careful about how you use your primary e-mail address, you're likely to find yourself covered up in spam before you can turn around. Once spammers lay their hands on your primary e-mail address, they will send you spam forever. There seems to be no "time-out" period, either. You can verify to a spammer that your e-mail address is "live" by purchasing something from a non-secure site, clicking a link to a Web site, or choosing the "unsubscribe" button at the bottom of an e-mail message.

The following sections tell you what not to do with your e-mail address and why. None of this is any guarantee that you won't get spam, or that spammers won't find you. But by following this advice, you can drastically reduce your spam problem.

GunkBuster's Notebook: Your Friends May Be Your Worst Enemy

No matter how hard you try to keep spam out of your In box, and no matter what strides you take to protect yourself from spammers, you can't control what your friends do. In fact, it may well be your friends that become your downfall. I had a spam-free In box once. That was before my friend JD used my address to get free movie tickets (if you offer up 15 or more e-mail addresses, you'll be sent a ticket good for a free pass). Leo gave my address to a Web site so that I could see some cute list about how to be happy (yeah, that made me *real* happy), and years ago John sent me a greeting card from a popular greeting card Web site.

Unfortunately, these well-meaning friends and their cute cards, schemes to get prizes, and funny jokes will only help spammers meet their goals. Once you're on one of these lists, you're on all of them. So when you get a new and pristine e-mail address, you're going to have to be tough with your friends and family. Make sure to tell your friends in no uncertain terms that this is your *private* address. They are not to share it with anyone.

Don't Use the Unsubscribe Option

Ever find it funny that a spam message rarely gives any information about who the spammer is, what company they come from, or the physical location of the company but that they almost always offer some legitimate-looking option to unsubscribe? If you believe hitting that unsubscribe button actually works to get you off lists, I've got some oceanfront property in Arizona I'd like to sell you!

The thing is, hitting the unsubscribe button only tells the spammers that they've reached a working address. Once they know that, you're doomed. Unsubscribing from a spammer's e-mail address is always a hoax. The sole purpose of the link is to verify the address. Now, you may actually run across a legitimate unsubscribe option every now and then, say from Amazon or Northwest Airline, but with unsolicited e-mails, unsubscribe options will never get you off the mailing list. Better than unsubscribing is blocking, creating rules, and using spam filtering utilities. Whatever you choose, keep your fingers away from the mouse and that unsubscribe button!

Never Post Your E-Mail Address on the Web— Except as a Graphic

Getting new addresses to spam is one of a spammer's highest priorities, and they go to great lengths to get them. In the late 1990s, spammers took a hint from Web search engines and created Web crawlers and Web spiders that simply go through page after page looking for the @ symbol. When they'd find one, they would harvest the address. If you've got your e-mail address on a Web page, you're sure to get spammed.

The lesson is clear: Do not post your e-mail address in "naked" form on your Web page. The spiders are still lurking around, all day, every day. Furthermore, make it clear to friends, family, and colleagues that they cannot post your e-mail address on their Web pages. This is a big problem for people who are publicly known for some reason, like a senator or congressman, or whose address is often used for a contact, such as one who serves on a committee.

If it's absolutely essential that your e-mail address be posted on a Web site, have it rendered in graphic form. You've probably seen this already—where someone's address is not character-based but designed into a graphic in a file. Spiders can't read the contents of graphics, so this is one way around the spiders.

E-Mail Addresses, E-Lists, Newsgroups, and E-Commerce

Just as there are spiders that look at Web pages to harvest addresses, there are spiders that look on Usenet newsgroups, in chat rooms, and at Web discussion boards too. Postings to newsgroups and boards often require the entry of an e-mail address of some kind. Some people simply post a phony address; that works. Others obfuscate their usual e-mail address so that those "in the know" can still contact them while spiders get lost in the Web.

The idea behind obfuscating is that the address is broken up in a way that a spider can't identify it as a phony address but a reasonably intelligent person can. For example, if your e-mail address is BobsAGreatGuy@mac.com you might try any of the following addresses:

√ BobsAGreatGuy@MacPULLTHIS.com

√ BobsAGreatGuy@MacNOSPAM.com

√ BobsAGreatGuy@MacSPAMSUCKS.com

Unfortunately, the spammers figured this out pretty quickly (seeing how all they have to do is note that an address has a block of uppercase type), so you'll have to be a little more ingenious if you really want to protect yourself:

√ BobsAGreatGuy@MacPuLLThIS.com

√ BobsAGreatGuy@MacNO$PAM.com

√ BobsAGreatGuy@MacSPaMSuCKS.com

Although it might take a minute to figure out what to remove, those users who participate in newsgroups regularly will be old pros and will know what you've done.

TIP: *It won't be long before you'll have to remove the word "spam" from your obfuscated address name. Spammers have figured that out too.*

Use Disposable Addresses for E-Commerce

The largest and best-known e-commerce retailers like Amazon.com can probably be trusted not to sell your e-mail addresses to spammers. (They have too much to lose if it ever came out, for way too small a financial gain.) Unfortunately, midsize and smaller retailers are another matter. When creating an account with online retailers then, no matter how big or small, always use a disposable e-mail address. These are e-mail addresses obtained from one of many free e-mail services that are everywhere on the Web. They cost nothing, and when an address inevitably becomes a spam magnet, it can be discarded and another one obtained easily.

Nearly all e-mail clients can support multiple e-mail accounts, and that includes Mail and Outlook Express or Entourage. Here are the general steps to follow:

1. Create and set up a separate account for each address you use.

2. When you check your mail, make sure it is set to obtain all of your e-mail from all of your addresses.

3. Create a filter or message rule that deposits all mail sent to your disposable address into a specific folder. Creating filters is specific to the mail client you use. In the next section, I'll talk about doing that in Apple's Mail. For other clients, read the associated help files.

If you limit the use of a disposable address to a single vendor, you'll be able to quickly find out if that vendor sold your address to spammers. If that happens, fire off a nasty letter, tell all of your friends, and boycott the vendor and its services. It's one way you can do your part to end spam!

TIP: You don't have to give Web sites a real address all of the time, especially if you don't need a registration code or verification. When asked for an e-mail address to enter a site, make one up like sales@puthecompanynamehere.com.

GunkBuster's Notebook: A New Way to Deal with Spam

There are services available that will ask for verification from a sender before their e-mail is forwarded on to you. The services ask the sender to input a few words to verify that they're an actual person, not a spammer. Once the sender responds, the e-mail is delivered to your In box. While these services eventually learn who your legitimate contacts are and actively reduce spam from reaching you by asking for this verification, ultimately (in my opinion), the services only cause headaches for the people that send you legitimate e-mail.

These types of services and spin-offs of them will continue to be available in the upcoming months and years, and each subsequent release will prove more and more effective. For now, keep in mind that your contacts will be inconvenienced by such a "service" and you may lose legitimate job offers, miss valuable contacts, and, well, simply cause more work for those who need to contact you quickly.

Services That Manage Disposable Addresses

There are online sites that offer paid services for creating and managing e-mail addresses, and they all work basically the same way. They allow you to create a self-destructing e-mail alias for your e-mail address. These aliases can then be sent to e-commerce retailers, and after a predetermined period of time or predetermined number of messages sent back to you at that specific address, the address self-destructs.

These services are pretty cheap. They charge from $10 to $20 a year, but not all of them work out quite as expected. Some allow you to make the mistake of replying to a message with your real e-mail address in the From field, completely negating the benefit of using their services. Because there are so many free services anyway, it all seems rather pointless in the long run. If you need a disposable address, just grab one from Hotmail, Yahoo!, BoxFrog, or any one of the multitude of other options out there and discard them as necessary. (Many self-destruct anyway after 30 or 60 days of inactivity.)

TIP: When filling out online forms, always remember to uncheck the option "Yes, send me exciting offers," or "Yes, send me offers from your partners." Even if this option is from your friendly neighborhood bank, I guarantee that within a month you'll have more offers for home refinancing, car refinancing, life insurance, medical insurance, and cheap vacations than you'll know what to do with.

Using Mail's Junk E-Mail Utilities

You can choose from a number of e-mail clients, and while there isn't enough room here to discuss all of them, I would at least like to introduce the spam filtering features of Apple Mail. Apple's Mail has a few tricks up its sleeve for protecting you from spam. One is the new Junk E-Mail Filter, which can be used to train Mail to decipher between legitimate mail and spam. Another is an option to create message rules. Mail also provides a Bounce Sender command that sends a junk message back to the sender, coded as if it had reached a non-working address. Spammers hate that! Let's talk about these three things in detail, and if you use Apple's Mail, follow along and incorporate these utilities.

Creating Rules

You can create rules to tell Mail what to do with specific messages. For instance, if your ISP warns you of spam by adding something to the Subject line (like mine does), you can create a message rule to send any message with that warning to a folder you've created. You can then look in that folder occasionally to make sure nothing important has been accidentally placed there. Look at Figure 8-2. Notice that the subject line of many of these messages has ✭✭✭✭✭POSSIBLE SPAM✭✭✭✭✭ added to it. That means that my ISP has caught this mail and tagged it as spam before it ever got to me. Now that's what I'm talkin' about!

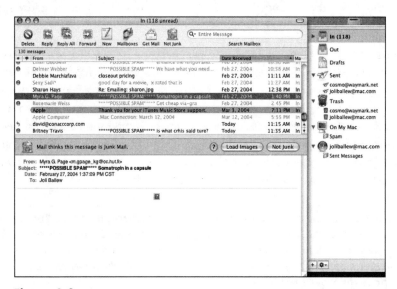

Figure 8-2

Some ISPs tag messages as spam.

You can also create message rules that filter incoming e-mail into folders if they are from a specific person (like your spouse, boss, or secretary), if the e-mail is from someone in your address book (or not), if the message is flagged as junk e-mail, if the message is to a specific person, and more.

TIP: Consider creating a rule that looks for the word "unsubscribe" in the body of the e-mail. Most spam has this word in it. Because the word "unsubscribe" is usually part of a live link back to the spammer and not a graphic, the rule will pick up most of these spam messages.

To create a new folder and a specific folder rule to send e-mail to it, follow these steps:

1. Open Mail.

2. Choose View>Columns and verify that Mailbox is selected.

3. In the Mailbox pane, Control+click the In box and select New.

4. Select a location from the choices. Choices will vary. Selecting a choice not already in the Mailbox pane will cause it to be added. Name the new folder. Click OK.

5. Choose Mail>Preferences>Rules.

6. Select Add Rule.

7. Use the options in the Rules dialog box to configure the rule; use the triangles to see the choices. Figure 8-3 shows how I've configured this rule to send anything that contains "POSSIBLE SPAM" in the subject line to the Spam folder I created earlier.

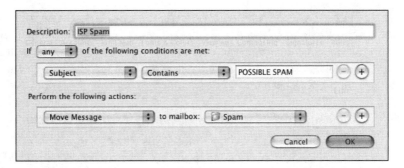

Figure 8-3
Adding rules allows you to filter incoming e-mail into folders you create.

8. Click OK to apply the rule. Close the Rules window.

Keep in mind that you don't have to work just on filtering spam; you can also filter any other type of messages. You can send messages from e-lists to a specific folder so you can read them at the end of the day, you can send messages from your spouse to a specific folder to read on your lunch break, or you can send e-mail that contains the characters "FW:" to a specific folder called Junk or Jokes. It's all about getting rid of clutter.

Using the Junk E-Mail Filter

The Junk E-Mail Filter appeared in Mac OS X version 10.2 and is likely here to stay. It has many features you're probably already aware of, including message titles appearing in color if Mail thinks the message is a spam message. Your job, for the first month or so, is to "teach" Mail what is and is not spam.

TIP: Make sure Junk Mail Filtering is enabled before continuing. Choose Mail>Preferences>Junk Mail. Verify that Enable Junk Mail Filtering is checked.

After you select a message to read, you can decide if it's junk or not. If Mail thinks it is junk mail and it is, do nothing. If Mail thinks it is junk mail and it isn't, click Not Junk, shown in Figure 8-4. If Mail does not think it is junk mail and it is, click Junk at the top of the Mail window.

Figure 8-4
Training Mail takes some time, but once it's trained it works pretty well.

It should take about a month to train Mail so that it becomes 95 percent accurate in identifying spam:

1.   Choose Mail>Preferences>Junk Mail.

2.   In the When Junk Mail Arrives choices, select Move It To The Junk Mailbox (Automatic). Don't forget to check this mailbox occasionally, as well as any other folders you've created, and delete the contents. You don't want to create gunk yourself!

GunkBuster's Notebook: Using Bounce Sender

When spammers send you messages, they're trying to do two things: First, they may want to sell you something, but more likely they're just harvesting e-mail addresses that they can then resell to other spammers. I assume you won't actually buy anything from spammers (at least I hope not), and I assume you won't click on any links in the e-mail. As for reaching a valid e-mail account, well, there hasn't been much you could do about that in the past, until now. Here, I'll show you how to use the nifty little Bounce To Sender command to irritate spammers and send them messages back that makes it seem as if your account is not valid.

TIP: Want to get rid of an acquaintance? Use Bounce To Sender every time they send an e-mail and they'll think your address is no longer valid!

To use the Bounce To Sender command to send a message back to the sender coded as though it has reached a non-working address, do the following:

1. Select the e-mail to bounce.

2. Control+click it and select Bounce.

3. Click OK to verify you want to proceed. Figure 8-5 shows what the response will look like to a user on the other end.

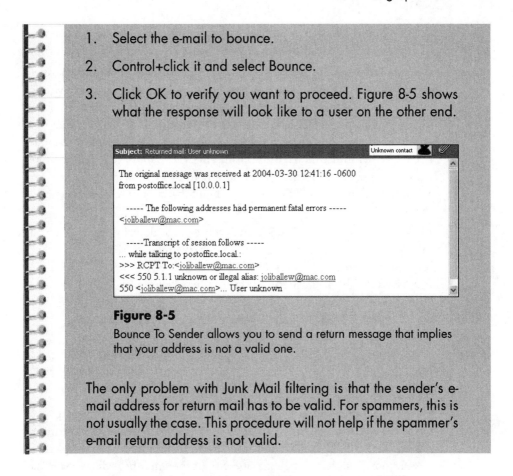

Figure 8-5
Bounce To Sender allows you to send a return message that implies that your address is not a valid one.

The only problem with Junk Mail filtering is that the sender's e-mail address for return mail has to be valid. For spammers, this is not usually the case. This procedure will not help if the spammer's e-mail return address is not valid.

Use a Separate Spam Filtering Utility

As hard as you try to stay out of the spider's Web and remain free of spam, you'll fail eventually. Even if you use an obscure e-mail address and Apple's Mail client and set up filters and create rules, you'll get spam. The only way to deal with that when it happens is to use some sort of spam filtering technology. Spam filtering is done when a program of some kind inspects an incoming e-mail message and decides whether it's legitimate or spam. How it does that is crucial, but how that decision is made is also highly technical and difficult to describe.

In the next section, I'll explain how spam filtering works and suggest how to use it to divide spam from legitimate e-mail.

A Short Spam Filtering Glossary

The best way to start is to define a few terms from the jargon associated with spam filtering. Most spam filtering products use more than one means to make the decision about whether an e-mail is spam or not. In order to get the most out of any spam filtering utility, then, you'll need to understand this jargon.

√ Bayesian filtering—With this method, spam filters learn how to spot spam using statistical analysis of the message length and the distribution of words present in the message. You receive e-mails and tell the filter whether or not each is legitimate mail. The filter uses statistical analysis to analyze what words tend to be in spam versus real e-mail. It then uses that information to guess whether future messages are spam or not. The more you train the filter, the better it gets. Unfortunately, it can only really be 90 to 95 percent accurate. You do have to be extremely careful that no real mail is deleted, though.

√ Blacklist—A blacklist is a list of e-mail addresses or domains from which all mail is to be considered spam and discarded. If a message's sender is on the blacklist, no further analysis is done and the message is deleted. Outlook Express and other mail clients call this the "blocked senders" list or the "banned senders" list.

√ False negative and false positive—When a spam message is mistakenly identified as a legitimate message, it is a false negative. When legitimate e-mail is tagged as spam and discarded, that's a false positive. False positives are far more harmful than false negatives, and false positives are the bane of spam filters.

√ Magnet—This is a term used primarily by POPFile, but other filtering technologies are beginning to accept it. A magnet is a user-defined term or address that "pulls" a message toward a spam classification or a non-spam classification. "Pulling" a message one way or the other helps filter spam and legitimate e-mail.

√ Mail proxy—Many of the best spam filtering utilities are mail proxies. They sit between your e-mail client and the POP server from which your e-mail is delivered. All of your e-mail passes through the proxy, which filters spam and deletes it or places it in some folder other than your inbox before it ever reaches you. Norton Anti-Spam acts as a mail proxy.

√ Whitelist—The opposite of blacklists, whitelists allow you to create a list of e-mail addresses and domains from which you will always accept e-mail. Your whitelist could contain your friends, family, and colleagues or newsletters and e-lists you subscribe to.

With the basic terms in mind, then, let's take a look at a few of your options for free, or low-cost, third-party spam filtering utilities. In the next few sections, you'll learn about three of my favorites: JunkMatcher, SpamSieve, and SpamSlam. (POPFile is also a great utility, and it's free too. Unfortunately, it's a little difficult for beginners because there's no clear-cut version for the Mac yet. However, it can be done, and if you want to give it a shot, search Google for "POPFile for Mac.")

JunkMatcher

JunkMatcher is free. It filters spam using queries against multiple blacklists, such as SpamCop.net, and uses other techniques such as e-mail property matching, which is used to defeat some of the tricks spammers use to obfuscate their spam messages. JunkMatcher's latest version allows you to launch it from inside Mail, and because it's free, it's well worth a try. Visit **www.cs.cmu.edu/** and search for JunkMatcher.

SpamSieve

SpamSieve, available at **www.c-command.com/spamsieve/**, offers a 30-day (or 20 launches) free trail period for combating your In box spam. If you decide to buy it, it'll cost you about $25 (U.S.). It automatically filters messages and claims to be so accurate that there are "almost no false positives." It integrates with the most popular e-mail clients and address books so that no legitimate e-mail from your own contacts is ever marked as spam. This utility is now fully compatible with Panther.

SpamSlam

This utility, available from iLesa (**www.ilesa.com**), helps rid your In box of spam for a mere $25 (U.S.). It uses a statistical content-based filter that automatically trains itself. Like other anti-spam utilities, you can configure a whitelist, configure preferences, and easily and automatically eliminate unwanted spam messages.

Avoid Triggering Other People's Spam Filters

Last but not least, you should try not to trigger others spam filters, especially those people who you know have strict spam rules in effect. Here are a few tips to keep your e-mail from looking like spam to others:

√ Avoid putting certain words in the Subject line. Avoid words like "free", "Viagra", "enlargement", "Xanax", and other words you see in the spam you get. If you actually sell mortgages or medications, try to keep those words out of the header.

√ Avoid using certain words in the body of the e-mail. Many people create rules that look for words such as "unsubscribe" and "limited time". If you include those words in the body of your message, it'll get trashed. If you send jokes with foul language, don't be surprised if you don't get a response. Many people filter and create rules based on obscene language as well.

√   Avoid putting images inside an e-mail. Many spam messages contain pictures and images. You've seen them. Some people filter out all e-mail that contains images so they don't have to look at all the pornography that comes through. If you must send an image, consider sending an introductory e-mail first stating that the next e-mail from you will contain an image.

√   Send text as plain text. Since most spam is sent as HTML, send your messages as plain text. They are less likely to get caught up on the spam filters.

√   Make sure your clock is correct. Some spam is sent with incorrect dates and time in the "Time Sent" field. Some major e-mail systems tag misdated messages as spam. If your Mac thinks its 1999, chances are good that some of your e-mail isn't getting through.

Summing Up

This chapter is about preventing spam from getting to your inbox. If you get enough e-mail, the sheer quantity can be sources of gunk all by itself, especially if you ever slip up even once and click a link to an unknown Web site. Processing through spam is a waste of time and your biggest e-mail problem. This chapter offers you several tools—including multiple e-mail accounts, spam filters, and mail proxies—to help reduce or eliminate spam. Remember to keep your personal e-mail address private and circulate through backup and disposable addresses as needed.

Cleaning Up E–Mail Gunk

Degunking Checklist:

√ Organize your Address Book.

√ Learn how to keep your current e-mail organized.

√ Create a folder hierarchy for storing e-mail you want to keep.

√ Get rid of unnecessary e-mail, including those with large attachments.

√ Create a system for backing up e-mail you want to archive.

√ Learn some tips and tricks for sending, opening, and color-coding e-mail.

In Chapter 8, you learned how to avoid and get rid of spam—that unwanted, unasked-for e-mail that always finds its way to your In box. In this chapter, we're going to talk about what to do with the legitimate e-mail you get. Even legitimate e-mail can become gunk. Think about all of the e-mail you've received and want to keep: funny pictures, digital receipts, passwords, client correspondence, artwork from friends, e-statements from your bank, personal Web page information, and similar items. You need a place to store that stuff in case you ever need to access it.

In this chapter we're going to deal with your e-mail gunk. That includes sorting out your Address Book and deleting non-working e-mail addresses, throwing out old messages, creating a folder hierarchy, and learning some miscellaneous pointers for better use of Apple's Mail. You'll also check your computer for fax gunk.

TIP: *I'll be using Apple's Mail client throughout this chapter. If you use another client, you'll have to stretch the directions a bit. The concepts still apply, although you may need to alter specific commands.*

Do You Know Who's in Your Address Book?

The Address Book can become a gunk magnet quite quickly, especially if you have a lot of contacts. Cleaning out your Address Book files is a great degunking task to take on. An organized Address Book will make it easier for you to find the addresses you want quickly, and it will reduce the chances you'll send an e-mail to an old account that isn't checked much or a non-working account that will bounce back your e-mail.

Think about the various types of gunk you might have that you don't need:

√ A contact has gotten a new e-mail address. You should delete the old one.

√ You no longer need to communicate with a contact. You can delete it.

√ You've had a major life change and no longer want anything to do with your boss, spouse, or ex-friend. You might as well get rid of these addresses. You don't want to accidentally send them a note later on.

√ A contact has a new phone number or address. You should edit their contact information so you can retrieve the correct information when needed.

√ You often forward jokes to the same group of people, or each person in the group of people you work with needs to see the e-mails you write to other members of the group. Create a group with those people in it so you only have to pick the group instead of having to add the names one by one.

Your Address Book will be much easier to navigate if you delete those addresses that are no longer wanted or that no longer work. It will also be much more useful if you update your contacts' information and much more efficient if you create groups for the people you send e-mail to most often.

Delete Unnecessary Addresses

Deleting unnecessary addresses is the fastest and easiest way to get rid of Address Book gunk:

1. Open the Finder, and choose Applications>Address Book. You'll see something similar to what is shown in Figure 9-1.

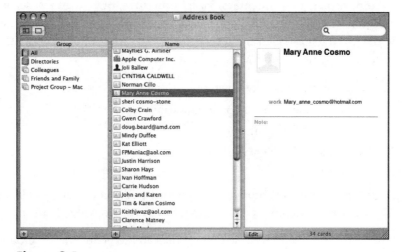

Figure 9-1
Here's an example of an Address Book.

2. Select a contact to delete.

3. Press Delete on the keyboard and then choose Yes in the resulting verification box.

TIP: If you have created groups and placed contacts in them and you delete a contact from the All folder that is also in another group, that contact will be deleted from the All folder and from any other group it's been added to.

Edit Contact Information

Editing contact information for contacts you want to keep is another extremely fast and easy way to get rid of Address Book gunk:

1. Open the Finder, and choose Applications>Address Book.

2. Control+click any contact name and select Edit Card from the resulting list, or click the Edit button in the Address Book interface.

3. Use the Tab key to move among the available information areas. Add information as desired.

4. When finished, click the Edit button in the Address Book interface to apply the changes.

Create Address Groups

If you send e-mail to groups of people—for instance, jokes to friends and family, project files to all members of a committee, or requests to senators and congressmen—you can create groups that contain those people. The next time you need to send an e-mail to everyone in that group, simply choose the group instead of typing in the names individually.

To create a group and add contacts to it, follow these steps:

1. Open the Finder, and choose Applications>Address Book.

2. Under the Group pane, click the + sign.

3. Type a name for the new group.

4. Select the All folder.

5. Drag contact names from the Name pane to the new folder you just created. The names will not be moved from this pane, only added to the new group.

The next time you need to send an e-mail to the people in the group, simply choose the group from the list when selecting the recipients of the e-mail or type the group name. Now that your Address Book is straightened out, let's take a look at all of that e-mail you've got hanging around.

Buy, Sell, or Hold?

As with spam, the best way to eliminate "real" e-mail gunk is to prevent it from piling up in the first place. This requires you to think about each e-mail that comes in. In general, there are three categories:

√ Mail with lasting value that should be retained indefinitely. (Buy)

√ Mail that can be read and deleted immediately. (Sell)

√ Mail associated with a project, committee, due date, end date, venture, or assignment that will be completed; the data can then be archived or deleted. (Hold)

Each time you get an e-mail, decide which type it is. Later in this chapter you'll learn how to organize and archive the mail you want to keep and delete the e-mail you no longer want.

GunkBuster's Notebook: The 100 Message Rule

Most people who depend on e-mail to make their living rack up quite a few in a single day. I get around 75 e-mails daily. As with most people in my position, I deal with some messages right away by responding and deleting, some are from e-mail mailing lists that I filter into another folder for reading when I have the time, some are messages that require lots of time and thought and therefore sit in my In box until they are taken care of, and some are items I need to keep and archive, such as receipts and bank statements or notes from clients or colleagues.

My goal is to never let my e-mail get out of control. I can't stand for my e-mails to extend more than one screen. If the list becomes longer than that, I begin to feel overwhelmed and generally head out with my PDA to my local Starbucks to gather myself.

Some people aren't quite so neurotic and adhere to a different rule—the 100-message rule. Basically, if you have more than 100 e-mails in your In box, stop what you're doing right now and start taking control! Get it down to 50, at the most, and strive to keep it that way. Any more than that and you're likely to be less productive, frustrated, and probably late on whatever projects you're working on.

Once Again, It's Psychology, Not Technology!

Deciding what messages to keep and what to get rid of is a matter of psychology rather than technology. You have to make your own decisions—technology can't do it for you. It's very easy to convince yourself that almost any message needs to be saved forever, but generally that's not true. However, that's the same as saying you'll never need those large, empty boxes you've kept stored in your garage the past three years; it's almost a given that the day you throw them out, your daughter will need those boxes to move in with her boyfriend.

So how do you decide? Well, that's really a judgment call on your part. If you just can't bring yourself to delete those two-year old messages, you can always archive them onto a CD or a back-up disk. I doubt you'll ever go back and read them, but hey, you never know.

If you're looking for some common-sense guidelines, do keep the following:

√ Financial records

√ Legal records

√ Genealogy records and notes

√ Unique technical advice

√ Client files

√ Statements from banks and online bill-paying Web sites

√ Receipts

√ Passwords for Web sites

√ Validation codes for downloaded software

√ Contacts and ongoing job opportunities

√ Agreements, compromises, negotiations, and concessions that, while not legally binding, will help you out of a jam if you find yourself in one

All this e-mail should be organized into your electronic filing cabinet. I'll discuss how to set up a folder hierarchy next.

Create a Folder Hierarchy

If you had a filing cabinet for your written correspondence, would you just throw all of the paperwork into the file cabinet's drawers and never create or label folders? Of course you wouldn't. E-mail is just another type of correspondence, except it's electronic. You'll want to keep your electronic correspondence in order just as you would your written correspondence.

The single biggest way to get and keep Mail's In box in shape is to create a hierarchy of folders and subfolders to hold and organize what you want to keep, just as you would with a real filing cabinet. Lucky for you, Mail comes with several folders already created: In, Out, Drafts, Sent, and Trash. Unfortunately, that's like saying you bought a filing cabinet and it has five drawers. You're going to need to create some additional folders if you want to get organized. Figure 9-2 shows a pretty unorganized situation using Apple's Mail client. There's been some attempt to create folders, but there's lots of unread e-mail, and the amount of spam in the In box is unbelievable. There are way too many e-mails in the In box too, and there are dual accounts configured. This is a mess, and you may have something similar going on in your computer.

If you want to prevent this kind of mess, you'll have to create subfolders and move the items you want to keep into them.

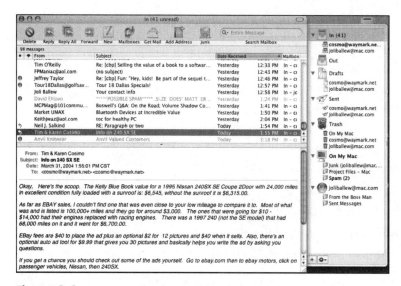

Figure 9-2
This is the "before" picture of an unorganized Mail client.

Keep Your New Folder Hierarchy to One Screen

The key to creating a folder hierarchy is not to have so many folders in the Mailbox pane that you have to scroll through them to see them all. Unfortunately for most of us, if something is out of sight, it is usually out of mind too. This means that if you create a folder named Photoshop E-Mail List and create a rule to tell Mail to send all e-mail from that list to that folder, you'll probably forget to check it on a regular basis if the folder is out of sight. This could cause you to get behind in your responses or, worse, create more gunk on your Mac by collecting and holding unnecessary e-mail!

TIP: If your new folders take up more than a single page and cause you to have to scroll, consider creating subfolders (nested folders).

Creating Folders and Subfolders

You'll have to decide which folders to create by looking at what e-mail you need to "buy" and "hold." Think about the types of e-mail you receive and what it contains, and don't think so much about who the mail comes from. When looking back for a saved e-mail, you might not remember who sent it, but you will remember what it was about. Folders should thus be about topics and not people. Here are some examples:

√   Mail from your employer or team members

√   Mail from clients

√   Mail from iTunes

√   Mail from a church or civic group

√   Mail from your child's school

√   Mail from friends and family that contains specialty items such as digital photos as attachments

√   Mail regarding hobbies and interests

√   Mail for a specific project

√   Mail related to financial transactions

√   Mail related to medical issues

√   Artwork created for specific clients

Once you have a folder hierarchy in you head, put it to use:

1. Open Mail. (If you're using a different mail client, you'll find similar options for creating folders and subfolders. These steps will probably, very generally, work for you.)

2. Verify that the Mailbox pane is showing. If it isn't, choose View>Show Mailboxes.

3. Control+click the In box. Select New. (Alternately, you could choose Mailbox>New from the menu bar.)

4. In the New dialog box, type a name for the new folder.

5. From Location, choose On My Mac if you want to create a folder for messages received from your ISP. If you have a .Mac account and you want to create a folder for filing messages from that account, choose the @mac.com option. Click OK.

6. Repeat these steps until all desired folders have been created.

TIP: You can also drag and drop a newly created folder on top of an existing folder to make it a subfolder (as you would in the Finder).

Follow these steps to create a subfolder inside a folder:

1. In the Mailbox pane, select the folder you want to create a subfolder in.

2. Control+click the folder and choose New.

3. Type a name for the subfolder and click OK.

Now, simply work through your In box, deleting items that are of no value, responding and filing those that do have value, and cleaning up that mailbox!

Figure 9-3 shows a much more organized Mailbox pane that contains folders named Clients, Experts, Family Matters, Fun Stuff, Golf Specials, Hacks, Project Files-Mac, Spam, and Studio B E-List for one account, and Apple and iTunes, From the Boss Man, and Junk for the other. The Project Files-Mac folder also has subfolders named Mac and Technical Reviews. The In box, even though it isn't shown, is clear.

Figure 9-3
This is the "after" picture of a newly organized Mailbox pane.

GunkBuster's Notebook: Use Message Rules to Filter Incoming E-Mail

In Chapter 8 you learned how to use Mail's rules to help filter out spam. You can also use rules to filter e-mail that you want but can't read right away. For instance, most e-mail list headers contain text that denotes the e-mail comes from a specific list. You can create a rule using that header information so that every e-mail from that list goes into a specific folder when it is received. This has a dual purpose. First, it helps keep your In box clean by not attracting tons of e-mail that isn't of high significance, and second, it allows you to put e-mails that do not need to be read right away in a folder that can be accessed later.

In addition to filtering e-mail such as this, you can also turn Mail into a personal secretary. Create rules that filter e-mail from your boss into a folder named Urgent, filter e-mails from your wife into a folder called Pick This Up on the Way Home, and filter e-mail from your country club into a folder called Golf Tournaments. Be careful to check all of these folders regularly, though, and delete their contents when appropriate. You don't want to acquire unnecessary gunk!

GunkBuster's Notebook: Managing Your Sent Folder

Every time you send a message to someone, a copy of it is saved in your Sent folder. You have to empty that folder occasionally if you want to prevent gunk from piling up. If you don't move sent messages or delete them, they'll be there forever. People who have used e-mail for a number of years are often surprised to find that thousands of messages have accumulated there.

Sent items are useful if you have a lousy short-term memory and need to recall if you actually sent an e-mail or didn't and what you said. Sent items are also useful if you need to prove that you actually responded to an e-mail. Those messages are date and time stamped and can be used as evidence. For that reason, I suggest keeping the Sent folder but deleting items as they reach the two-month-old mark. Chances are good that if you haven't been called on something in that amount of time, you won't be.

There is one thing to look for regularly, though, and those are items that you sent that had attachments. Attachments are generally large and can be project files, art files, pictures, or even music or video. For more information on how to sort e-mails by attachment and delete unnecessary e-mail that contains attachments, read the next section.

Watch Out for Those Attachments

E-mail attachments are items that you add to an e-mail such as a picture, a sound file, a video, or some sort of document, spreadsheet, or presentation. Attachments can sometimes be quite large. How e-mail clients handle attachments varies. Most clients allow you to store the attachment on your hard drive or open it directly, without saving, and most denote an attachment with a paperclip icon.

Whether you save the attachment to your hard drive or not, the attachment still remains in your In box. If you delete it, it still remains as a file in your Trash folder. If you forward it, it'll also be inside your Sent folder. Since some attachments, such as video, may be 2 MB or larger, having several copies of it in different folders can really eat up disk space. You need to be pretty careful with attachments.

Before we get too much further into the whole attachment conversation, let's make sure that the attachment column is displayed in Mail:

1. Open Mail and select the In box.
2. Control+click the bar that contains the From, Subject, and Date Received headings and check Attachments. This is shown in Figure 9-4.

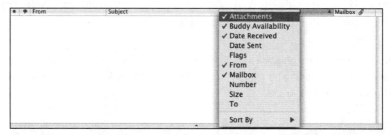

Figure 9-4
Add Attachments to Mail's headings.

3. Notice the new paperclip icon among the header choices.

You can now sort your In, Drafts, Sent, and Trash folders (and any others you've created) by clicking the new paperclip. All of the e-mail with attachments will be grouped together.

What to Watch Out For

Attachments are potentially dangerous, besides hard drive space hogs. Here are some useful guidelines for dealing with attachments:

√   Do not use Mail as a storehouse for attached files. When a message appears with an attachment, immediately save the attachment to a separate location on the hard drive if is to be retained. If not, delete it.

√   Don't open an attachment unless you know what it is. If you don't know who it came from, don't open it! This is how viruses propagate.

√ Don't open attachments from Apple; Apple won't be sending you anything like that. The same is true of your ISP. If in doubt, visit the company's Web page for verification.

√ Keep an eye out for attachments in your Sent folder. If you've forwarded a message that contains a large attachment, that message and attachment will remain in your Sent folder until you delete it.

√ If you can't open an attachment, drag it to the StuffIt Expander icon in the Applications>StuffIt folder. This utility almost always opens any attachment. You might also drag this utility to the Dock if you use it often.

√ Use Mail's Message>Remove Attachments to send unwanted attachments to the Trash. Periodically review your Sent folder and delete any messages with attachments. If you are pressed for time, look for the messages that have the biggest attachments.

My mantra is delete, delete, delete. Delete e-mail with unwanted attachments from your Sent folder, delete unwanted attachments from folders you've created, and finally, delete what's in the Trash.

TIP: You can sort your messages by file size. Just Control+click the bar that contains the From, Subject, Date, and Received headings and check Size. Click the new heading to sort your e-mail by file size.

GunkBuster's Notebook: Don't Attach It; FTP It

E-mail is so easy to use and so accessible that most Mac users I know fall into the habit of trying to send everything by e-mail—huge photos, video clips, presentations, big projects for clients, and so on. Knowing this, most ISPs have size limits for how large an attachment can be, thus limiting our use of this technology. Many users I know would try to send something as big as a car if they could via e-mail. But e-mail was really intended to be a system for sending short, text-based notes. As with many technologies, it has just grown and grown to the point of becoming one of the biggest gunk magnets on the planet.

You can do yourself a big service (and a service for all of your friends and business associates) if you get in the habit of transferring your files by using FTP instead of by e-mail. FTP stands for File Transfer Protocol and it provides a very simple system for transferring files to other users who use the Internet. With the power and flexibility of FTP, you can send and store files just as if your Mac is connected to a network right inside your home or office.

To use FTP, you'll need an FTP client and an FTP server. The FTP client is software that runs on your Mac. The FTP server, on the other hand, is a server (a computer with a very big hard drive) that is connected to the Internet at all times. The FTP client I recommend for Mac users is CuteFTP (**www.cuteftp.com**). It's fast, powerful, and easy to use. You can even download a free trial if you want to give it a whirl before buying it. To transfer a file, you simply run the FTP client and upload the file (or set of files) to an FTP server. You can then give the address of the FTP server to your friends and business associates and they can log into the FTP server and retrieve the files that you have uploaded. This might sound like a big deal, but it is very easy to do.

If the company you work for has an FTP server set up, you'll simply need to find out the address and add it to the appropriate field in your FTP client. If you don't have direct access to an FTP server, you can sign up for a service and use someone else's FTP server. There are various companies that offer FTP services like this. To find a service, you can use Google and search for "ftp service" or "ftp hosting." You can find a range of services to work with; some are free or very inexpensive and others charge a little more but provide a few professional-level services. Here are a couple of the more popular services that you can explore:

www.zftp.com/ - Provides basic packages for $5.99 (U.S.) per month where you can sign up and store up to 500 MB.

www.hosting4less.com/filehosting.html - Very professional service that charges $25 per month. This is a good service if you do a lot of professional work in areas such as graphics production and you need to transfer a number of large files.

The pricing on these services is typically determined by the amount of data that you can store.

GunkBuster's Notebook: Spring-Cleaning Your E-Mail

If you send and receive any significant quantity of e-mail—and especially if you have a folder hierarchy to store it in—you should budget one day a year for "spring-cleaning" to make sure gunk isn't quietly accumulating in the far corners of your e-mail machinery. As with all e-mail management, it's less technology than psychology. That hardest part is setting aside the time to do it.

Here's a simple checklist for your annual e-mail spring-cleaning:

1. Schedule at least three hours for it. This might sound like a lot of time, but if you let your mailbase get away from you and accumulate a bunch of gunk, you will spend a lot more time than that straightening things out and looking for lost messages in the morass.

2. Before you do anything else, take a stab at the number of messages in your mailbase. You can resize the window so that 25 e-mails show at a time and then click, count, and click again to get a fair idea of how many e-mails you're saving. Keep this number in a safe place, and next year, compare it to what you had this time around.

TIP: If you'd rather not manually count the messages in each folder and you are using Apple's Mail client, use the Apple Mail script Count Messages In All Folders. This gives a detailed list of all mail boxes, read and unread messages, and deleted messages—a good overview of what you're starting and ending with.

---

3. Open the Sent Items folder. Delete everything that's older than two months or so. If you can't bring yourself to do this, at least delete what you can and move the rest to folders for saving and archiving.

4. Next, go through your In box and either delete or classify anything beyond the 100-message rule limit. Force yourself to deal with anything unpleasant or difficult that's been awaiting action. If you're convinced you can't bring it down to fewer than 100 messages, you're fooling yourself. See if you need to add a folder or two for new interests or topics that have generated e-mail but don't fit in any existing folders. Whatever you do, do your best to get it down to less than 50 messages.

5. Delete or archive. Pour yourself a cup of coffee, start at the top of your folder list, and see what you no longer want or need in each folder. No longer interested in radio-controlled cars? Archive or delete the entire folder. Sometimes a message that looked like a keeper last year isn't needed anymore. Let it go. Sometimes messages that you thought you wanted to keep forever were really time limited. Be ruthless. It's the only way to stay ahead of your mailbase.

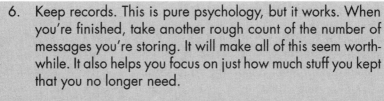

6. Keep records. This is pure psychology, but it works. When you're finished, take another rough count of the number of messages you're storing. It will make all of this seem worthwhile. It also helps you focus on just how much stuff you kept that you no longer need.

Between forcing yourself to deal with old problems that are unresolved—and deleting pointless archived e-mails, old news, older jokes, and a lot of e-mail clutter— you will soon find yourself working faster and more efficiently. Cleaning up your e-mail will be worth it!

Miscellaneous Pointers

Beyond what has previously been introduced in this chapter and the preceding section, there are a few odds and ends to think about in terms of e-mail gunk. These are pretty minor compared to sifting through and organizing your e-mails and attachments, but nonetheless, they are useful in terms of degunking your Mac.

Send E-Mail as Plain Text

There are two kinds of e-mail you can create when using Apple's Mail program: plain text and rich text. The rich text format allows you to send e-mail using special fonts, colors, and text sizes. Rich text uses word-processing controls such as paragraph alignment, bold, italic, and underline. Unfortunately, sending e-mail in this format might cause the e-mail to open more slowly on the recipient's end, and depending on who receives what you send, the message might lose its formatting altogether. Your recipients won't be able to read the e-mail in the font you send it in, either, unless they have the font you used in your e-mail installed on their computer. Because of this, consider sending rich text e-mail using familiar fonts such as Arial, Times, and Courier.

Plain text messages are faster to send and can be opened and viewed by virtually anyone. You can still attach files, though, making it a good choice when you need to send a file quickly. You can change the type of formatting Mail uses by default from Mail>Preferences>Composing.

Have Your E-Mails Read to You

If you'd like for your e-mails to be read to you, they can be. Select the text to be read, and Control+click it. Choose Speech>Start Speaking from the resulting menu. To stop this function, repeat these steps and choose Stop Speaking.

Color-Code Messages

One of the really neat features of the newest version of Mail is that you can color-code messages you receive. Even when you move the message from one folder to another, it retains the color-coding that you've applied. If you're the type of person who keeps close to 100 or so messages in the In box, this might just be what you need to help you get organized. Consider the following color-coding options:

√ Green—Use to denote messages that contain job or money-making opportunities.

√ Red—Use to denote messages that require immediate attention.

√ Blue—Use to denote message that pertain to recreational activities, such as your summer vacation or movie recommendations.

√ Yellow—Use to denote funny e-mails that make you laugh.

√ Purple—Use to denote messages you want to forward.

√ Black—Use to denote messages that contain bad news.

To color-code any message, select the message, choose Format>Show Colors, and select a color from the Colors dialog box. (You can also flag a message using Message>Mark>As Flagged.)

Archive Messages

For many people, deleting old e-mail that may contain an ounce of something that may be needed later is unthinkable. If you're one of those people, that's okay, as long as you know how to save that data and store it somewhere else so that it doesn't become gunk. In addition, everyone at some point in time will want to create a backup of their mail. That's certainly important if you use e-mail daily and your job depends on it, as mine does.

As you know, I've talked a lot about archiving your e-mail in this chapter, but I've yet to discuss how to actually do it. Now that you've gotten Mail pretty much under control, I'll teach you how. Before we get into the nitty-gritty of archiving, though, let's first take a look at how mail is actually stored on your Mac. Open Finder>*your home folder*>Library>Mail>Mailboxes and take a look at what's in there. Figure 9-5 shows mine.

Double-clicking any mailbox that currently exists in your Mail setup opens Mail and the folder that corresponds to the mailbox. Because there's an icon for each mailbox folder here, you can easily drag and drop to another drive to copy the information and archive it. Here's an even quicker way to archive a particular mailbox folder:

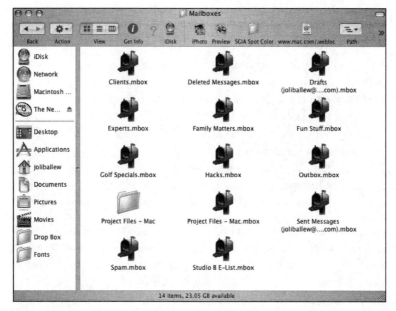

Figure 9-5
Here's a sample Mailboxes folder.

1. Open Finder>*your home folder*>Library>Mail>Mailboxes.
2. Decide what mailbox folder to archive and Control+click it.
3. From the resulting drop-down list, select Create Archive Of *"folder name."*
4. Drag the new ZIP file to the area of your hard disk (or external hard disk) where you keep archived files.
5. If you ever need to use those files again, unzip them. Then, drag the file back to the Mailboxes folder. (If necessary, rename the mailbox before dragging.)

How often you should archive your e-mail depends on how much e-mail you get, how important it is to you, and how much you save (just in case you ever need it). I'm guessing my mother will never need to archive her messages since she mostly gets jokes and spam, and occasionally a note from me. Since she prints out anything important from doctors, banks, and similar contacts and then files them in a filing cabinet, the whole archiving thing is unnecessary. However, if you keep a lot of e-mail and if your livelihood depends on having that e-mail as a backup, you should archive regularly. Consider archiving weekly if this is the case. For most people, the monthly archiving system mentioned in the GunkBuster's Notebook will suffice.

> ## GunkBuster's Notebook: Create an Awesome Archiving System
>
> With Mail, it's easy to create an archiving system that works and is easy to maintain. You don't need a third-party utility, and you don't have to be a genius! Every month on the first of the month, just create a folder with the date inside of Mail's hierarchy system, January 2005, February 2005, March 2005, and so on. Each time you come across an e-mail that you know you'll want to save, move or copy it to this folder after reading it and responding. At the end of the month, just archive this file. It's easy, it's painless, and you have an automatic archiving system that'll be easy to use.
>
> Because the folders have a different name each month, they're easy to locate and restore. You won't have to worry about writing over existing e-mail or disrupting any other folders if you ever have to access them. With this system, each archived folder is unique and easy to organize in a complete backup and archiving system.

TIP: Don't Forget about Fax Gunk! Your Mac can be set up to send and receive faxes. By default, when receiving faxes, the faxes are stored in the Macintosh>Users>Shared>Faxes folder. You can also have faxes sent to your e-mail address. When cleaning up your fax gunk, make sure you check both places.

Summing Up

Keeping your e-mail client organized and degunked is important to maintain your efficiency, work speed, and sanity. The e-mail you receive is no better than spam if it only turns into gunk on your Mac. Learning to deal with e-mail as it arrives, organizing what you want to keep in folders, and learning to let go of e-mail you no longer need is important.

In this chapter, you learned how to get and keep your Address Book organized, how to take control of your In box, how to filter incoming e-mail, and what to watch out for when dealing with attachments. You also learned some neat tricks for sending and saving e-mail, including color-coding e-mails and having your e-mail read aloud to you.

Ultimately, it's up to you to keep this up. Devote a little time daily to keeping things under control, and once a year be prepared to do some annual spring-cleaning of your e-mail folder. Learn to archive what you want to keep, and be prepared to throw stuff out!

Optimizing OS 9

Degunking Checklist:

√ Understand why moving to OS X is important.

√ Get rid of common gunk that accumulates in OS 9.

√ List problem applications and devise a plan to resolve the issues.

√ Resolve common Classic problems.

√ Rebuild the OS 9 desktop.

√ Create a plan to move to OS X.

I f you're reading this chapter, you are one of two kinds of people. Either you have a Mac OS X machine, Classic opens regularly to run your programs, and you need to optimize that aspect of your Mac; or you have a Mac OS 9 machine (with no version of OS X at all) and it's all gunked up. Whatever the case, this chapter can help.

NOTE: I've chosen to write this chapter using a Mac OS X machine with an available Mac OS 9 Classic environment so that I can make the chapter interesting and applicable to as many readers as possible. (If you only have a Mac OS 9 machine, you can still use this chapter to degunk your Mac, as is true of the entire book.)

The differences between OS 9 and OS X are complex and many, and because they are so vast, the new technology of OS X has forced Apple to offer a hybrid operating system to get people (and software manufacturers) through the move. For programs that are not yet OS X compatible, OS X offers a Classic environment that kicks in when older programs need to be run. The complex changes to the OS may thus require you to use both operating systems for a while, or at least until software manufacturers catch up with all of the changes Apple has made and you purchase the upgrades! In this chapter, I'll focus on optimizing this OS 9 area of your Mac.

Understanding the Differences Between OS 9 and OS X

To make the differences between the OSes easier to understand, consider the differences between VCR players and DVD players: they are used for the same purpose, but they use completely different technologies, the latter is superior to the former, and they are not directly compatible. As with OS 9 and OS X, you'll probably keep both a VCR player and a DVD player. You can't watch your old VCR tapes in your DVD player, but you can't watch the newest movie releases on your VCR because they're only available on DVD. You'll have to ultimately make the move from one to the other, though, including transferring your VCR tapes to DVD; eventually manufacturers will stop producing VCR tapes and tape machines altogether and only offer DVD technology.

It's important to understand the VCR-DVD analogy because the same thing is going to happen with OS 9 and OS X. You have to seriously begin making the move from the former to the latter. There will come a day when OS 9 products are no longer available, and eventually your OS 9 machine will give out. In fact, Apple has dropped OS 9 and is not developing any new technologies or products (although maintenance updates are still offered). As time passes, there will also be fewer and fewer reasons to maintain OS 9 inside OS X. There's a ton of OS X–compatible software available, and more and more programs and apps are appearing every day. However, as with your older VCR, you may still be forced to use the Classic environment to work with your older programs until you can obtain the newer versions. If that's the case, you can at least optimize OS 9 by getting rid of common gunk and begin preparing to move to OS X permanently.

TIP: If you have a brand-new Mac, there's a good chance you might not even have OS 9 folders. If this is the case, you can skip this chapter.

Classic Gunk

A house is a house is a house, and no matter how old your house is, it still attracts dust bunnies. In fact, older homes probably attract more. Both OS X and OS 9 can get gunked up. You can have unnecessary files and fonts, unnecessary or problem applications, and the same general batch of issues you have with OS X. If you've been following along with this book from the beginning, you may or may not have directed your energies to your System Folder or your Applications (Mac OS 9) folder. Don't worry if you haven't, though, because we'll revisit those concepts here.

Degunking System Preferences

You might have created your own level of gunk by incorrectly configuring System Preferences for OS 9. Just to double-check and to see how your OS 9 configuration is set up, open System Preferences, and under System, click the Classic icon. You'll have several choices from your Mac OS X machine:

√   Start/Stop—The Classic environment can be started here. You can also configure it to start automatically when you log on, to warn before starting Classic, and to show Classic status in the menu bar. You can also force-quit Classic from here. None of the options is checked by default. If you don't want Classic starting when you begin, don't configure it to; in my mind, that defeats the purpose of having OS X. I think it's important to know when and why OS 9 starts. Remember, your ultimate goal is to move to OS X. However, if you use OS 9 every day, go ahead and configure it to start when the computer boots. Then, it'll always be available.

√   Advanced—Here you can configure the startup and other options, such as turning off extensions, opening Extensions Manager, and configuring a key combination to start Classic. You can also configure when Classic goes to sleep, and you can rebuild the desktop. For now, leave the Startup And Other

Options set to Turn Off Extensions and let Classic go to sleep after 5 minutes of inactivity. I'll come back to rebuilding the desktop and disabling extensions later.

√ Memory/Versions—Here you can see the running applications and their memory use. You can also choose to view background applications.

Manually starting Classic from here allows you to run a program in the Classic environment if that's necessary. However, opening a program that is a Classic program will cause Classic to open as well. For now, just make sure you haven't created your own gunk and that OS 9 isn't starting unnecessarily when you boot your Mac.

Removing Unnecessary Files

Open your Macintosh HD and take a look around. You will probably see two folders that relate to OS 9, the Applications (Mac OS 9) folder and the System Folder. Both can contain gunk, and more than likely you'll find things in the Applications (Mac OS 9) folder you can get rid of.

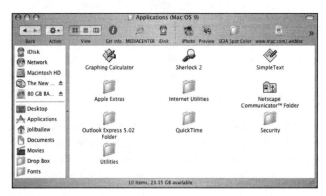

Figure 10-1
The Applications (Mac OS 9) folder contains applications you probably don't need.

In the Applications (OS 9) folder, shown in Figure 10-1, consider tossing these things:

√ Documents, pictures, and other files you no longer need.

√ Applications you've installed but no longer use, such as older Office applications, graphics applications, or specialty tools such as gardening or genealogy applications.

√ Applications that have been replaced with newer technologies, such as Internet Explorer 5 (replaced by a newer version in OS X) or Outlook Express 5, which you don't use because you use Apple's Mail program.

√   The Security folder contains one file, Apple File Security, that you can toss. OS X has much better security that OS 9 did, and AFS is not needed.

√   Unnecessary Internet browsers such as Netscape Communicator.

The ideas behind degunking the personal aspects of OS 9 are virtually the same as the ideas behind degunking OS X. You want to get rid of unnecessary files and applications, organize what you want to keep, and see if you can speed up OS 9. Following the degunking principles offered in this book, this first step was to get rid of things you created and no longer want. If you need to, refer to Chapters 3, 4, and 5 for more information on organizing your files and applications.

Fonts

In Chapter 7 you learned how to get rid of fonts you don't want and how to move fonts from OS 9 to OS X. If you didn't read that chapter and you'd like to optimize your Fonts folder in OS 9, go back to that chapter and review it. You can move, organize, disable, enable, and delete fonts quite easily.

Problem Applications

If you have any applications that you have problems with, perhaps the application that you created your first resume with or the first music program you acquired to create a composition, consider trashing them. Also consider getting rid of programs that hang up, that cause OS 9 to freeze, or whose manufacturers have gone out of business. There are lots of applications out there that are better. Sure, there's the learning curve, but it's well worth it to run an application in OS X without the nagging problems of unsupported or out-of-date programs.

Classic Issues

There are some problems that seem to be common to OS 9. For one, I keep hearing that OS 9 is more prone to crashing than any other operating system. I don't know if I believe that, but there are certainly steps you can take to reduce the chances that OS 9 will conk out on you while you're in the middle of an important project.

In the following sections, I'd like to introduce some tools you can use with OS 9 to enhance how it performs, including third-party utilities (such as Norton Utilities 8.0) to recover from and avoid more serious problems and defragment the drive. I'll also show you how to disable startup items that are unnecessary and rebuild the desktop to make certain the Classic environment runs efficiently.

Use Symantec's Norton Utilities 8.0

Symantec's Norton Utilities 8.0 maximizes your computer's performance. Sure, it's about $100 (U.S.), but it's worth every penny. You can run the program to do system checks, use the program to optimize your hard drive by defragmenting on a schedule, and boot into Mac OS X or Mac OS 9 to repair your hard disk if you ever have to. It can also be used to recover lost data, improve system performance, and repair computer problems. I highly recommend this program or one similar.

TIP: If you aren't into Norton, check out Alsoft's DiskWarrior ($80 U.S.).

Defragment Your Hard Drive

As mentioned in Chapter 5, it's important to defragment your drives occasionally. If you haven't done that, revisit that chapter and use a disk optimization utility soon. As mentioned in the previous section, Norton Utilities 8.0 offers such a tool.

Startup Items

Startup items are programs that start automatically when you boot your computer. You may or may not want these items to start each time you turn your computer on or access the Classic environment. If you always use the program, that's one thing, but if you downloaded a specific utility or application from the Internet and it placed an alias of itself in the Startup folder without your knowledge, then it's just slowing down the boot-up process. If you have items in your System Folder's Startup Items folder, you can remove them—here's how:

1. Open the Macintosh HD>System Folder.

2. Open the Startup Items folder.

3. Drag unnecessary items to the Trash.

Rebuild the Desktop

Another way to make sure your system runs efficiently is to rebuild the OS 9 desktop file regularly. The desktop file is what keeps tabs on all of the documents and applications you use, and it can become damaged. A damaged or corrupt desktop file can cause the computer to respond slowly, or it can cause applications to fail to open. You might also see some odd things like icons changing or warnings that particular files or applications can't be found. Whatever the case, if you use the Classic environment quite a bit, you should rebuild the desktop file monthly.

Since I'm assuming you have OS X and are using the Classic environment when needed, here I'll show how to rebuild the desktop file using OS X's System Preferences. If you aren't using OS X, you should consult the Help files for assistance in rebuilding the desktop. To rebuild the OS 9 desktop using OS X, follow these steps:

1. Open System Preferences.

2. In the System section, open Classic.

3. Click Advanced.

4. Select Rebuild Desktop, as shown in Figure 10-2.

5. Select the volume for rebuilding, and click Rebuild.

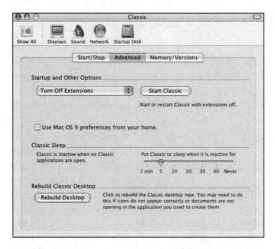

Figure 10-2
Rebuild the desktop once a month to avoid common problems associated with corrupt desktop files.

GunkBuster's Notebook: Uncheck Extensions

If you do not configure OS 9 to start when you boot the computer (this slows down the boot process), and if you don't use OS 9, you don't need to read this GunkBuster's Notebook entry. However, if you use the Classic environment, you can enhance how fast it opens and how stable it runs by disabling some of the extensions and control panels that load when OS 9 opens.

Extensions and control panels are software programs that load into memory when OS 9 starts. You don't need a lot of these because Mac OS X now offers many of these functions already. Turning them off then make OS 9 more stable and speeds up the startup process. This can also be performed on an OS 9 machine.

Here's the lowdown:

1. Open System Preferences>Classic>Advanced.

2. From the Startup And Other Options area, select Open Extensions Manager; then click Start Classic.

3. In Extensions Manager, shown in Figure 10-3, select Duplicate Set.

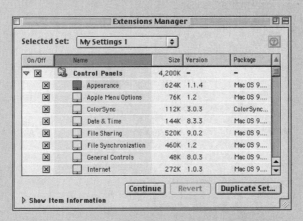

Figure 10-3
The Extensions Manager can be used to enhance how the Classic environment works.

4. Name the new set Enhanced Classic Startup, and click OK.

5. You can disable many of these items because they are already taken care of in OS X's settings. For instance, there's no point in leaving the Modem control panel enabled because the modem is already dealt with in OS X. The same holds true for Energy Saver and similar items. If you have configured your Internet settings in OS X, there's no need to enable that control panel here too. You can safely disable the following control panels:

√ Energy Saver

√ File Sharing

√ Internet

√ Modem

√ Monitors

√ Mouse

CAUTION! *Don't disable General Controls or Startup Disk. You'll receive errors when OS 9 needs those items.*

---

6. Scroll down to the extensions. Depending on how you use the Classic environment, you can turn off several of these:

    √ If you access the Internet from OS X, turn off anything with a modem name, the LDAP extensions, NBP PlugIn, and NetSprocketLib.

    √ If you don't use OS 9's speech tools, turn off Speech Manager and Speech Recognition.

    √ If you aren't part of a network, turn off AppleEnet, AirPort extensions, AppleShare, File Sharing Library, and Network Setup Extension.

    √ If you aren't going to print from OS 9, turn off all print extensions.

7. Scroll down to Startup Items and see if there's anything to disable that you recognize.

8. When finished, click Continue. You should see improvement in how fast Classic starts.

Without getting too technical as to why and what other extensions and control panels can be turned off or disabled, I will say that this is just a start. You can disable many more items, but if you do and you find out later they are needed, you'll have to go into Extensions Manager again and enable them. Although this isn't difficult, it can be time consuming. If you are up to the task, disable and enable to your heart's content and experiment. You can always revert back to the original settings if you mess it up too badly!

Get Rid of OS 9

If you don't use OS 9 at all, there's no point in keeping it around. That's the consensus of many, anyway, but you have to really want to do some serious degunking to trash the System Folder and the Applications (Mac OS 9) folder. If you do decide to get rid of these folders, it's easy; however, I don't recommend it.

To delete these folders, make sure you aren't running the Classic environment (and that you'll never need to), and drag the OS 9 folders to the Trash. Empty the Trash and you'll be done with OS 9. If you encounter problems deleting the System Folder, open the System Folder and choose Edit>Select All. Send all of those files to the Trash, rename the System Folder, and restart the computer. Toss the newly renamed folder and empty the Trash. No more OS 9.

Just Say No

A better choice than trashing the OS 9 folder altogether is making a saner move to OS X using tried-and-true techniques. You want to move away from OS 9 and on to OS X and you want to stay there because OS X is far superior to OS 9. It's supported by all the latest software manufacturers *and* Apple. It's more secure, supports multiple users, and allows you to be much more organized with far less effort. Just remember two things: You don't want Classic to open, and you don't want Classic running in the background. Making the move to OS X will take a little time, just as it'll take some time to get rid of your VCR. It's a long road replacing all of those tapes with DVDs, copying home movies from VCR tapes to DVDs, and cataloging and organizing what you've done. It's also difficult tossing out the VCR+ codes you spent three days inputting. The same is true here, and I understand. For that reason, let's look at this from a purely pragmatic perspective and see what we can do to make this move less painful.

A Saner Way to Move to OS X

You want to move to OS X. Your ultimate goal is (or it should be) to use your Mac the way it should be used, with all programs running smoothly in OS X and with OS X performing as a healthy, happy OS. There are several steps involved in making that move, though, including taking inventory of the software and hardware you use often, purchasing new programs when necessary, and even adding RAM. Let's take a look:

1. Take a survey of what software you use that causes Classic to open. If you configure System Preferences so that Classic does not start automatically when you log in and it warns you before starting Classic, you'll be able to see this easily. If the program that causes Classic to open is an older version of Outlook Express, get an upgrade or move to Outlook or Entourage. If it's Internet Explorer, consider using Safari. If it's Photoshop 6.0, save your money and purchase Photoshop CS, or use and learn another graphics program that does work with OS X.

2. Take inventory of your hardware. Does your Web cam hardware and related software open Classic? If so, save up for an iSight, or see if your hardware manufacturer has an upgraded driver and software. Does your bargain-basement printer open Classic? Same thing there—look for an updated driver or purchase another printer. That'll teach those manufacturers to keep up when a new version of the OS is released!

3. Purchase new tools (such as Norton Utilities 8.0) to keep the system running smoothly. Your old OS 9 applications aren't going to do the trick. You can also look for freeware or shareware to optimize performance. Check out **www.versiontracker.com** for the latest.

4. Consider adding RAM. RAM is the single best way to increase the performance on your machine and may in fact become necessary after upgrading your applications and hardware drivers and adding new programs.

5. Transfer your favorite fonts from OS 9 to OS X, just in case you get a wild hair and want to trash the OS 9 folders some day.

6. Gather up any documents, pictures, music, artwork, or movies from your OS 9 folders and move them to your OS X folders. Put them in the appropriate folders, such as Documents, Music, Pictures, and Movies.

Once you have everything running the way you want it to, leave the OS 9 folders in place for another month or so. You never know what might come up. Then, if you're up to it, drag those OS 9 folders to the Trash and say goodbye to OS 9 forever!

Summing Up

In this chapter you learned the importance of moving from OS 9 to OS X and some ways to do that. You also learned why OS 9 is available in Panther and how to optimize it if you rely on it daily. It's extremely important to consider making the move to OS X, though, and doing so will probably require you to purchase new software, download new device drivers, and move data around. For now, use OS 9 only when necessary and keep it optimized just as you would OS X.

Optimizing Your Hard Drive

Degunking Checklist:

√ Degunk the startup process by configuring System Preferences.

√ Explore various startup options.

√ Clean up your account's Startup Items settings.

√ Understand what can cause a startup failure so that you can prevent a failure from happening in the first place.

√ Locate freeware and shareware performance tools.

√ Enhance hard disk performance with updated drivers, non-intensive screen savers and backgrounds, and more.

√ Perform miscellaneous performance tweaks.

I know many of you turn your computer on the day you bring it home and leave it on indefinitely. That's what's great about the Mac and maybe one of the reasons you chose it over a PC; it just doesn't need to be rebooted that often (*especially* compared to PCs). Others of you may turn your computer off every night, hoping to keep down your electric bill or because company rules and standards (or your spouse) enforce such a policy.

Whatever the case, *I* believe it's a good idea to reboot your machine often, at the very least once a week, if only to reset the RAM and release any stored temporary files. It also gives you a chance to make sure you haven't deleted anything that the startup process needs or installed any incompatible software or hardware that will affect your Mac's performance. You should really give your Mac a chance to regain its composure once in a while.

So, when you do reboot, whether it's once a week, every morning, or only after installing an update that requires it, your Mac ought to start as quickly as possible, open up what it is you want to use, and not open things you don't. After it's booted, it should also run as smoothly and efficiently as the day you bought it. In this chapter, that's what I'll discuss: degunking the startup process and optimizing the hard drive so that your Mac runs as efficiently as possible.

Degunk the Startup Process

How long does it take to start your car? It shouldn't take long. You should be able to turn the key and have the car start immediately. Sometimes, though, it takes a little longer. Maybe you left the headlights on and it has to struggle a bit, maybe the air conditioning is set to maximum, or maybe it's just too cold or too hot to start properly.

You can also have problems with the startup process on your Mac for a number of reasons. Fortunately for you, there are ways to tweak the startup process so that it works as it should and remains trouble-free.

In the following sections, you'll learn some of the tricks for getting a clean, effective, and fast boot-up, including selecting a default startup disk, configuring System Preferences so unnecessary applications don't use system resources on startup, logging on automatically, and other miscellaneous performance tweaks. I'll also discuss what can make a good startup go bad (just like leaving your headlights on all night), such as bad RAM, problem hardware and software, and outdated firmware.

Select an Optimum Startup Disk

The default startup disk is the disk that is configured to start when you turn on your Mac. You may have several to choose from, perhaps a network startup disk, a CD restore disk, a disk with another version of the operating system, or a CD you've created with a System folder for backup purposes. Only one disk can be functional at a time, so you have to choose one to be the default.

Follow these steps to select (or see what is) the default startup disk for your Mac:

1. Open System Preferences.

2. Select Startup Disk from the available choices at the top of the dialog box.

3. Select the appropriate startup disk or select another. One will be selected already; that is the default. Figure 11-1 shows these options.

4. Close this dialog box.

Figure 11-1
Select a default startup disk from System Preferences>Startup Disk.

If you ever want to boot to another available startup disk, repeat these steps, choose the disk to boot with, and click Restart. The computer will restart using the selected startup disk. If for some reason you can't boot to the default disk and access System Preferences, refer to the GunkBuster's Notebook "Use the Startup Manager to Choose a Different Startup Disk" for information on how to choose another disk while the computer is booting up.

GunkBuster's Notebook: Use the Startup Manager to Choose a Different Startup Disk

There may come a time when you have problems with the startup process and the problems are so severe that you can't boot to your default volume. If you have more than one disk that has a System folder on it and you'd like to boot to that disk instead of your default disk, simply hold down the Option key as soon as the computer begins to boot. You'll see the Startup Manager, where you'll be able to choose a viable startup volume. Once the watch has turned into an arrow, select the disk to start up with and press the arrow key on the screen.

Choosing a startup volume in this manner is helpful when you need to resolve disk startup problems, when the computer doesn't boot to the default disk properly, when you want to boot to the OS X CD, when you want to boot to a restore CD, or when you simply want to boot to another available disk. (You can also hold down the C key to boot to the CD if desired.)

Degunk Your Startup Items

Some programs start by default when your Mac boots. Some might be unwanted items, such as the iCalAlarmScheduler (especially if you don't use iCal), while some might be warranted, such as .VirexLogin (an anti-virus application). The more items you have configured to boot automatically, the longer the startup process will take. In contrast, the fewer items you have, the faster startup will finish. To degunk the startup process, then, let's take a look at what you have configured on your computer to start up automatically:

1. Open System Preferences>Accounts.

2. Select your account, as shown in Figure 11-2.

Figure 11-2

Cleaning up startup items starts with the System Preferences dialog box; first choose an account to manage.

3. Select Startup Items.

4. Notice what items are in the list. Figure 11-3 shows an example. These items will start automatically when your Mac boots.

Figure 11-3

Startup Items start automatically each time you boot the computer.

5. All of the items in the list will start and open automatically, but you can remove the check mark beside any item to hide the application when you log in.

6. To change the order in which applications start, click and drag the item to a new area of the list.

7. To remove an item from the list, select it and choose the – sign to delete it. Removing an item from this list prevents it from starting when your Mac boots.

Adding Startup Items You Need

You can also add to the list startup items that you need and use every day. Although this may seem like it's the opposite of degunking, it can actually be a good thing. Sure, it'll take a little bit longer to boot and load all of those programs, but if you restart the computer only once a week, it's really not that big of a deal. In fact, you may save time by letting your Mac open the programs you use.

Here's how to add an item to the Startup Items list:

1. Open System Preferences>Accounts.

2. Select your account, as shown earlier in Figure 11-2.

3. Select Startup Items.

4. Click the + sign and browse to the Applications folder; then select any application you'd like to add. Repeat this step as necessary.

5. Click the + sign and browse to and select any folder or document you work with daily. Repeat this step as necessary.

6. Figure 11-4 shows how my account is set up. I let my anti-virus software, Mail, iTunes, Drop Box, and the Degunking Mac folder open when my Mac boots up. I also open and hide iPhoto.

7. Close the Accounts window.

Figure 11-4
Here's how my startup items are configured.

GunkBuster's Notebook: Other Startup Options

In the GunkBuster's Notebook entry earlier in this chapter, you learned how to open the Startup Manager during startup to select another startup disk. That works well in emergencies. There are some other startup options you should be familiar with though. Keep these in the back of your mind, just in case you ever need them:

√ Command + X—Holding down the Command=X key during startup will force OS X to start. This is useful if you have another version of the operating system set as the default.

√ Option+Command+Shift+Delete—Holding down this key combination during startup will force your Mac to bypass the primary startup volume and look for a startup volume on a CD or external disk.

√ C—Holding down this key during startup will force your Mac to start from a CD (if the CD has a System folder).

√ T—Holding down this key during startup will force your Mac to start in FireWire Target Disk mode. (This lets you turn your Mac into an external hard drive for another Mac. It's great for exchanging information between laptops, iPods, and similar devices. For more information, refer to Chapter 13.)

√ Shift—Holding down this key during startup will force your Mac to start in Safe mode. This disables unnecessary kernel extensions and login items.

√ Command+S—Holding down this key combination during startup will force your Mac to start in Single-User mode. This is the command line.

√ Command+Option+P+R, hold until you hear the startup sound a second time—Holding down this key combination during startup will force your Mac to reset its PRAM. PRAM, or parameter RAM, is a small amount of RAM that stores settings of several control panels and system software. This includes the date and time, the choice of startup disk, and similar information. If you suspect your PRAM is corrupt because these settings are not retained after a reboot, use this key combination to "zap the PRAM."

√ Command+S, then type /sbin/fsck -fy at the prompt—This key combination will force your Mac to run some basic file system checks at startup. This is a good tool to use when the computer is "acting funny" and when first starting troubleshooting tasks.

√ Command+Options+O+F, then type eject cd at the prompt— This key combination will force your Mac to eject the CD.

Save Time: Log On Automatically

Another way to shave a few seconds off the startup process is to log in to your account automatically. This is a good option for people who don't share a computer with others. You can still use it if you *do* share the computer with others, but you'll be leaving yourself open to intrusion and reducing your level of security. In addition, you'll probably frustrate anyone who restarts the computer and needs to log on themselves!

If you do decide to configure the computer to log on automatically using your personal user account, follow these steps:

1. Open System Preferences>Accounts.

2. Click Login Options. Figure 11-5 shows the dialog box that appears when you do.

Figure 11-5

Configure a user for automatic login from System Preferences>Accounts.

3. Check Automatically Log In As and select your account as the one who is chosen to log on automatically.

4. Inform users that if you are logged in and they need to access their account, they should not restart the computer; that will only log you back in again. Tell them to select the Apple menu and Log Out <*your user name*> instead and then they will be able to log in successfully.

Things That Can Make a Good Startup Go Bad

Although you probably won't see many major problems with startup procedures, if you do and you get a multilingual error message that states, "You need to restart your computer. Hold down the Power button for several seconds or press the Restart button," you have yourself a kernel panic. Kernel panics are rare and are generally caused by hardware problems. This could be a problem with memory, a graphics card, SCSI gear, a digital camera, or a similar device. If restarting doesn't help, you'll have to try to find out what is causing the problem and get rid of it. Recovering from kernel panics have been the subject of many a book, and in Chapter 14 you'll learn a little about troubleshooting these problems, including using Disk Utility to verify and repair disk permissions or your OS X CD to access Disk Utility (OS X) or Disk First Aid (OS 9), programs that scan your startup disk looking for problems.

TIP: In the following sections, I'll talk about what causes common startup problems so you can avoid creating your own startup issues. In Chapter 14, I'll talk about available troubleshooting tools and techniques to use when problems do occur.

Firmware

Firmware is the embedded and burned-in software that controls the internal circuitry of your Mac. This isn't the software you use to upload digital pictures, get your mail, or configure your Internet connection; this is software that your Mac uses to start up and run. Firmware is generally a computer program that is stored on a read-only memory (ROM) chip or an erasable programmable read-only memory (EPROM) chip, the latter of which can be modified and updated.

Every once in a while, Apple offers firmware updates. You should get notices regarding these updates automatically if you have your Software Update settings configured as suggested in Chapter 12. Depending on what you have installed, you might have to update firmware for various devices. As this book is being written, the Apple.com support pages offer firmware updates for the following:

√ Wireless Keyboard/Mouse Firmware Update 1.1

√ AirPort Firmware Update 4.0.8

√ AirPort Extreme Firmware Update 5.3 (Dual Ethernet)

√ Bluetooth Firmware Updater

There are also updates for those who want to upgrade from OS 9 to OS X and various updates are available for FireWire drives and similar hardware. The moral of the story? Keep your Software Update settings configured to check for updates weekly (System Preferences>Software Update) and you'll always have the latest updates.

Incompatible Hardware

Another thing that can cause you startup headaches is incompatible hardware. There are several ways to avoid this problem; the most important is verifying that your computer meets the hardware's recommended requirements before purchasing and installing it. This type of degunking will avoid problems before they start. You can also avoid common problems by checking for the latest drivers when purchasing a new piece of hardware, avoiding used hardware (it's frequently outdated), and avoiding the first-kid-on-the-block-to-have-it syndrome. Wait a couple of months before rushing out to buy the latest printer-scanner-fax-camera-phone machine. Let someone else work the bugs out!

TIP: You can avoid common problems by reading the hardware's Read Me files and manuals and by checking Apple's Support files for known problems. Make sure you've configured your Mac with the correct settings too, including resolution settings.

Fixing Problem Software

Software can be a problem too. Problems caused by software often arise shortly after installing it or while using it, although this doesn't always have to be the case. Problems often occur because the software is installed on a computer that does not meet minimum requirements, has as an incompatible version of the operating system, or lacks sufficient RAM or CPU resources. Or the software is just buggy—which is often the case. As with hardware, always verify that your computer has the necessary resources before installing it—no matter who it's from.

If you suspect that software is causing startup problems, uninstall it, or at least look for an upgrade. Most software problems can be solved by upgrading to a newer version or by performing a clean install of the suspected application. You can also search Apple's Support files for known issues, as you can with hardware.

Repairing Bad Memory

One of the reasons I suggest restarting your computer on occasion is that you give the computer a chance to reset its RAM. RAM is random access memory, and this memory stores data temporarily so that you can retrieve it quickly when needed. It stores files for you until you can formally save them using the Save or Save As command. It also stores data that you send to the printer, as well as instructions and code for opening and running applications. When RAM goes bad or when you run out of available memory and receive memory error messages, you're sure to encounter problems. Those problems generally manifest into issues with startup or with general computing tasks such as editing or printing.

TIP: My eMac came with an Apple Hardware Test CD. This CD can be used to verify that the RAM is functioning correctly.

If you think you're having memory problems, see if your computer came with a hardware test CD. There are also other options:

√ Restart the computer.

√ Verify that there aren't too many programs configured to open when your Mac boots.

√ Close unnecessary open programs.

√ Run a system hardware test.

√ Replace any RAM that is damaged.

√ Add RAM if necessary or if you do not have enough required by system hardware or software.

GunkBuster's Notebook: Finding Performance Utilities on the Internet

It isn't always necessary to purchase the most expensive utilities; much of the time you can find what you want for practically nothing. Some of my favorite performance enhancers include the following:

√ Speed Download—This shareware application, around $20 (U.S.), ensures that you'll always get the fastest download speed from your Internet connection each time you download a file, no matter what browser you use.

√ DBoost—This shareware application, around $10 (U.S.), redistributes CPU time to give the frontmost application 20 to 30% more processor time than it normally gets.

√ Pacifist—For around $20 (U.S.), this utility allows you to extract individual files and folders out of package files. This is useful if an application that is installed by the operating system accidentally gets removed or is corrupt and needs to be reinstalled. With Pacifist, you can do that without reinstalling the entire operating system.

√ Dashboard 1.2—This freeware utility provides an extensive readout of system performance data, including CPU load, memory statistics, network bandwidth, and more. You can even use this utility to search for memory problems.

√ CodeTek Virtual Desktop—For around $30 (U.S.), this utility allows you to set up as many as 100 desktops for separating multiple tasks.

There are literally thousands more available, and many are freeware. Want to find out more? Just go to **www.versiontracker.com** and search for freeware. You'll be amazed at what's available. While you're surfing, try **www.apple.com/downloads/macosx/ system_disk_utilities/**.

Enhance Hard Disk Performance

You can enhance your Mac's hard disk performance in a number of ways, including the obvious ways such as having the latest device drivers and updates, but also in not-so-obvious ways such as using ShadowKiller (a freeware utility) to disable window shadows. Although it may not seem like you'll get that much of a performance boost by disabling window shadows (you won't), combined with other small tweaks, performance enhancements will eventually add up.

It's like this: Say you're saving your money for a new car and you want to cut corners everywhere you can. You start taking your lunch to work (saving a dollar a day), you increase the deductible on your car insurance (saving $100 a year, or about 30 cents a day), you refrain from eating out (saving $10 a week, or a little over a dollar a day), and you roll up all of your change instead of spending it (pocketing 50 cents or so a day). Although each of these little savings improvements won't be enough to pay for your new car by itself, together you can probably get together the down payment pretty quickly. That's what we're going to do here: we're going to make small changes to improve performance, and these changes will eventually add up to a noticeable performance improvement.

Get the Latest Device Drivers and Updates

As mentioned earlier, you should always have the latest device drivers and updates. You should have Software Update settings configured to get updates weekly, and you should always make sure you have the most up-to-date software and device drivers possible. If you are ever in doubt about the status of your system, from the Apple menu choose Software Update. Figure 11-6 shows two software updates and an iSight update. For more information on updates, upgrades, and device drivers, refer to Chapter 12. Degunking by staying updated is one of the easiest and surest way to guarantee that your computer is secure and properly maintained.

Figure 11-6

Check for software updates often or configure Software Update to check for updates weekly.

Choose Non-System-Intensive Screen Savers and Themes

One of my favorite screen savers is Holding Pattern from Idle Time; a sample is shown in Figure 11-7. I downloaded it from **www.Apple.com/downloads/ macosx** and I absolutely love it. I've also downloaded and installed some cool

Figure 11-7

Screen savers and themes can use valuable system resources.

icons, including Dust Bunnies Icons 1.0, and larger themes such as the LeoDesk ThemePacket. Holiday themes are always a welcome addition, too, as I just love decorating my Mac with colors and icons to match my mood. Unfortunately, these programs can rob your machine of valuable CPU and RAM resources quickly, and if you run system-intensive themes and screen savers, you will certainly notice a performance hit.

If you're looking to increase the performance of your hard drive, disable or remove system-intensive screen savers, themes, and desktop backgrounds that you've downloaded. Use the basic Apple backgrounds, desktop images, and screen savers, and stay away from third-party sites that offer the cool stuff.

TIP: Besides eating up valuable resources, third-party utilities such as screen savers and themes might contain code that is not well written and running these programs may use more resources than you think. Some can even cause system crashes or freeze-ups.

To choose a new desktop background or screen saver, open System Preferences, choose Desktop & Screen Saver, and click Desktop and then Screen Saver to make your choices. Choose a system choice for both. To completely remove any third-party screen savers you've added to your computer's hard disk, follow these steps:

1.   From the Finder, open your personal Users folder.

2.   Open your Library folder, and then the Screen Savers folder.

3.   Drag any screen saver to the Trash.

While you're here, check your personal Library folder for other third-party items you might have added. I have items in a folder named Application Enhancers, a FruitMenu Items folder, and several other third-party applications. If you see something you downloaded and added but no longer use, trash it.

Optimize Your Display Settings

Some applications, such as games, will run faster and cleaner if you lower your display settings. Some graphics programs run better if you raise your display settings. It's all about reading the information that comes with the program. If you aren't getting the desired results from a game or a graphics program, check the Read Me files for the proper display settings. A lower display setting will create a faster "redraw" of the screen and can enhance performance.

I leave my resolution at 1024x768, which is generally fine for most games and for programs such as Photoshop. This setting reduces the work OS X has to do to offer the graphics up on the screen, especially after changes have been made to something on the screen, such as a complicated change to a complex image.

Here's how to raise or lower the display settings on your Mac:

1.   Open System Preferences.

2.   Choose Displays.

3.   Select a new resolution based on the needs of your applications.

Optimize Your Hard Drive Easily

You can noticeably improve system performance by tuning Internet and file caching settings, eliminating duplicate or orphaned Login Items, automating common maintenance chores, deleting virtual memory swap files, clearing archived system logs, customizing hidden Mac OS X settings, and scanning preferences files for inactivity and corruption. Unfortunately, these are not easy tasks to do on your own.

I've found a great program that does all of this for you, or at least lets you do these things easily. It's called the Panther Cache Cleaner, and for only $8.95 (U.S.), it's quite a steal. You can get it from Version Tracker's Web site or Northern Softworks (**www.northernSW.com**). Figure 11-8 shows the interface and some of the options.

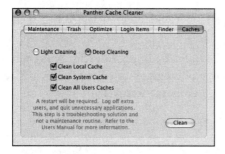

Figure 11-8
There are some really good and inexpensive utilities available that make enhancing performance a breeze, including Panther Cache Cleaner.

Other Ways to Tweak Your System

Besides the things that create noticeable improvements, such as getting updates for software or hardware device drivers, disabling system-intensive screen savers and themes, choosing the appropriate display for your Mac, and obtaining and using a third-party performance enhancer, there are little things you can do too. While most of these tweaks won't offer any noticeable improvements on their own (except for adding RAM), together they will speed up the performance of your Mac.

Check out these performance tweaks:

√   Don't use TinkerTool's "suck in" minimizing feature. It requires more CPU power than Apple's Scale or Genie effects. Of the latter two, the Scale effect is faster.

√ Disable menu fade-outs by downloading and installing FruitMenu. Menus will snap in instead of fade in, saving a millisecond or two.

√ Use ShadowKiller (a free utility) from **www.unsanity.com** to disable windows shadows.

√ Disable file sharing if you don't need it (System Preferences>Sharing).

√ Deactivate Remember Recently Used Items (System Preferences>Appearance).

√ Disable Font Smoothing (System Preferences>Appearance).

√ View pictures in iPhoto by roll.

√ Turn off extensions in Classic that you don't need (Chapter 10).

√ Disable fonts you don't use (Chapter 7).

√ Change the spring-loaded folders and windows delay to Short (Finder>Preferences>General).

√ Disable Calculate All Sizes in the Finder windows (View>As List, then View>Show View Options).

√ Avoid using iTunes to play music while also trying to perform a system-intensive task such as editing a large photograph or editing a movie. There just might not be enough power to do both effectively.

√ Install more RAM.

√ Continue degunking.

These tweaks can be seemingly insignificant when performed separately, but they can really add up when combined.

Summing Up

There are several ways to optimize your hard drive to enhance how fast the computer boots and how efficiently it runs. There are lots of options for starting up your Mac, including starting from additional disks, logging on automatically, and booting from the OS X CD. There are also ways to ensure that your startup processes will remain in good shape, including verifying that the computer meets minimum requirements before installing any hardware of software, keeping the computer's software and firmware updated, and avoiding third-party performance hogs such as screen savers and themes. Once you've started, you can keep your Mac healthy and enhance performance by learning and employing multiple performance tweaks, which, when combined, really add up to enhance your computer's performance.

Staying Organized and Up-to-Date

Degunking Checklist:

√ Set Software Update preferences to ensure that your Mac is always up-to-date.

√ Understand how Energy Saver works and configure optimum settings.

√ View system information with System Profiler.

√ Obtain upgrades for your Mac.

√ Learn about .Mac accounts and why you should have one.

√ Get up-to-date information from Apple's newsletter.

√ Explore Exposé and manage a crowded desktop.

You can get more out of your computer—including better performance, better security, and enhanced media capabilities—by keeping it up-to-date with the latest upgrades and updates. Degunking is about getting your computer to run faster, better, and more securely, and you can't do that if you don't pay attention to what Apple sends out in the way of updates! You know already that you can clean up the computer, do routine maintenance, stop unnecessary programs from starting on login, and tweak your Mac to your heart's content. But it's also important to maintain and increase the security of your computer by keeping it up-to-date with Software Update and by configuring Software Update to work automatically.

In this chapter, you'll learn about Software Update as well as available software upgrades. You'll learn how to use System Profiler to get information about your computer's hardware and software and how to configure Energy Saver for optimum performance. And you'll learn about some other tools for maintaining an up-to-date computer. I'll also introduce the .Mac account and state my case for why I believe you should have one, how and why to sign up for Apple's newsletter, and how to use Exposé to organize your desktop when multiple windows and applications are being used. Are you ready to get up-to-date and organize your desktop? Let's go!

Set Software Update Preferences

With Software Update, you can enhance performance and security by configuring your Mac to automatically download and install updates both for the operating system and for critical system components such as AirPort, iPod, and iSight. Of course, not all updates apply to all computers, and Apple will tailor its suggested updates around what you have installed. For the most part, you should always install what Apple suggests for your particular setup because those updates will generally enhance performance and increase security. Updates and upgrades will solve known problems too, such as a glitch in a software program or a bug in a prior update, and may even contain updates to drivers or firmware, necessary to keep your computer running smoothly.

Let's take a look at how your Mac is set up to obtain software updates, and then let's configure them to their optimal settings. To view and set Software Update Preferences, follow these steps:

1. Open System Preferences>Software Update.
2. Verify that Update Software is selected, as shown in Figure 12-1.
3. Select Check For Updates and choose Weekly from the list. (You can also choose Daily or Monthly, but I think Weekly is the best choice.)

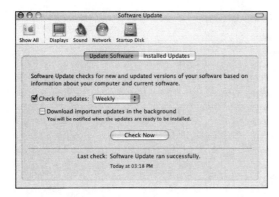

Figure 12-1

Configure Software Update to check for updates at least weekly.

4. If you would like Software Update to download the important updates in the background instead of informing you when updates are available so you can manually choose to download the important updates yourself, check Download Important Updates In The Background. You'll be notified when the updates are downloaded and ready to be installed.

5. Select Installed Updates. Here you can see what updates you've already installed. As shown in Figure 12-2, several updates have been installed on this computer, including a security update on April 13, 2004. *Security updates are extremely important and should always be installed!*

Getting the updates automatically using Software Update is the best way to stay on top of the update issue. However, you can get updates manually from the Apple menu by choosing Software Update. Either way, when updates are available, Software Update will offer up a notice like the one shown in Figure 12-3 and you'll have to choose which updates to install.

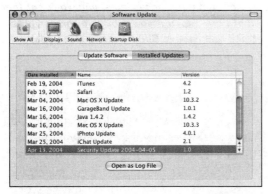

Figure 12-2

You can see which updates have been installed from the Software Update dialog box.

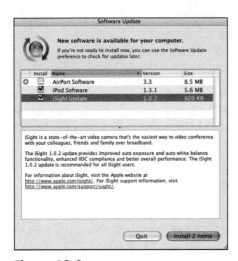

Figure 12-3
Software Update will offer various updates and make suggestions about what you
should and should not install.

Choosing What to Install

As mentioned previously, deciding what updates to install is pretty easy. For the
most part, you should simply install whatever Software Update has selected. In
Figure 12-3, two of the three available updates are selected, iPod Software and
iSight software. That's because I have both of those pieces of hardware. AirPort
Software is not selected because I do not have a wireless AirPort network set up
and thus do not need this particular update. You can make decisions such as
these when updates are offered to you.

TIP: *Your Mac looks for updates in the middle of the night, early in the morning, and on
certain days, and if your computer is not on during those times, you won't get them. If
you don't leave your computer on all of the time, or if you configure the computer to
sleep at night, read the section entitled "Let Atomic Bird Macaroni Get Updates for
You" later in this chapter.*

GunkBuster's Notebook: Store Software Updates

It's highly unlikely that you'll ever need to reinstall your Mac OS,
but if you do, you'll have to start completely over with the software updates as well. You'll be forced to download and install
them all over again, and this can be quite a time-consuming task.
If you are the type of person who always prepares for the worst,
you can start saving those software updates to your hard drive

as they arrive and back them up to a CD. Then, if you ever have to reinstall, you'll at least have them backed up somewhere and you can use that CD to reinstall the updates quickly.

The next time you get a notice of a software update, select the update(s) you want and then choose Update>Install And Keep Package from the menu bar. This will cause the package to be saved to your hard drive in the Macintosh HD>Library>Packages folder. Burn this folder to a CD for backup purposes and then you can reinstall them anytime you need to.

Energy Saver

Creating times when the computer, monitor, and/or display goes to sleep can help prolong the life of your computer and its hardware. Energy Saver is a utility in System Preferences that allows you to configure when, if ever, the computer should go to sleep, when the display should go to sleep, and when the hard disks should go to sleep. You can also use Energy Saver to create a schedule for when your Mac will shut down and start up and to set more advanced options such as automatically restarting the computer after a power failure.

Configuring Energy Saver settings is the same as configuring any other setting in System Preferences: simply open System Preferences, open Energy Saver, and make the appropriate changes using the Energy Saver dialog box. Figure 12-4 shows a few of the options.

The only problem in configuring Energy Saver to put your computer to sleep at night is that Software Update gets its updates in the *middle of the night*. If the computer is asleep (or off), you won't get these important updates and you'll have to remember to get them manually. So even though you may have configured Software Update to get its upgrades automatically, if you have Energy Saver configured incorrectly, you might not be getting all of the updates you need. It's important then to understand how to configure Energy Saver properly and also what third-party utilities can help you get the updates you need.

Configuring Energy Saver Properly

Since daily software updates are acquired in the wee hours of the night, your computer needs to be awake during those times to get the required updates.

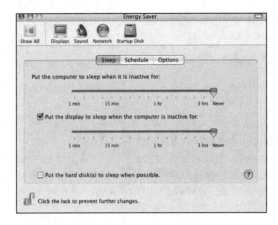

Figure 12-4
Energy Saver allows you to put the computer, display, and hard disks to sleep as desired.

With the new scheduling features in OS X you can now configure your computer to automatically turn itself on and off at these times. For the most part, your computer needs to be on from 2:00 A.M. to 6:00 A.M. every day, so scheduling the computer to turn on and off during these times may actually be counterproductive, causing unnecessary wear and tear on your computer. You don't want to gunk up your machine if there's a better alternative.

If you'd rather not leave your computer on all night, every night, if you want your computer to sleep at night, or if you simply turn your computer off when you're finished working with it, you have two options for keeping up with the required updates. Either you can try to remember to get them manually from the File menu or you can download and obtain a third-party tool to obtain the updates anytime the computer is on and idle.

Getting them manually is easy, if you can remember to do it. Just choose File>Software Update. Having a third-party utility do it for you is even easier, and a good one is Atomic Bird's Macaroni, detailed next.

Let Atomic Bird Macaroni Get Updates for You

Atomic Bird's Macaroni will let you put your computer to sleep at night or turn it off completely and still keep up with the updates without lifting a finger. You can get a 35-day free trial at **www.atomicbird.com**; just scroll down to the Macaroni Disk Image link and download the program. If you like it, it's well worth the price tag, currently under $10 (U.S.). Once installed, Macaroni can be accessed from the System Preferences dialog box under Other. Figure 12-5 shows that the Macaroni application is on and working.

Figure 12-5

Macaroni is on and working.

Obtaining Upgrades for Your System

In addition to updates, you can also get upgrades. (Sometimes these terms are used interchangeably.) Upgrading your applications, such as upgrading iLife to iLife 04, can enhance the programs you have installed on your computer and make working on your Mac a more productive experience. Other upgrades, such as the ones available for office applications, graphics programs, and Internet browsers, also become available and are generally worth the effort to obtain. Some are even free, especially Web browser upgrades. Finally, third-party software that enhances the Mac's operating system can also be quite useful. Occasionally you'll run into an upgrade of the operating system or components too. Just recently I *upgraded* from OS 10.3.2 to 10.3.3. (This might have been referred to as an update by Apple, but in my mind it's an upgrade.) The upgrade was well worth the small effort it took to get it; I know the computer is now more secure than it was and that some of the known issues have been resolved. That's the reason they put it out. I'll continue to install upgrades as they become available, and you should too.

Although there are and will continue to be upgrades of every kind, and there is absolutely no way to know what is on the horizon, you need to know that they are available. In the following sections, there are a couple I'd like to mention. I'd also like to steer you in the right direction for finding upgrades on your own.

Schubert's Free PDF Browser Plug-In

Accessing a PDF file on the Web can totally slow you down. You have to download it, open it, see what it contains, and then decide if you can use it. It's terribly inefficient. For a better approach to PDFs on the Web, download and install Schubert's free PDF Browser Plug-in, available from **www.schubert-it.com/pluginpdf/**. You can use it to open PDFs in any default PDF viewer or in Safari, and it offers options for zooming and printing. (See the section entitled "Plug-Ins" later for more information on what plug-ins do.)

iLife Upgrades

The iLife 04 suite includes updates for three of the popular iApps and includes a completely new application, GarageBand. iLife 04 offers five tools to help you be creative, and they work together seamlessly. For instance, you can use GarageBand to create a song and save it to iTunes. You can then use that song in iMovie or burn it to a DVD using iDVD.

TIP: You can find upgrades to other software from www.apple.com/software.

Plug-Ins

Plug-ins are program modules that you can add to almost any software, including Web browsers, graphics programs, Sherlock, multimedia applications, and mail clients. Much of the time, you can get plug-ins for free. These modules offer added functionality and allow you to do things you can't do with just the original program. There are a number of plug-ins for Netscape Navigator, for instance, that enable it to display different types of audio and video. Flash and Shockwave Player are examples.

To find out if plug-ins are available for your programs and applications, visit **www.google.com** and type in the name of the application followed by *plug-in*. A search for *Photoshop Plug-ins* yields almost 300,000 results. These particular plug-ins allow you to get more from Photoshop, including the ability to perform image processing, automate tasks, create 3-D shadows, perform extensive color corrections, and add page curls or other special effects. You can find similar plug-ins for the programs you have.

TIP: Visit www.apple.com/software, type in plug-ins, and check out what plug-ins are available for your Apple products.

GunkBuster's Notebook: Explore System Profiler

Apple's System Profiler is a tool that gives you a snapshot of your system, the software you have installed, and system resources. It can tell you if your hardware is working, if your new RAM is showing up, the serial number of your Mac, the versions of various software, and more. You can find out virtually anything about any hardware or peripheral attached to your Mac, such as wireless keyboards and mice, USB ports and what is connected to them, and Ethernet connections and their IP addresses. You can also find out what model modem or DVD drive you have, including who manufactured it. This information can help you locate new device drivers, replacement parts, or replacement equipment. You can even view information about preinstalled software, including third-party utilities that may be on your machine.

Besides simply accessing the information, you can create a printout of it by simply choosing File>Print once System Profiler has gathered the information. Having this information will prove useful if you ever can't get your Mac to start or if you have to replace any of the internal parts, such as the modem, PCI cards, or memory. A technician will sing your praises if you hand over your dead Mac and this printout at the same time!

To access System Profiler and view and print the available information, use the following steps:

1. Open Finder>Applications>Utilities>System Profiler.

2. Expand the Hardware and Software trees.

3. Select any item to view its properties. Figure 12-6 shows the properties for the modem on my eMac. Notice the firmware

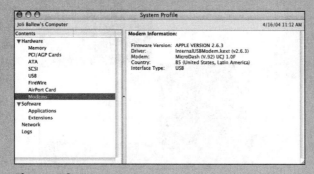

Figure 12-6

System Profiler offers various system information.

version is available in addition to the driver manufacturer, the name of the modem, the country, and the interface type (USB). This information will help me resolve problems with the modem if they ever occur.

4. Choose File>Print. Verify that the correct printer is chosen and that Pages: All is selected, and click Print.

5. Click System Profiler>Quit System Profiler after the print job has completed.

Explore Exposé

Exposé is a feature included with Mac OS X that allows you to quickly shift open windows around on the screen so that you can immediately access any window that contains the data you need. This will put an end to the clutter you have to sift through to find the window you want when you have several programs running and multiple documents open. Exposé offers three modes: All Windows, Application Windows, and Desktop, all of which have customizable views.

Although it would seem like Exposé would be available from the Applications folder, it isn't. You access Exposé through System Preferences, and you use Exposé by selecting the appropriate function key. Figure 12-7 shows an

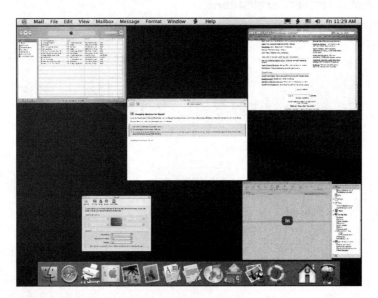

Figure 12-7

Exposé lets you view all windows at the same time.

example of how Exposé works in All Windows mode; pressing F9 offers this view. Selecting any window maximizes it and brings it to the front. You can also press F11 to clear the desktop of all windows and press F10 to show the frontmost application.

Accessing Exposé in System Preferences isn't necessary unless you want to change its properties. From the Exposé dialog box you can create active screen corners and/or change the keys used to access the different views. Active screen corners can be set to allow you to click on a single, specified area of the desktop (say the top-left corner) and have something open automatically—such as the desktop, all application windows, or all windows—or even start the screen saver.

GunkBuster's Notebook: Create a Desktop Printer

Another way to get organized is to create a desktop printer. When you create a desktop printer, your Mac creates an alias to the print queue on your desktop. It works quite efficiently—just drag documents onto the icon to print them. You can even move the print icon to the dock!

If you print quite a bit and think a desktop printer would make a good addition to your desktop, follow these steps:

1. Open Applications>Utilities>Printer Setup Utility.

2. In the Printer List dialog box, choose the printer to use.

3. Choose Printers>Create Desktop Printer.

4. In the Save As window, type a name for the new desktop printer.

5. Verify that Desktop is selected in the Where choices.

6. Click Save and close the Printers window.

The new printer will appear on the desktop. Figure 12-8 shows mine.

Figure 12-8
The new desktop printer is really just an alias to the print queue.

Get a .Mac Account

When I purchased my last Mac, I was encouraged by the salesman to purchase a .Mac account also. It's $99 (U.S.) regularly, but with the new computer it was only $69 (U.S.). Although I was skeptical, I joined up. Now I can't imagine not having that account, and I want to encourage you to consider it as well.

After signing up for a membership (and you can sign up for a free trial if you'd like), you gain access to the .Mac area at **www.mac.com**. There, you have access to the following:

√ Feature Updates—Updates for all Apple products can be found here.

√ Apple Training—Much of this free training is in the form of QuickTime movies, making learning fun, easy, and accessible.

√ Games and Puzzles—Download free games and puzzles.

√ Themes—Download themes that you generally have to pay for, for free.

√ Free Access to Other Services—At the time this book was written, .Mac members could sign up for a free VersionTracker Plus subscription. VersionTracker Plus touts, "Never mess an important software update again!." This subscription normally sells for $24.95 (U.S.).

√ Mail Account—Get a free e-mail address. Mine is JoliBallew@mac.com if you ever want to write.

√ HomePage—Create your own home page for free with your .Mac membership.

√ Backup—Get free backup software and a storage area on the Web.

√ iDisk—Get 100 MB of space on Apple's Web servers, which is a great place to store data that you can access from anywhere.

√ Discounts—Get discounts on Apple and third-party products.

I'm not associated with Apple or .Mac. I've just found that the updates, the iDisk storage area, the discounts, and the free software are well worth the .Mac membership price. Since we're talking about staying up-to-date and organized, this seems to fit right in. Go ahead and check it out; you'll probably agree.

GunkBuster's Notebook: Stay Informed

Finally, staying up-to-date and organized can also mean staying in touch with Apple, including staying abreast of new updates and products. You can get the latest news at **www.apple.com/enews**, where you can also subscribe to various newsletters. The site **www.apple.com/enews/subscribe** offers several options.

Summing Up

Keeping your computer running efficiently and keeping it degunked requires you to be vigilant about staying updated. In this chapter you learned the importance of keeping your Mac up-to-date with the latest updates and upgrades. You also learned how configuring Energy Saver to put your computer to sleep at night can impede getting these updates regularly. You learned where to get updates and upgrades and how to stay abreast of the latest developments at Apple.

The Best Hardware for Mac Degunking

Degunking Checklist:

√ Purchase and install extra RAM to enhance the performance of your Mac.

√ Add a backup device to perform regular backups and store them off-site.

√ Add a second monitor to extend your desktop and make room for all of your running applications.

√ Add a second hard disk or a Universal Serial Bus (USB) hub to expand the capabilities of your Mac.

√ Physically clean the computer.

√ Purchase a new computer and transfer only those files that are needed.

√ Learn how to use FireWire Target Disk Mode.

This chapter introduces you to the different types of hardware you can acquire to beef up your system. Here, you'll learn how having the right hardware can help with the degunking process. Doing things like adding RAM will speed up the computer, and adding a USB hub will allow you to keep all of your USB devices plugged in at the same time. No more swapping them out because you don't have enough ports! You'll learn how to configure and take care of your existing hardware, too, so that you can get the best possible performance from what you already have.

Beyond adding physical hardware, though, you'll learn that keeping the computer clean is important as well. You'll learn how to clean the monitor, keyboard, and mouse and the outside and inside of the case and why this is important. Finally, I'll talk about what to do if all of this degunking still doesn't give you the performance you want. If you decide to purchase a new computer, you'll want to know what to save and how to recycle the old computer.

Why Add Hardware?

Have you ever thought you'd like to add a room onto your house or turn your garage into a game room? I think about that a lot, and it isn't because my house is falling down or in disrepair or that I need to buy a new one; I just need more room! In fact, I think I could live in this house for another 10 years if I added that room, got a storage place, and gave the place a makeover with some new paint and carpet. The same is true of your Mac.

No matter how much degunking you do, there will come a time when you realize you're simply out of space. You'll need more RAM so the computer can handle GarageBand, Final Cut Pro 4, and all of those other fancy programs you've installed. You might need a larger (or another) hard disk, a separate backup device, or a USB hub to house all of your USB devices. These items can give your computer new life and enhance how it performs. The easiest and fastest way to give your computer a performance boost is to add RAM, though, so let's look at that first.

Add Memory

My eMac came with 128 MB of RAM. That worked out quite well. For about a week. RAM stands for random access memory, and RAM is where your Mac stores data until it needs to perform a task such as printing a document, performing a calculation, or receiving and opening an e-mail. You'll also use quite a bit of RAM to render a movie, create a song, copy and paste a large chunk of data, or perform an edit in a graphics program like Photoshop. In fact, the recommended amount of RAM for Photoshop's Creative Suite for Macintosh is 256 MB. Anything less, or the minimum of 192 MB, is going to cause the program to barely drag along. If you have only 128 or 192 MB of RAM, *everything* is going to take longer than if you had more.

Physical Installation

So, just how hard is it to purchase and install extra RAM? It isn't difficult at all! These days, you simply figure out what kind of RAM you have, walk into your nearest Apple store, and purchase it from one of the sales representatives. (Apple's made it easy to install.) You can also order it online from one of many e-retailers like **www.crucial.com** and **www.ramjet.com** (my favorite way to go). The first step in adding RAM is to find out how much you already have and what type you need. There are many different kinds of RAM, and you need to have that information before you head out shopping. Once you know what you need, you must decide if you have an open slot available for more and how and where you're going to get it.

Finding the Right Memory for Your Machine

Here's how to see how much memory is installed in your Mac and if you have any available slots for adding more:

1. Open Applications>Utilities>System Profiler.

2. Expand Hardware and choose Memory.

3. Write down the information given. Figure 13-1 shows an example of what may have come installed on your computer; in this example there are 128 MB installed and an open (empty) slot that can hold more.

Next, find out what type of machine you have. You can get this information from System Profiler too; just click Hardware. This particular machine is an eMac with a PowerPC G4 processor and a 1GHz CPU speed. You will probably be asked for this information when you purchase your RAM.

TIP: *To find our how much RAM you can add, refer to the user's manual that came with your computer. The computer referenced in this section can have up to 1 GB of RAM, installed in two 512-MB memory models. If you don't have that manual, refer to the GunkBuster's Notebook "Using the Web to Decipher Your RAM" for more information.*

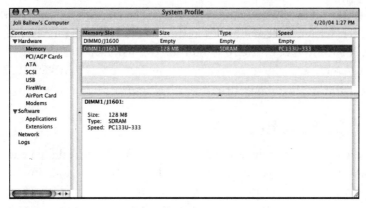

Figure 13-1
Use System Profiler to find out what kind of memory you have and if you have open slots where more RAM can be added.

Installation Instructions

Although the process for adding memory can differ from machine to machine, it's pretty much the same. You have to open up the machine, find the empty RAM slot(s), and put the new RAM in. The process of installing additional memory in an eMac and other Apples is similar:

1. Turn off the computer.

2. In the case of the eMac, carefully place the computer on a soft, clean cloth or towel, monitor side down. You'll have to decide how to position the other models based on their size.

3. Use a Phillips screwdriver to loosen the screen on the memory access panel; then remove the panel. Other models may have a door or similar panel.

TIP: Always consult your user's guide before opening up the case, just to make sure you're adding the RAM correctly.

---

4. Touch any piece of metal inside the case (something that is not a computer part) to make sure you won't shock the inside of the case and cause damage to the electrical components. Avoid doing anything that would cause you to build up static electricity, such as walking around on carpeted floors while working.

5. Disconnect the power cord from the computer.

6. Insert the new memory module into the open slot. The "ejectors," what holds the memory in, should be open. After you place the memory in the slot and push down, the ejectors will lock automatically.

7. Turn the computer right side up, plug it in, and turn it on.

8. Once the computer boots, choose the Apple menu and then About This Mac. Verify that the new memory is recognized. You can get more information from System Profiler.

TIP: With OS X, memory and virtual memory settings are configured automatically. There's no need to do anything else.

GunkBuster's Notebook: Using the Web to Decipher Your RAM

If you are confused about what memory to buy, how much can be installed, where to buy it, or who to trust, look no further than this GunkBuster's Notebook entry. You don't even need your user's guide! Here's the skinny on finding the RAM that's perfect for your machine:

1. Open the Safari browser or another Web browser and go to **www.crucial.com**.

2. Locate the window that helps you find what memory you need, and choose Apple from the list. Click Go To Step 2.

3. Select your Apple product line from the list, and click Go. (You can find this information in the System Profiler under Hardware.)

4. Select your Apple model and click Go. (You can find this information in the System Profiler under Hardware.)

5. View the compatible memory. You can click Buy if you decide to purchase. Also notice on this page that Crucial tells you the maximum amount of memory you can add, what is recommended for your machine, and how to decide what to buy.

When your memory arrives, it will contain instructions on how to install it. Crucial even has a tech support line if you're still feeling uncomfortable.

TIP: Although it's generally more expensive, you can always order directly from the Apple Store—there you just click on which computer you have and it displays the available/compatible RAM. If you're a little nervous about using third-party sites, go this route.

Add a Backup Device

To protect yourself from a disaster such as a failed hard drive, unrecoverable kernel panic, a spilled cup of coffee, or a lightning strike, you'll need to back up your data regularly. Even though Chapter 16 is all about backing up your files, here I'd like to talk about selecting and adding a physical backup device.

External Hard Drive

My favorite backup device is the external hard drive because I can connect it to my Mac via a USB port, do a backup, connect it to my other Mac, do another backup, and then unplug it and store it in a safe place until the next major backup is scheduled. It's important to be able to remove the backup device from the physical area where the computer is in case of flood, fire, power surge, or another unexpected event. It doesn't do any good to have a backup of all of your important data on a device that can be destroyed by the same cup of coffee you spill on your computer! Make sure the backup device can be stored in another room or even another building.

External hard drives can be purchased from almost any computer store and are generally easily installed. Just plug it in to the USB or FireWire port, plug it in, and turn it on, and it's right there as another drive on your desktop. Figure 13-2 shows an example of an 80-GB backup device connected to my computer network. Backing up to this device can be done using third-party backup software or by simply dragging and dropping.

TIP: If you want to add a second internal hard drive or remove the one you have and install a larger one, head to your local Apple store. You'll want an Apple technician to handle that job for you.

Figure 13-2
Here's an example of an external backup device attached to the Mac.

Backing Up Using CD and DVD Burners

If you have a recordable or rewritable CD or DVD drive, you already have a pretty solid backup device. These kinds of devices allow you not only to back up your data by dragging and dropping, but also to archive data you no longer use in order to degunk (or keep your machine degunked) on a regular basis. Once you've backed up what you need to, you can store the backup in a safe place. Archiving old data is necessary so that your hard drive isn't filled up with data you no longer access but want to keep.

TIP: If you don't have a CD or DVD burner on your Mac, you can add one. It's easier to purchase an external burner than it is to install one internally. Visit your local Apple store for more information.

Other Storage Options

You don't have to stick with the tried-and-true backup options like CDs and DVDs and external hard drives. There are several other options, including flash drives, smart battery backups, Zip disks, FireWire hard drives, and more. For everyday backups of your latest document, letter, or picture, consider a Zip disk. The newest Zip disks can store anywhere from 250 MB to 750 MB of data. That's perfect for last-minute backups at the end of the day or for those of you who don't have that much to back up.

You might also consider a USB flash drive. These are small devices that plug directly into a USB port and are small enough to fit in a shirt pocket or on a key chain. This offers a quick way to back up data and take it with you to another computer or to work. These devices used to only hold 64 MB of data but are fast becoming a viable option, with more expensive models holding much more data. (Your iPod can also store different types of data, including music, calendars, and text notes. Watch for improvements on that front soon.)

Get a .Mac Account

If you are a .Mac member and have an account—it's generally $99 a year (U.S.)— you have 100 MB of space on Apple's servers that you can use as an online backup. Although 100 MBs doesn't seem like much, you can drag and drop quite a few files there and you can retrieve them from just about any computer on the planet. Talk about degunking the backup process!

Figure 13-3
iDisk offers an innovative way to back up data.

Figure 13-3 shows my desktop with three disks. The first is my Macintosh HD, the second is my 80 GB external backup device, and the third is my iDisk, part of my .Mac account with Apple. I can drag and drop to Apple's iDisk just as I would with any other.

TIP: If you really want to go high tech, visit www.apple.com/store and search for hard drives. I found an awesome Apple drive module—a 250-GB drive that is hot-pluggable for $500 (U.S.).

Add a Second Monitor

If your monitor is all gunked up with running programs and you constantly have to toggle between open windows, consider adding another monitor and extending the desktop to it. Adding a second monitor can be beneficial for those people who use multiple programs and have to access multiple open windows, such as day traders, programmers, moviemakers, or artists.

Unfortunately, not all Apple models allow the desktop to be "extended." For instance, while you can use the Video Out port on an eMac to connect to an external monitor or projection device that uses a VGA connector, the eMac only mirrors what's on the screen and does not extend it. This won't be of much help if you need more screen real estate. However, it might be helpful if you're a teacher or presenter and need to show what you see on your desktop computer on a projection screen for the entire class to view.

To connect an external display or a projector, follow these steps:

1.   Turn off the computer.

2. Connect a video cable (and an adapter, if necessary) from the video output port on your computer or graphics card to the video input port on the second display. (You'll need an adapter if your second display is a television or similar device.)

3. Verify that the connections are solid.

4. Turn on the computer and the second display.

5. Once the new display is connected, you can configure it in System Preferences>Display.

6. If your computer supports an extended desktop, click Arrangement. Follow the on-screen instructions.

7. If you computer does not support an extended desktop, click Arrangement and select Mirror Displays.

TIP: *To find out if your computer supports an extended desktop, refer to your user's guide or the manual that came with your computer.*

Add Additional USB Capabilities

As time passes, you're likely to acquire more and more USB hardware. These might consist of USB keyboards and mice, cameras, scanners, card readers, and iPods, just to name a few. You may not have all of the ports you need, though, and you may find yourself unplugging your digital camera to plug in your external backup device or unplugging your PDA's synchronizing base to plug in your scanner. That's no good. You can resolve these problems by purchasing and installing a USB hub and then you can leave everything plugged in all the time.

There are several places to purchase USB accessories, including Apple's store at **www.apple.com/store**. I've had better luck with other options, though, including my local computer store and online retailers. One of my favorite sites is **www.keyspan.com**, which offers hubs that work on the Mac at reasonable prices.

What Should You Buy?

Although there are several USB alternatives to increasing the available ports on your computer, some are easier to install than others. The more difficult solution includes purchasing USB cards and installing them inside your computer's case. Adding a card involves verifying that you have an available PCI slot, opening the case, installing the card, closing the case, and then installing the driver for the card. That's pretty complicated, and many of you won't have the available slots anyway, or you won't have access to the inside of the computer case.

A simpler solution is to purchase a USB hub.

USB hubs offer a simple and reliable way to connect multiple devices at once. Just plug the hub in to one USB port and the hardware device then offers you four or more new ports. In addition, most hubs allow you to continue to add on other hubs—up to 127 USB devices!

Physically Clean the Machine

I'm not going to imply that if you physically clean your machine you'll get better performance, but I will say that if you do, it'll likely last longer than if you never cleaned it. And a big part of the practice of degunking is to extend the life of your machine as much as possible! Maybe the mouse won't hang as often, or you can get a few extra keys to be less sticky, but for the most part, cleaning is a maintenance issue. There are parts of your computer that just collect stuff—your keyboard likely has crumbs in it, your mouse has lint around the ball (if you have that kind of mouse), and your monitor has fingerprints and grime. If you smoke, if you have cats or dogs, or if children have access to your computer, the problem is certainly worse. If you have the ability and the nerve to open the computer's case, you'll find all kinds of dust and dirt. You'll be surprised what you find while working through this section.

TIP: If your Mac came with instructions on how to clean it, read those instructions now and follow them to the letter. While I might tell you to turn the keyboard over and shake it, if you have a laptop that definitely isn't the best way to go! So, before you get carried away here, see if you can locate in your user's guide any specific directions for cleaning your Mac.

Cleaning Keyboards, Mice, and Monitors

Your keyboards and mice will work a little better if you give them the once over and remove excess particles hanging around in there. Monitors will look better if you do some dusting once in a while too. Depending on what type of Mac you have, you might be able to use a light cleanser on them too, which will help loosen stubborn gunk.

Degunking the Keyboard

Perhaps this is going to sound silly, but pick up your keyboard, turn it upside down, and give it a couple of good shakes. What fell out? A few eraser bits, a piece of bread, cat hair, a lost hamster, paper clips, and other odds and ends. This might seem like a primitive way to clean, but it works. You can use compressed air to get out the stubborn pieces, and your vacuum cleaner works too. (You can get compressed air at your local computer or hardware store.) With the big pieces out, take a bit of liquid bleach cleanser on a clean, lint-free rag, and gently wipe off the keys. Use Q-tips to get into the cracks if necessary, but be careful not to drip any cleanser anywhere. You want only enough on the rag to clean the stains; you don't want to immerse the keyboard in cleanser.

TIP: *For a long time, Macs came with black keyboards, which hid most dirt and grime. The newer Macs have white or silver keyboards that don't hide the dirt so well. If you'd rather not clean the keyboard, find one of those old black ones!*

If you need to clean the keyboard of your laptop, open up the computer and set it on a sturdy surface. Locate the two small tabs and plastic lock at the top of the keyboard. Use a small flat screwdriver to unfasten the lock, and then pull down the tabs and tilt the keyboard toward you. Make sure you don't pull the keyboard away from the flat cable that holds it together. Now, blow compressed air through the keyboard, making sure not to blow the gunk up onto the display. Once you're finished, put the keyboard back in its place and use a damp cloth to clean the outside of the keys.

Degunking Mice

The mouse that came with my Mac didn't have a ball in it. However, I've replaced it with a mouse that does because I like the feel of it and I like my mice to have two buttons. If you have a mouse without a ball, an optical mouse, you only need to clean the outside of the mouse with a gentle cleanser. You can also take a dry cotton swab and clean the bottom of the mouse, where the light is.

If your mouse has a ball in it, flip it over, turn the backing to get inside, and take out the ball. Use a Q-tip and alcohol to carefully clean the ball and the rollers. You might have to reach in there to pull out the gunk that comes off. Make sure the ball and its components are dry, and then replace the ball and clean the outside of the mouse with a cleanser. While you're degunking, consider replacing that worn mouse pad too; it can have snags or uneven spots that cause the mouse to hang. Once you fully clean your mouse like this, you'll be amazed at how well it works.

TIP: *The Q-tip and alcohol technique is a common one for cleaning the inside of a printer. Make sure your printer manufacturer agrees before proceeding though. Oh, and don't forget to see what's hiding under that printer too!*

Degunking the Monitor

The monitor may be really gunked up with fingerprints, kitty prints, or kid prints, or it might just be covered in a layer of dust. Whatever the case, you should clean the monitor occasionally to keep it sparkling clean. When cleaning the monitor, turn off your Mac and disconnect all of the cables. Then dampen a clean, lint-free cloth with water and wipe the screen. You should avoid spraying anything directly onto the screen or using any cleaners that contain alcohol. If you can't get a spot clean using water, spray a little window cleaner (nonalcohol) onto a clean, lint-free rag and gently scrub the offending spot.

Degunking Outside of the Case

You can also clean the outside of the case using a lint-free cloth and nonabrasive cleaner. As always, turn off the computer and disconnect all of the cables, spray the cleaner onto a cloth, and gently wipe down the computer. Never spray the cleaner directly on the computer; it could run down and drip inside the case and short something out. Also, eMacs, iMacs, and Power Mac G4's have a pretty sensitive case, so rub gently and carefully to avoid scratching it. Finally, use compressed air to get rid of excess gunk that is stuck in depressed areas of the case where dirt and grime can gather.

TIP: *If you have a G4 or G5 tower, you may also want to open the tower and clean inside the case using compressed air or a vacuum with a soft brush attachment to run over the non-circuit-board parts (such as fans and hard drives). Read your owner's manual, though; opening up an eMac to clean out its insides will void the warranty! Don't open it up and perform this degunking task unless your user's guide says to.*

GunkBuster's Notebook: Using iSkin

Your iBook or PowerBook G4 keyboard sits on top of all of the important parts that keep your laptop working properly. If anything gets underneath those keys, the electronics hidden under there are at risk.

If you're serious about the health of your computer and you want to make sure nothing can get underneath the keyboard and cause damage to the internal parts, consider purchasing an iSkin from **www.MacSales.com**. The iSkin is a cover that fits over your keyboard to protect it from spills, dust, food particles, and so on.

The iSkin is precisely molded to the keyboard so you hardly know it's there. It's washable and goes on and comes off easily. It's also available in various colors, making it a nice addition to your laptop. If you really want to protect that new laptop, consider purchasing this add-on.

Purchase a New Computer

Although I'll stress that this is a measure of last resort only, you might have reached the limits of what degunking can do for you if you have encountered the following situations:

√   You've removed all of the extra files and programs you can, but your system still runs and boots too slowly.

√   You've maxed out how much RAM you can add, and it isn't enough for the programs you want to run.

√   Your system has to be rebooted often and you can't figure out why. Neither can tech support.

√   You system is out of warranty and to repair it would be almost as costly as buying a new one.

√   Your hard drive is too small for your needs and upgrading is too expensive and difficult.

√   Your computer isn't repairable because you've spilled coffee on it, it's been dropped, or a lightning strike destroyed it.

√   You want to upgrade to OS X but your system doesn't support it.

√   You need to use an application but your computer doesn't meet the minimum requirements.

So what's a degunker to do? You might have to purchase a new computer if these problems exist. When you do though, don't gunk up the new machine with old files and programs you don't need or applications or hardware that aren't compatible. Be a savvy computer user. Make sure what you take over to your new computer you really need.

Transferring Files and Settings

If you think your computer is about ready for the junkyard (but it's still alive and kicking), be smart and gather up the information you need before the computer dies for good. Purchasing a new computer consists of much more than just walking into the Apple store and plopping down your credit card. It may also entail purchasing an upgrade of your favorite program, or it may mean you need to say goodbye to that old printer and splurge for a new one. You'll also want to find out if your existing peripherals are going to be compatible with your new computer and if there are drivers available for them from the manufacturers.

Here are some things you should write down and back up before your computer goes kaput and before you go out shopping for a new one:

√ Back up all of your important documents, pictures, music, movies, and other files to a CD, DVD, or external drive. Remember, though, just because you back it up doesn't mean you have to put it on the new computer. Only transfer what you need to the new computer.

√ Write down your printer name and model, scanner name and model, camera name and model, and so on, and visit the manufacturers' Web sites to verify that there are updated drivers for these devices. If there aren't, seriously consider not installing these items. You don't want to gunk up your new machine with an incompatible piece of hardware.

√ Write down the applications you plan to install on the new computer, and visit those manufacturer's Web sites to verify that they will work properly on your new system. Look specifically for Cocoa applications—those written specifically for OS X or higher. Avoid installing problem applications, and try to stay away from applications that will cause OS 9 to kick in (if your new computer even supports OS 9).

√ Make a note of your display settings; they're configured this way for a reason. Either a program requires it or you prefer it. Either way, they're important.

√ Write down your Internet connection data. That includes the phone number you dial or TCP/IP address you access, dialing options, security settings, custom settings, type of servers for POP3 and SMTP and their names, account names and passwords, e-mail addresses, address book, and messages. If you use dial-up, this may be a good time to move to DSL or cable.

√ Write down any network configuration settings such as workgroup or domain name, computer name, passwords, and so on.

√ Make a note of firewall or anti-virus programs and settings.

√ Make a backup of your Preferences folder.

If you think your computer is about to die, back up all of the data you want to keep to CDs or DVDs. You might have to install the data manually from that media if your computer poops out before you get a new one. If you manage to purchase a new computer while your old computer is still working, there is a way to hook up your new computer to your still-working one and transfer the data more easily. That's called FireWire Target Disk Mode, and it is detailed next.

FireWire Target Disk Mode

FireWire Target Disk Mode is a well-kept secret and a powerful way to transfer data or salvage a dying computer. This feature lets you turn your Mac into an external hard drive for another Mac. Turning the computer into a simple hard drive lets you transfer data with ease, which is valuable in multiple circumstances. If you want to transfer data from your laptop to a desktop Mac, copy data from an old computer to a new one, or transfer data quickly between laptops, you can use this mode to do it.

Let's say you have an older Mac and you just purchased a new one. You want to transfer your data directly from your old computer to the new Mac quickly and painlessly. Here's how:

1. Shut down your old computer and start the new one.
2. Connect the two computers by connecting their FireWire jacks using a 6-pin FireWire cable. (If you have an iPod, you can use that cable.)
3. Turn on the old computer and press the T key immediately after the chime.
4. On the new computer's desktop, notice the new hard drive. It's your old computer!
5. Copy the files you want, being careful not to gunk up your new machine.
6. When you're finished, turn off the old computer and then disconnect the cable.

Remember, this nifty trick isn't just for transferring data from an old computer to a new one. You can also enable FireWire disk use for your iPod and use your iPod as a second hard drive or transfer files between laptops at conferences and meetings.

Summing Up

In this chapter you learned that enhancing your computer's performance with hardware and physical upgrades can really spark new life into it. You learned that adding memory is the easiest and fastest way to enhance a computer's performance and that an extra 128 or 256 MB of RAM can provide a surprising boost. Other hardware tweaks, like adding backup devices or a second monitor and physically cleaning the machine, can also boost productivity and performance.

If performance is just about as good as it's going to get, if you have ongoing problems that can't be solved, if the computer is maxed out on the amount of RAM you can install and you need more, you might need a new computer. If that's the case, remember that you don't want to gunk up your new machine by bringing over data you don't need or programs or hardware that aren't compatible. Remember, too, that you can continue to use your old computer as a second hard drive.

Maintenance and Troubleshooting Tools

Degunking Checklist:

√ Maintain your Mac by checking for and repairing file system errors.

√ Clean up your Mac by deleting library caches.

√ Use Disk Utility to verify and repair permissions.

√ Use the OS X CD to scan the startup disk for errors and repair them.

√ Use Disk First Aid to find and repair problems with OS 9.

√ Zap the PRAM when strange crashes and errors cannot be explained or repaired.

√ Create a new user in case of an emergency situation.

√ Learn about good third-party applications that can help you maintain and troubleshoot your Mac.

If you own a house, you've probably had it sprayed for termites. If you have a dog, it probably wears a flea collar. If you have a car, you regularly have the oil changed. If you do what your doctor tells you, you go in once a year for a checkup. You do these things to prevent problems, catch problems early, and deal with problems as (or before) they arise, hopefully finding small problems and fixing them before they become even bigger ones. You need to take that same kind of care with your computer.

In this chapter you'll learn what tools are available to help you maintain your Mac and what tools can be used to search for, find, and fix errors with hard disks, permissions, and similar issues. You'll learn how to create a new account that can be used to log into your computer if for some reason your own account becomes corrupt. I'll also introduce my favorite freeware and shareware that's available to help you maintain your Mac in the background and assist you in keeping your newly degunked machine, well, degunked.

Check the File System for Errors

If you've been following along from the start, your Mac is now running better than ever. You rarely (or never) receive error messages, use Force Quit, or reboot. Your Mac seems stable and healthy, and you figure you've got it made. Because of this, you're probably thinking you don't need to check the file system for errors and that you can skip this section (and maybe even the chapter). Don't do that though, because there may be problems lurking in the background that you can't see. Just as it's a good idea to go to the doctor once a year even if you feel great, you need to give your Mac the once-over every once in a while too.

Although you could purchase expensive third-party utilities to search your hard disk for errors and repair them, your Mac OS X machine comes with a built-in utility called File System Check that you can use to do the same thing. File system checks are run using Single-User mode by typing in a simple command. You should perform these checks monthly. To run a file system check now, follow these steps:

1. From the Apple menu, choose Restart.

2. As your Mac boots, hold down the Command+S key combination to start the computer in Single-User mode. (Make sure to press this key combination right after the chime; otherwise, you won't get in.)

3. At the command prompt, type */sbin/fsck –fy*. There's a space before the –fy. This command tells your Mac to run File System Check, force the check (f) and answer yes (y) to any and all questions regarding fixing, repairing, or

salvaging information. Apple says this is the optimal approach because answering no to any question causes fsck (File System Check) to stop running.

4. If the File System Check finds errors, run it again until no more errors are found. You'll know errors were found if you receive the message "FILE SYSTEM WAS MODIFIED". You'll know when all errors have been repaired when you see the message "The volume Macintosh HD appears to be OK".

5. Type *reboot* once all of the errors have been found and repaired.

TIP: *Third-party utilities perform more extensive system checks. If you continue to have problems, you might want to consider a utility such as Alsoft's Disk Warrior or Norton's SystemWorks.*

Delete Library Caches

A cache is where OS X stores data it needs to access often (such as extensions and icons). Storing data in cache makes your Mac run faster because it can obtain the data quickly. Sometimes the cache gets corrupt, though, because of software updates, conflicts, and unexpected quits, and this can cause problems. You might experience application or system crashes or see seemingly random problems that don't appear to be caused by anything in particular. To prevent the cache from becoming corrupt, you should delete everything in the Caches folders once a month, about the same time you run the file system checker mentioned in the previous section.

Here's how to clean your caches:

1. Choose Users>*your user name*>Library>Caches.

2. From the Menu bar, choose Edit>Select All.

3. Drag all of the items to the Trash.

4. From the Macintosh HD, choose Library>Caches.

5. Choose Edit>Select All, and drag the items to the Trash. You'll be required to type in an administrator's password.

6. Restart your Mac.

TIP: *Again, third-party utilities can handle this task, and even perform it on a schedule you set, as well as offer many more utilities, such as Panther Cache Cleaner, available from www.northernsoftworks.com.*

Run Disk Utility to Verify and Repair Permissions

For some reason, Macs have a tendency to forget who can open, read, or write to what file or folder and who has what permissions. You might have even seen errors relating to this yourself, with your Mac complaining that a specific file doesn't belong to you when clearly it does. Whether you've seen these errors or not, you can prevent them from ever occurring and resolve them if they have occurred by using Apple's Disk Utility.

You should run Disk Utility two or three times a year for prevention's sake and whenever you receive a permissions error. To run Disk Utility, follow these steps:

1. Open Applications>Utilities>Disk Utility.

2. Select your startup disk from the list, as shown in Figure 14-1.

3. Select the Disk First Aid tab and then click Verify Disk Permissions.

4. If you receive errors, click Repair Disk Permissions. (You can just as easily skip step 3 and go directly to Repair Disk Permissions.)

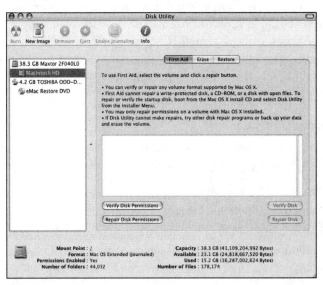

Figure 14-1
Verify permissions two or three times a year to prevent permissions problems.

Scan the Startup Disk for Errors

You can boot your Mac using your Mac OS X CD and access the Disk Utility too. There, you can use Disk First Aid to verify permissions and also scan the hard disk for errors. Disk Utility checks the Overflow files, the Catalog file, multi-linked files, and the Catalog hierarchy. It also checks volume information and can be used to repair problems it finds.

You should scan the hard disk for errors once a month. Here's how to do that:

1. Place the OS X Install Disk 1 or your Software Install and Restore CD 1 in the CD drive and restart your Mac.

2. When you hear the chime, hold down the C key to boot to the CD.

3. From the Installer menu, choose Open Disk Utility.

4. Choose the First Aid tab and select your startup volume from the list.

5. Select Verify Disk and wait for the results.

6. Select Repair Disk and allow Disk Utility to repair any problems it finds.

7. Close Disk Utility.

8. Select Installer>Quit Installer. When prompted, choose Startup Disk to restart your Mac.

9. If necessary, choose your startup disk from the list of available options and click Restart.

Zap the PRAM

Zap the PRAM sounds like a character out of Douglas Adams's *Hitchhiker's Guide to the Galaxy*. It isn't, though; PRAM is a component inside your Mac's case that remembers stuff like how loud your speakers should be when the computer chimes and what startup disk to choose. The PRAM (parameter RAM) is a small portion of RAM that remembers what time it is and similar system data. PRAM is powered by a battery, and that's how it remembers this information even when the computer is turned off. If the PRAM becomes corrupt, all kinds of things can go wrong, including failure of the system to boot properly or the system not booting at all. You'll recognize PRAM problems when the time and date are wrong, if the color scheme is wrong, or if you can't print or connect to the Internet for unknown reasons.

You should *zap* your PRAM every three or four months, just to make sure it hasn't become corrupt, or whenever the computer starts to behave strangely. Zapping the PRAM is easy (and safe—don't be scared):

1. From the Apple menu, choose Restart.

2. Hold down the Command+Option+P+R keys.

3. The computer will restart, at which point you can let go of those keys.

TIP: *Once you zap the PRAM, you may have to reset system data like the date and time and the default startup disk.*

GunkBuster's Notebook: Create a New User for Emergencies

Another preventative measure is to create a separate account with administrator privileges just in case your user account becomes so corrupt that you can't log in. If you're ever in this predicament, you can log in with a different user account, fix the problem, and be back on your way. Without that account, you'd be out of luck.

Follow these steps to create a second administrator account:

1. Open System Preferences>Accounts.

2. Click the + sign under Login Options to create a new user.

3. Type a name for the user, create a short name, create a password and verify it, and optionally, create a password hint. Figure 14-2 shows what you'll see after doing so.

Figure 14-2

Create a new user with the Accounts options.

4. Select the Security tab. Select Allow User To Administer This Computer as shown in Figure 14-3.

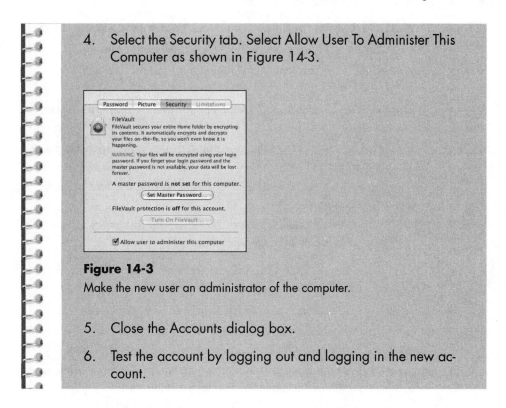

Figure 14-3
Make the new user an administrator of the computer.

5. Close the Accounts dialog box.

6. Test the account by logging out and logging in the new account.

Incorporate Third-Party Applications

You can do quite a bit with the free tools that come with your Mac. Scanning the startup disk for errors, correcting permissions, deleting caches, and zapping the PRAM are excellent ways to make sure your Mac always runs at its best. However, these free tools are no match for the tools and utilities you can find on the Internet and in your local computer store.

Get Awesome Freeware and Shareware

Freeware and shareware are abundant on the Web, and third-party utilities can be purchased to automatically perform maintenance tasks, make your computer more secure, and work to keep your Mac in tip-top shape. To see what's available in the way of freeware and shareware, visit **www.versiontracker.com**. Search the site for "freeware" and see what you can find to assist you with maintaining your Mac. On a recent visit I found the following free utilities:

√ Permanent Eraser 2.0—This one allows you to securely delete your files.

√ PsyncX 2.1.1—This is a free backup utility.

√ RsyncX 2.1—Use this free utility to sync, back up, distribute, and schedule files.

√ PW-Creator 1.0—This is a free utility that creates secure passwords.

√ Data Keeper 1.05—This free utility allows you to create, edit, and view encrypted documents.

√ TCstripper 1.1—This one checks your files for bad file types and Trojan horses.

√ Anti-APPL 1.0—You can use this to combat Trojan horses. It checks files to ensure that they aren't applications.

√ Virus 7 Scripts 1.0.6—This utility offers scripts to scan the hard drive and update virus definitions.

√ Primedius Total Privacy and Security 1.12—Use this free utility to anonymously chat, surf, instant-message, and more.

I also found the following shareware utilities (they're cheap and good) that can help you with your degunking-related tasks:

√ Déjà vu 2.6.3—This utility allows you to schedule backups, clone your system, and sync folders.

√ Lights Out 2.2.3—Customize Energy Saver settings for individual applications.

√ Xupport 2.0—A great utility that optimizes your system, performs maintenance tasks, deletes unnecessary invisible files and folders, and more.

√ LogMaster 5.2.1—View, search, and monitor system log files.

√ Pacifist 1.6.3—This is a custom installer for package files.

√ Data Rescue X 10.4.1—Use this to recover data from crashed disks.

There are many other utilities available that are free or extremely inexpensive. Before buying anything from your local computer store, make sure there's nothing similar on the Internet that's a better deal and offers the same things.

Great Commercial Software

Finally, check out these more expensive utilities you can purchase at your local computer store or on the Internet. They all enhance performance, provide maintenance options, secure the computer, repair problems, and more:

√ Tech Tool Pro 4

√ Norton SystemWorks

√ Norton Utilities

√ Spring Cleaning 6.0

√ DiskWarrior X

√ Mac Washer X

Summing Up

An important part of degunking your Mac requires running routine maintenance tasks such as cleaning out Caches folders, zapping the PRAM, using Disk Utility to scan the startup disk for errors and check permissions, and preparing for a disaster by taking some similar preventative measures. Taking care of your Mac by finding and fixing small problems before they become bigger ones can certainly prolong the life of the Mac as well as enhance its performance.

Improving Security

Degunking Checklist:

√ Protect your Mac by incorporating some simple security measures such as using screen saver passwords and turning on OS X's built-in firewall.

√ Purchase, install, and configure anti-virus software.

√ Understand Safari's security options.

√ Let friends use a visitor account if they need to use your Mac.

√ Turn on FileVault if necessary.

√ Understand encryption and when to use it.

√ Set up a firmware password for really tight security.

S ecuring your Mac is just as important as enhancing its performance. It doesn't do any good to clean up, maintain, and organize your home or garage if you're going to leave the door unlocked for anyone and everyone to drop in without your permission. The same situation is true of your Mac. Don't go to all of the trouble of getting it running efficiently, organizing all of its files and folders, and performing maintenance tasks when you've left a door open to malicious coworkers, uninformed visitors, viruses, spyware, or thieves, all of which can really gunk up (or destroy) your Mac.

TIP: *If you are the only one who ever accesses your Mac and it is in your home, some of these security measures may be overkill. You don't have to employ all of the security measures introduced here; they are simply options for you to choose from.*

Basic Security Tasks

The first thing you think of when securing your home is installing locks on all of the doors. You might also think about installing a burglar alarm to protect other entry areas, such as windows or garage doors. However, you have to be a little more creative to think about shredding your documents before you put them in the outside trash container or installing a sprinkler system in case of a fire. Those things are a little "outside the box." In this chapter you're going to learn a few "outside the box" ideas for securing your Mac, things you might not have thought of before.

Physical Security

Let's start with the obvious. Your Mac should be *physically secure*. By that I mean if it's in an office, you should be able to lock your office door at night, and your cleaning staff, if you have one, should be bonded, insured, and drug tested. The computer should also be on a secure desk and in a clean environment (not in an extremely dusty or smoky room), and backup devices should be far enough away that a spilled soda can't destroy both your Mac and your backups.

You should also make sure that when you leave your desk, coworkers, visitors, or children don't have access to your personal data. That may require you to lock your door or log out of your Mac before leaving the room. One malicious coworker with a grudge could very easily walk into your office and send an e-mail from your account. If the e-mail is sent to the right person and contains just the right amount of evil, it can destroy a career. I know. I've seen it happen. Make sure your Mac is physically secure.

Secure the Login Process

One extremely easy way to secure your Mac is to create a login screen that requires the user to input both the user name and the password. This requires the would-be-intruder to know both instead of knowing only the password or getting that handy automatic login we all have come to love.

To change the way you (or others) log in to your Mac and to create a more secure environment, follow these steps:

1. Open System Preferences>Accounts.
2. Click Login Options.
3. In Display Login Window As, select Name And Password.
4. Although it isn't necessary, deselect the Automatically Log In As option. Figure 15-1 shows an example.
5. If you want to prevent anyone from changing these settings, click the lock.

Figure 15-1
Configure the login options to require a user name and password.

Hide the Restart and Shut Down Buttons

If your Mac is running and some no-good evildoer wants to, they can restart the computer and bypass the login options you just set in the previous section. How? All they have to do is boot to a Mac OS X CD, boot in FireWire Target Disk Mode, or restart in Single-User mode. They can do all kinds of damage in all of those places. To prevent this from happening, you can hide the Restart and Shut Down buttons so that they aren't available. (Now, a truly determined evildoer can simply unplug your Mac and plug it back in, so it isn't foolproof, but it can't hurt. Later you'll learn about setting a firmware password to cover this security loophole.)

To change these settings, repeat the steps in the previous section and check Hide The Sleep, Restart, And Shut Down Buttons. This option is shown in Figure 15-1.

Create a Screen Saver Password

When you leave your desk, you leave your Mac open for intruders. Anyone can walk up to your Mac and steal your latest ideas or delete an important file. Worse, they may even have access to your personal e-mail, diary, calendar, or similar items. To make sure this doesn't happen to you, configure your Mac to use a screen saver and to require a password after the screen saver has engaged.

Follow these steps to configure a screen saver and then configure a password to be used with it:

1. Open System Preferences>Desktop And Screen Saver>Screen Saver.

2. Select a screen saver from the list and move the slider to have the screen saver engage after a specific period of time.

3. Click Show All, and then select Security.

4. Check Require Password To Wake This Computer From Sleep Or Screen Saver. Figure 15-2 shows this screen.

5. Close System Preferences.

Figure 15-2

Configure a password-protected screen saver.

Log Out Automatically

Another option in Figure 15-2 is the option Log Out After ___ Minutes Of Inactivity. This may be a good option for you if you want to completely log out after a specific period of time but don't want to have to be there to do it.

TIP: Notice the other security options in Figure 15-2. You can require a password to unlock each secure system preference, and you can disable automatic login. Make the choices you feel are appropriate for your environment.

Use Mac OS X's Built-In Firewall

Did you know your Mac OS X comes with a built-in firewall? It isn't turned on by default, though, so you'll have to do that manually if you decide you need it. Firewalls should be configured because they monitor what types of data come into and out of your network and eliminate almost all possibility for attack. Being a Mac user, you know your chances are slim that you'll ever get attacked, but if you have an always-on Internet connection or a wireless network connection, I'd suggest turning it on anyway.

Here's how to turn on Mac OS X's included firewall:

1. Open System Preferences>Sharing>Firewall.

2. Click Start to start the Firewall.

3. You'll notice, as shown in Figure 15-3, that the services you've already configured to run are listed (with description and port) and checked. If you need to add other ports, click New. In the dialog box that appears, you can choose items such as MSN Messenger, ICQ, IRC, Retrospect, and others.

4. Add what you need and click OK. Close System Preferences.

Use Secure Empty Trash

When you carry your trash out to the trash can behind your house, you probably realize that there's a risk that people might rummage through it and recover bank statements, credit card numbers, or similar items. You might shred those types of documents before you carry them out. That's certainly a good idea. You can "shred" the items in your Trash folder too, using Secure Empty Trash. In Chapter 5 I included a GunkBuster's Notebook entry entitled "Secure Empty Trash" that explains how that works. The idea bears repeating here, though; when you're ready to empty your Trash and you know you'll never need what's in it again, choose Secure Empty Trash from the Finder menu.

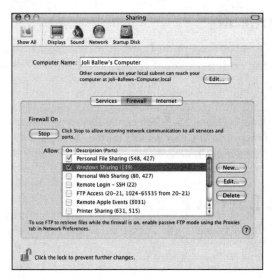

Figure 15-3

Configure OS X's firewall from System Preferences>Sharing.

Create and Enable a Visitor Account

If you're planning on having company soon and your visitors will require the use of your computer, create a visitor account for them to use. They don't have to use yours. It's pretty easy to create a standard account named Visitor and place any restrictions and limitations you want on it. This will help protect your Mac from unintentional harm and from others viewing your personal files.

To create a Visitor account, follow these steps:

1. Open System Preferences>Accounts.

2. Click the + sign to add a new account.

3. Name the account Visitor and create a password that they can use to log on.

4. Select the Limitations tab and click Some Limits.

5. Deselect any item you do not want your visitors to have access to. Figure 15-4 shows this screen. Make sure to uncheck Change Password.

6. Check This User Can Only Use These Applications (if desired), and configure what applications the user can access.

7. Click Simple Finder.

8. The Simple Finder has a simplified Dock and allows the user to directly use only those applications showing in the My Applications folder in the Dock. Again, choose what to allow and disallow.

9. Close the window.

Figure 15-4

Create a visitor account that places strict limits on what a user can and cannot do and access.

GunkBuster's Notebook: Secure Your Laptop

If you carry a laptop, you're more vulnerable to attacks than if you had a desktop computer. Laptops may be configured to use wireless networks (which can be very insecure) and they can be stolen and their contents pilfered. To secure your laptop requires that you do all of the security tweaks mentioned religiously, including keeping the computer physically safe at all times, securing the login process, enabling a firewall, and using Secure Empty Trash, but you can do even more to protect yourself.

Consider these additional security measures:

√   When going through airport security, never take your eye off your laptop. If possible, allow a traveling companion to go through before you, and watch your laptop as it comes through the scanner.

√   Purchase a good, sturdy carrying case that locks.

√   If you're on the road a lot, consider purchasing a nondescript carrying case; one that does not scream,'"Hey, look! I've got a laptop over here!"

√   Don't leave your laptop on your front seat when you go inside somewhere; lock it up in the trunk.

√   When in a hotel room, physically secure the laptop to something large in the room if possible.

√ Label your laptop with gusto. Consider having information etched onto the back of the case or applying a large sticker with your name on it.

√ Encrypt your Home directory. You'll learn more about how to do that later in this chapter.

√ Create a firmware password, also detailed later.

√ Purchase tracking software from a third-party vendor, such as LapCop or Stealth Signal's XTool Computer Tracker. When thieves logs on to the Internet with your machine, their location is tracked and hopefully the police can find them.

Use Anti-Virus Software

Using anti-virus software, when it's kept up-to-date, is the easiest way to protect your Mac from Internet risks like viruses and hackers. Anti-virus software is easy to install too, and a snap to keep current. If you don't have anti-virus software now, get some! (If you have a .Mac account, just download Virex from the .Mac Web site.) Figure 15-5 shows how simple the interface can be. This particular anti-virus program is Virex 7.2.

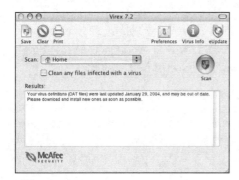

Figure 15-5
Anti-virus software is a snap to use and configure.

Anti-virus software can protect against lots of different Internet threats, not just viruses and hackers. It can protect against unauthorized connections and privacy threats. It can repel unwanted cookies and Java applets and scan incoming and outgoing e-mail. Many products also include a personal firewall, which offers additional protection. There are lots of anti-virus software manufacturers to choose from; to find them visit **www.apple.com/store** and search for "anti-virus software."

Common Configuration Techniques

Once it's installed, the software must be configured so that it offers the most protection with the least interference possible. For instance, you might configure preferences so that the updates are obtained at night when you aren't using your Mac. You might also want to have the computer run full system scans during that time so that you are never disrupted by the software.

For the most part, consider the following configuration choices for your anti-virus software (if they are available):

√ Set the anti-virus program so that it automatically protects your Mac. This may slow down the boot-up process, but it's worth it.

√ Let your anti-virus program automatically repair any infected files it finds.

√ Perform a complete system scan once a week. With the new spyware and adware threats, it never hurts to be overly protective.

√ Scan incoming and outgoing e-mail for viruses.

√ Enable protection for your instant messaging software.

√ Enable automatic and scheduled downloads on new virus definitions weekly.

√ Automatically delete infected files.

Configure Safari for Security

Safari is a pretty cool Web browser, and it's secure for the most part. You just don't hear too much about Mac users getting hacked or having Internet Explorer–like problems on the Web. Safari does have a few security settings you can tweak though, and they are well worth a look.

Explore the Security Options

To see what security options are available, open Safari and choose Safari>Preferences from the menu bar. You'll see several tabs, as shown in Figure 15-6. From these tabs you can set preferences such as what home page you'll use, where to save downloaded files, how plug-ins and cookies should be handled, what to do about pop-ups, and more.

I don't want to go through every tab and option that Safari offers; you can do that on your own. Instead, I'd like to point out a few things you should take notice of and perhaps configure to further secure your Web experience.

From the General tab:

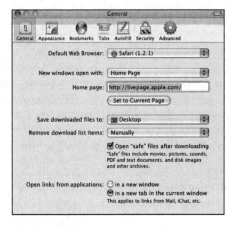

Figure 15-6
Safari offers a few ways to tweak the security settings.

√ Save Downloaded Files To—Instead of saving downloaded files to the desktop, the default, create a folder inside the Finder and then use this option to browse to it. It will keep your desktop clean and allow you to organize all of your downloaded files.

√ Remove Download List Items—Instead of manually removing downloaded list items, automatically remove them by changing the defaults here.

√ Open "Safe" Files After Downloading—If you don't want to trust Safari to decide what is a "safe" file and what isn't, uncheck this box. You'll then have to manually open all downloaded files.

From the Appearance tab:

√ Display Images When The Page Opens—By default, this option is checked. If you don't need or want to see images on a Web page when it opens, uncheck it.

From the AutoFill tab:

√ AutoFill Web Forms: Using Info From My Address Book Card—By default, your address book information is automatically added to most Web forms as you fill them out. You can edit what information is offered by editing your Address Book card. Just click Edit by this option. You can also uncheck this box to disallow the automatic insertion of data. That is a good idea if you share a computer with others and you don't log on and off before surfing the Web. If information is automatically added to forms, anyone using your computer will have your private information.

√ AutoFill Web Forms: User Names And Passwords—By default, this option is not checked. Checking it will automatically input user names and passwords at Web sites you've previously logged into. Again, this is not highly secure if others have access to your Mac.

√ AutoFill Web Forms: Other Forms—This lists Web sites you've previously logged into and automatically inputs information as you access the site. Click Edit to remove any Web site information or uncheck it to disallow data to be automatically input.

From the Security tab:

√ Web Content—By default, plug-ins, Java, and JavaScript are enabled. These are components of Web pages that are generally harmless and are used to display information. If you turn off these features, you may not be able to view Web page data. However, you may want to turn off certain types of content because you find it annoying. Block Pop-Up Windows does just that, and I'd suggest checking this item.

√ Accept Cookies—Cookies are little pieces of text that Web sites place on your computer to remember your preferences when you visit their Web pages. Almost all cookies are harmless. Many sites require you have cookies enabled to view content on their site. For the most part, the default setting, Only From Sites You Navigate To, is the best option. If you ever want to remove the cookies on your machine, select Show Cookies and delete to your heart's content.

√ Ask Before Sending A Non-Secure Form To A Secure Web Site—Leave this checked so you'll always be informed about sending private information over a non-secure transmission.

Scan through the other options available so you know what is offered. Remember, the goal is to maximize security while minimizing disruption. Disabling Java, for instance, may mean your Mac is more secure but it will cause your Web surfing experience to suffer a performance hit because pages won't display as expected.

Lock Keychain When You Leave Your Desk

When you log in to Mac OS X, you offer a password to identify yourself. You also have to enter a user name and password to visit certain Web sites. Before long, you have a list of passwords as long as your arm! Apple knows this is a problem and created Keychain, a program that remembers your passwords for you. It's a no-brainer; you log into your Mac with a single password and it verifies you are who you say you are and offers up your other passwords automatically.

The problem with Keychain though is this: If you leave you desk and don't log off your Mac, anyone and everyone who wanders up to it has free reign to your passwords. That's security gunk! To avoid this, you can lock the Keychain manually when you step away from your desk or automatically after a specific period of inactivity. Here's how to do both:

1. Open Applications>Utilities>Keychain Access.

2. To lock your Keychain manually, click Lock at the top of the window. You can see this in Figure 15-7.

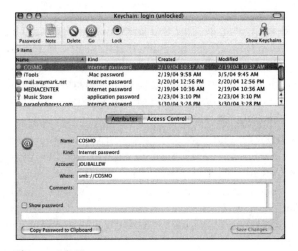

Figure 15-7
Lock the Keychain manually using the Lock button.

3. To lock your Keychain automatically, from the Menu bar, choose Edit>Change Settings For Keychain "Login."

4. Check Lock After ____ Minutes Of Inactivity and/or Lock When Sleeping. Configure the number of minutes of inactivity. Click Save.

5. Close all windows.

TIP: Because the Keychain Access utility is so secure, consider adding other personal information here. Choose File>New Secure Note Item from the menu bar and configure as warranted.

Use FileVault

FileVault is one of Apple's best and newest features. It allows you to encrypt your Home folder using a 128-bit Advanced Encryption Standard (AES) encryption scheme. Encryption scrambles the data in your home folder so that the information is secure if your computer is ever lost or stolen. It automatically encrypts and decrypts your data on the fly, and you won't even know or notice that it's happening. So, what's the big deal with that? Well, 128-bit encryption protects your data like a large, ugly ogre sitting in front of a one-lane bridge asking for the answer to a ridiculously difficult riddle before you can cross. You're just not going to get through without the right answer (password), even if you sit there and plead with that ogre for years!

You should use FileVault if your Mac contains sensitive information that would ruin you or your company if it was ever stolen. In addition, I think anyone with a laptop should seriously consider it. Unfortunately, using FileVault can interfere with scheduled backups or access to shared folders, and it might not be for everyone.

TIP: Apple's online Help files are amazingly helpful on this subject. If you'd like more information on FileVault, check there.

To use FileVault, follow these steps:

1. Open System Preferences>Security.
2. Read the information regarding FileVault. Pay special attention to the warning "Your Files Will Be Encrypted Using Your Login Password. If You Forget Your Login Password And The Master Password Is Not Available, Your Data Will Be Lost Forever." If you're willing to take that chance, select Set Master Password.
3. Fill out the required information in the Security dialog box and click OK. This will require you to input and verify a master password.
4. To turn on FileVault, select Turn On FileVault. This is shown in Figure 15-8.

Figure 15-8

Turn on FileVault to encrypt and protect your data.

5. Input your administrator password, click OK, and then click Turn On FileVault from the new Security dialog box.

6. The computer will restart.

GunkBuster's Notebook: Set an Open Firmware Password

This entire chapter focuses on ways to improve security on your Mac. Unfortunately, there are several loopholes that allow enterprising evildoers to still gain access to your Mac, even if you follow all the guidelines in this chapter. Any intruder can hack into your Mac by restarting it and holding down the proper key combinations. Someone could restart your Mac by using the Restart command or by simply unplugging and plugging back in the machine. During the restart process, intruders can boot to a CD, boot up in FireWire Target Disk Mode, start up in the Unix console, and more. Think of the damage one could do if an intruder connected his or her laptop to your Mac, and booted it up in FireWire Target Disk Mode! If you really want to secure your Mac, you have to block this security hole.

To keep intruders from gaining access to your Mac in this manner, you'll have to create an open firmware password. Creating the password blocks intruders from using these key combinations to get to your Mac. You have to input the open firmware password to use these alternate boot methods. Creating this password is serious business; if you forget the password you create, you'll be in deep trouble. You won't be able to use these alternate boot methods either. Even Mac support can't get you out of this mess.

With those cautions in mind, if you're ready to create an open firmware password, follow these steps:

1. Visit **www.apple.com** and select the Support link.

2. In the Search box, type *Set Open Firmware Password* and click Go.

3. Locate, download, and install the Open Firmware Password program that matches your Mac version.

4. Once it's installed, open the Open Firmware Password application.

5. Click the padlock to authenticate yourself and enter your administrator password.

6. Click Change.

7. Select the check box Require Password To Change Open Firmware Settings.

8. Type your password in the Password and Verify boxes.

9. Click OK and confirm your decision.

10. Click the padlock to prevent further changes.

11. Choose Open Firmware Password>Quit to close the application.

Summing Up

In this chapter you learned how important it is to secure your Mac and what built-in and third-party utilities and software are available to help you. You learned how to employ some basic security tasks such as using a password protected screen saver or using Mac OS X's built-in firewall to keep your Mac free from harm. You learned about Safari's security options, how to encrypt data, and how to keep out even the most resourceful hackers. Security is certainly a part of degunking; if your computer is compromised by a hacker, intruder, or malicious coworker, you'll certainly have more gunk than you know what to do with!

Backing Up Precious Files

Degunking Checklist:

√   Create a backup plan.

√   Choose from several backup techniques.

√   Learn what to back up and how often.

√   Store backups in a safe place.

One of the most important tasks for a computer user to remember to do is to back up data regularly. And as you become more diligent about degunking your Mac on a regular basis by using the degunking maintenance tasks outlined in this book, you'll need a good backup strategy. After all, degunking your Mac properly involves deleting documents and programs as well as moving files around on a regular basis. If you have a regular backup strategy in place, you'll feel more confident about getting rid of files and programs you don't use because you'll be able to restore them later if you decide you need them. The worst kind of degunker you can be is the "packrat degunker," the person who is afraid to throw anything away for fear they'll need it again later. Usually this fear comes from having a lousy backup strategy.

Backing up data is especially important these days because we store everything from family videos and pictures to music and important documents and records all on a single hard disk. Image how much could be lost by a single hard drive crash. Even a good backup on an external drive could be destroyed by a house fire or flood.

In this chapter you'll learn a little about backing up data, with the emphasis on creating a backup strategy and sticking to it. It doesn't matter to me if you purchase an expensive tape backup system or if you back up your data once a week to a Zip disk or a CD. I just want you to do *something,* and I want you to do it on a schedule. I also want you to learn what to back up, how often, and options for performing that task regularly.

Backup Techniques

Your Mac came with installation CDs that you can use to restore your system if you ever need to. That's all well and good, but they won't restore your personal data, the fonts you've acquired over the years, your preferences files, the folders you've created, the music you've downloaded, the movies you've made, your Internet cookies, your Keychain entries, your mailbox files...well, you get the idea. If something happens, you need to have all of that backed up.

It's going to be pretty hard to back up, on your own, every single thing you'll need to recover from a hard drive crash. It'll even be harder to try to keep these backups up-to-date. If you can afford it, let me suggest that you purchase a third-party backup utility to help you; the Mac doesn't come with a dedicated one. Sure, there's Disk Copy, but it's not really a backup program, and it isn't going to really do what you want in the way of backups.

Popular Backup Programs

There are lots of programs you can purchase to assist you in backing up regularly, and they range in price. Take a look at these options, and visit **www.apple.com/store** for others. If you want to try to find some freeware to help you back up your data, visit **www.versiontracker.com**. I've listed a few I found there later in this chapter. You never know what you might find!

Using iDisk

If you are a .Mac member, you can download and use the backup program that comes with it. This backup program, called Backup, allows you to schedule backups to iDisk or to an iPod, a FireWire hard drive, or CDs or DVDs. The .Mac membership runs around $100 (U.S.) a year.

Personal Backup X

For around $60 (U.S.), this software will let you run a backup automatically at shutdown or at defined intervals and perform complete folder and volume backups. It gives you complete control over what is backed up.

Retrospect Desktop

For around $130 (U.S.), this program allows you to set up and configure scheduled backups for your network of up to three computers. As with other backup programs you can schedule, when those backups occur, save them to various devices and restore from backup easily.

Available Freeware

Although freeware has a long way to go, there are some pretty neat utilities available from **www.versiontracker.com**. Here are just a few:

√ iBlog Backup—Back up your iBlogs.

√ Safari Backup and Restore—Back up important Safari user files.

√ Backup Script—Back up your AppleScripts.

√ SmartTools—Back up your Home folder.

√ PsyncX—Mirror part or all of your hard drive to a FireWire drive, a disk image, or a network drive.

√ LaCie SilverKeeper—Back up files and create bootable backups.

If you're used to working with freeware, go ahead and give a few of these a shot. You'll have to visit **www.versiontracker.com** regularly though and look for updates, but if you're looking for something that's free, that's just part of the job!

TIP: If you try a freeware program and don't like it, don't forget to drag it to the Trash.

Copy to CD as a Backup Option

If you're not interested in purchasing software or installing freeware on your Mac, you can always use the old and reliable drag and drop option. Just pop in a CD-R, drag the files over, and select Burn. It's simple and effective. It can even be more effective if you do it once a month and remember to make backups of items other than your personal folders (Documents, Movies, Music, Pictures, and so on). When making a backup using the drag and drop method, remember to copy these folders too, all located in your personal Library folder:

√ Application Enhancers

√ Calendars

√ Cookies

√ Favorites

√ Fonts

√ FontCollections

√ Keychains

√ Preferences

√ Printers

√ Receipts (located in the HD>Library folder)

√ Scripts

√ Screen Savers

In addition, don't forget your Shared folders, Drop Box, Faxes folder, Desktop, and similar items. When you take the time to manually back up items like these, you're getting close to creating a "full" backup, a backup that can be used to restore your computer in case of a disaster. While third-party software utilities can create a real, full backup, if you don't go that direction, at least you can get pretty close here.

Other Backup Devices

Finally, if you just don't dig the drag and drop to a CD thing and you don't like the idea of scheduling backups to occur automatically with purchased software, you can always use a Zip disk; copy data to a network drive, iPod, or flash drive; or purchase a dedicated backup unit. Whatever you decide, make some sort of decision now.

How are you going to back up your data?

Recommendations for the Home User

Just in case you get gunked up with a virus, forget your open firmware password, spill a cup of coffee on your computer, or have an unrecoverable kernel panic, make sure you have a good, solid backup. If you are a casual home user, consider performing a full backup that includes Fonts, Preferences, Cookies, Keychains, and similar folders two or three times a year. Store those backups in a safe place, preferably in another room or another building. Then, at least once a month, create a backup of your Documents, Music, Movies, and Pictures folders, plus any personal folders you've created. Store those in a safe place as well.

If and when you need these backups, you'll have them. Beyond that though, creating a backup CD once a month allows you to more freely degunk your machine when needed. If you decide later you'd really like to see the picture of your Mom's dog in a dress again, look no further than last year's March backup.

More About How Often to Back Up

If you don't consider yourself a casual home user, you'll need to back up more often than mentioned in the previous section. You will have to develop your backup strategy based on how much data you can stand to lose. I perform a daily backup (sometimes called a normal backup) at the end of each workday, but I make quite a few changes every day to the data on my hard drive and I consider my data (take this chapter for instance) quite valuable. I don't want to rewrite this chapter tomorrow if a lightning strike destroys my computer tonight! Table 16-1 sums it up.

Table 16-1	Choose a Backup Schedule That Is Right for You.	
If you are a:	**Perform normal backups:**	**Perform full backups:**
Casual user who only turns on the computer twice a week to check your e-mail	Once every two weeks or anytime you create anything you just can't lose	Twice a year
Home user who works on your computer every day	Two or three times a week or anytime you create anything you just can't lose	Four times a year
Home user and digital media enthusiast or someone who runs a business out of your home using your computer	At the end of each day or once a day	Twice a month or once a week
Small business owner	At the end of each day	At least once a week

Regardless of how much you use your Mac, you should have a pretty comprehensive full backup and several normal backups. I think you should make a habit of performing some type of backup weekly, even if it's dragging your recent files over to a Zip disk or external hard drive.

About Storing the Backups

A spilled soda that lands on your Mac and then spills over onto your backup devices will destroy both, so placing your external hard drive, with your backups on it, on top of your G5 tower doesn't make much sense. In the same vein, a flood or fire could destroy devices in the same building or room, so keeping full and monthly backups there doesn't make that much sense either.

Just to be on the safe side, consider keeping backup CDs in another room, in a safe deposit box, or at your mom's house. You might also use an external drive, which can be physically moved as well. It's a hassle, but you'll thank me if you ever have to recover from a disaster. Your pictures, music, movies, tax records, bank statements, and personal documents can't be replaced.

Summing Up

Your data is important, and keeping it safe is the last (and possibly the most vital) part of degunking your Mac. It's extremely important to protect your valuable personal data, pictures, movies, music, tax records, and similar items because those things are not easily replaceable, if they are at all. Good backups promote good degunking habits too. If you know you have good backups, you're more likely to experiment with the degunking techniques introduced in this book. There are lots of ways to back up your data, including using third-party software, freeware, CDs, external hard drives, and more. Whatever you do, just do it!

Appendix: Troubleshooting Your Mac with Degunking Techniques

If you are having specific problems that are slowing you down or keeping your Mac from running as it should, you can apply specific degunking techniques to solve many common problems you are likely to encounter. This appendix lists the most common problems Mac users get as the result of accumulated gunk. This section will help you if your time is limited and you don't have several hours to degunk your machine completely as outlined in this book, specifically in Chapter 2. The Degunking Sheet at the front of this book is also useful; it will help you perform various degunking tasks with the time you have.

To get the most out of this appendix, you should first try to identify the problem and then search the appendix for it (or locate the problem that is most similar), performing the corrective action recommended. You'll be surprised how many problems can be solved by referring to this list and simply doing the right degunking task. If this doesn't work or you can't find the problem you're looking for, check the index to this book.

After you solve your specific problem, put a little time aside later to more fully degunk your Mac. For example, if you encounter the problem of not being able to save your latest movie because you're out of hard drive space, and then fix the problem by deleting some large and unnecessary files, return later to this particular degunking task and take some time deleting other unnecessary files. This way you can keep this problem from happening again. Experience shows that if you encounter a problem, it will likely continue to happen unless you put some type of maintenance plan in place.

Operating System Problems

Problem: The boot process is really slow.

Your Mac may simply have too much to do on startup. To speed up the process, limit what programs open when you boot your Mac (Chapter 11), and check the file system for errors (Chapter 14). If problems persist, check to see that you have the latest firmware (Chapter 11).

Problem: After installing new hardware or software, your Mac is booting slowly or running poorly.

It's likely that something is wrong with the new hardware or software; it is probably incompatible in some way. Visit the manufacturer's Web site for driver updates for your hardware (Chapter 11), get the latest Apple software updates (Chapter 12), and verify that the software is compatible and your system meets minimum requirements. If the software does not meet minimum requirements related to memory, add more RAM (Chapter 13).

Problem: The computer won't boot at all.

If your computer will not boot, disconnect all hardware from the computer and try again. If the computer boots, add the hardware back in one at a time until you find the culprit. Once the problem hardware is found, look for a newer driver for it (Chapter 11). If this is not the problem, zap the PRAM (Chapter 14) and then run Apple's Disk Utility program from the CD (Chapter 14), typing fsck at the command line (Chapter 14).

Problem: Your Mac freezes and requires a Force-Quit randomly.

You most likely have a hardware or software problem, although you could be lacking enough RAM to perform the tasks required of the system. To troubleshoot the former, in order of preference: look for a software update (Chapter 12), restart the application, delete the application's Preferences file (Chapter 4), restart the computer, and reinstall the application. For the latter, see if it's possible to add more RAM (Chapter 13).

Problem: You get a request to send an "error report" to Apple.

When a problem occurs and an error message appears, you'll likely be asked to report the problem to Apple. Go ahead and click OK; they won't be acquiring any personal information from you. It'll help them find answers to common problems and offer those solutions in a future update.

File Management/Hard Drive Problems

Problem: You have accounts configured you no longer need.

There's no reason to keep user account gunk on your computer for users who no longer access it. Delete excess accounts from the System Preferences pane (Chapter 3).

Problem: You can't find the picture you just uploaded from your digital camera, and you have problems locating other files when you need them.

You need to organize your files and folders by type, name, date, or using a similar filing system. Chapters 3 and 5 detail ways to do this. Consider creating a color-coded system, renaming files and folders so they accurately represent their contents, and keep folders small enough to easily make backups and archive when necessary. Set aside some time to do this properly, and you'll forever be organized.

Problem: Your hard disk is getting full and you are having problems running applications and saving data.

You need to manually delete as many files, folders, and applications as you can to free up hard disk space (Chapters 3, 4, and 5). You need to empty the Trash on the Dock, from iPhoto, and from iMusic (Chapter 3); clean up your saved e-mail (Chapter 9); and, finally, run a third-party disk defragmenter utility (Chapter 5).

Application Problems

Problem: Your graphics program opens really slowly.

There are several things at work here. You may have installed and uninstalled so many applications that your hard drive is fragmented, in which case you need to defragment it (Chapter 5), you have too many fonts and they need to be culled down and organized (Chapter 7), the program opens in Classic mode and that particular part of your computer has yet to be degunked (Chapter 10), or you have too many programs open and need more RAM (Chapter 13).

For the most part, though, it has to do with gunk. Too many fonts, too many applications, too much stuff saved to your hard drive. If you continue to see problems such as this, you really should work through the book from the beginning, entirely degunking your computer.

Problem: The application requires you to use Force-Quit often.

You most likely have a software problem, although you could be lacking enough RAM to perform the tasks required. To troubleshoot the former, in order of preference: look for a software update (Chapter 12), restart the application, delete the application's Preferences file (Chapter 4), restart the computer, and reinstall the application. See if it's possible to add more RAM (Chapter 13). If problems persist, check the drive for errors (Chapter 14).

Problem: The application opens in Classic Mode, and it seems to take forever.

First things first: optimize OS 9 (Chapter 10). Then, make a decision about the application and its future. Is there an upgrade or has the company gone out of business? If the company is no longer in business, learn another program so that you can eventually remove the old one. If there's no company, there's no support. If an upgrade is available, purchase it.

E-Mail and Web Browsing Problems

Problem: When you try to send an e-mail, it seems to take an exceptionally long time and sometimes never sends.

Your e-mail system might be so overloaded with saved e-mails, sent items, and deleted items that it can't send out or receive e-mail. This, of course, depends on who your ISP is and what e-mail client you are using. Clean up your e-mail client (Chapter 9).

Problem: You have only one e-mail address, and you are getting so much spam you are having difficulty getting your legitimate e-mail.

Set up different e-mail accounts for different circumstances, set up a spam filtering utility to assist you in getting rid of spam, and configure Mail's junk e-mail options to avoid spam (Chapter 8).

Problem: You send e-mail to friends or colleagues, but they don't receive your messages.

If you aren't receiving messages that your e-mail bounced due to a misspelling in the e-mail address, your e-mail is probably triggering others' spam filters. Learn what sets off these triggers (Chapter 8).

Problem: Your e-mail client opens slowly.

It's likely that your combined set of e-mail in boxes and out boxes is really large and contains lots of things you don't need or want. Check all folders and delete what you don't need, taking special note of e-mail with large attachments (Chapter 9). Try to delete as many sent e-mails with attachments as possible.

Problem: While surfing the Web with Safari, you encounter problems viewing images on Web pages, or you get errors relating to cookies.

Make sure cookies are enabled, Java is enabled, and your security settings are not too restrictive (Chapter 15).

Security Problems

Problem: You are concerned that Web sites are collecting information from you or that intruders are trying to gain access to your computer.

Enable OS X's firewall, install anti-virus software, and configure the security settings available from your Web browser (Chapter 15).

Problem: Your anti-virus program isn't running automatically anymore.

Keeping your anti-virus program running and up to date is crucial because you don't want viruses to sneak onto your machine. If your anti-virus program is no longer running automatically, your registration might have expired. Many are set to only run for a year, and their registrations must be renewed (Chapter 15).

Problem: You think someone else may be accessing your computer while you are away from your desk.

This is the easiest of all security problems to solve. Lock your office doors, log out when you leave your desk, configure a password-protected screen saver, hide the restart and shut down buttons, and disable AutoFill in Safari (Chapter 15).

Problem: You want your laptop to be as secure as possible, and if it's ever stolen, you don't want hackers to be able to access the sensitive data stored on it.

Enable FileVault and create an open firmware password (Chapter 15).

Hardware and Peripheral Problems

Problem: You don't have enough memory to run an application, run multiple applications at once, or open an attachment.

You'll need to add additional RAM (Chapter 13). You can do this by using System Profiler to find out how much RAM you have and how much more you can add. There are many different types of RAM, so use the instructions in that chapter to get the right kind. If your Mac can't accommodate additional RAM, you should consider buying a new one, or you will need to be ruthless in degunking your current computer.

Problem: A new hardware device is causing the computer to run poorly.

You may need a new and updated driver for the device. Visit the manufacturer's Web site for information (Chapter 11).

Problem: Keys stick on the keyboard and there are fingerprints on the monitor.

You can improve the performance of the keyboard by cleaning it, and the monitor can be cleaned with a moist cloth (Chapter 13).

Index

100 Message Rule, 149